POLITICS AS SOUND

MUSIC IN AMERICAN LIFE

A list of books in the series appears at the end of this book.

POLITICS AS SOUND

The Washington, DC, Hardcore Scene, 1978–1983

SHAYNA L. MASKELL

UNIVERSITY OF
ILLINOIS PRESS
Urbana, Chicago, and Springfield

Library of Congress Cataloging-in-Publication Data
Names: Maskell, Shayna L., 1979– author.
Title: Politics as sound : the Washington, DC, hardcore scene,
    1978–1983 / Shayna L. Maskell.
Description: Urbana : University of Illinois Press, 2021. | Series:
    Music in American life | Includes bibliographical references
    and index.
Identifiers: LCCN 2021009990 (print) | LCCN 2021009991 (ebook) |
    ISBN 9780252044182 (cloth) | ISBN 9780252086229 (paperback)
    | ISBN 9780252053122 (ebook)
Subjects: LCSH: Punk rock music—Washington (D.C.)—History
    and criticism. | Hardcore (Music)—Washington (D.C.)—
    History and criticism. | Punk culture—Washington (D.C.)—
    History.
Classification: LCC ML3534.3 .M382 2021 (print) | LCC ML3534.3
    (ebook) | DDC 781.6609753—dc23
LC record available at https://lccn.loc.gov/2021009990
LC ebook record available at https://lccn.loc.gov/2021009991

Contents

Acknowledgments

A huge thank you to my family who have been my cheerleaders, my editors, my diet soda distributors, and my therapists: my parents, Jack and Geri, my brother David, and my sister-in-law, Sylvia. Sending special love to my husband, Jesse, who has, with only minimal complaint, suffered through years of spirited arguments about the definition of hardcore but has always been my source of unconditional love and support. To Huck and Jude, my incredible, beautiful boys who made me question whether the birth of twins is harder than publishing a book.

A big thanks to all the people who agreed to be interviewed about DC hardcore—a special shout out to the '80s DC Hardcore Scene Kids Facebook Group and to Ian MacKaye, who has been unbelievably generous with his time, memories, and Dischord House tours.

I also owe an enormous amount of gratitude to my dissertation adviser, Dr. Nancy Struna, without whom I can with certainty say I would have never been able to finish this manuscript or turned it into a book. And thanks to the University of Maryland American Studies faculty and cohort, who were a constant stream of knowledge, humor, and guidance.

Thank you to my integrative studies friends and colleagues at George Mason University, particularly Pam Garner and Graziella McCarron, for their amazing encouragement and friendship.

Introduction

Rock 'n' roll is a language that can say whatever it wants, a kind of socially sanctioned anarchy. As Greil Marcus wrote, rock can "divine all truths, reveal all mysteries, and escape all restrictions."[1] Emerging from the democratically inclined tentacles of popular culture, rock 'n' roll represents a particular set of social and aesthetic attitudes. Rock is a challenge. It is aggression, liberation, entitlement, resistance, transcendence, obscenity, pleasure, and hedonism—all in the form of guitar, drums, bass, and vocals. Rock is the embodiment of cultural contradictions: art and schlock, tradition and rebellion, the crude and the complex, black and white, poor and rich. It is Little Richard kicking out his piano bench and gleefully attacking the piano; Elvis inducing panic and lust with the roll of his hips, pompadour perfectly in place; the Beatles causing young girls palpitations and then breaking out of their musical mold again and again; the Rolling Stones' Mick Jagger strutting around stage, spandex tightly hugging his legs, lips pursed; James Brown falling to the ground, only to arise with his royal cape around him; David Bowie transforming into alien-cum-sex-icon Ziggy Stardust; Jimi Hendrix licking his guitar, setting it aflame. Rock is riding around your car, going nowhere, singing at the top of your lungs; sneaking out in the middle of the night; dancing in front of the mirror, at the back of a concert hall, in the hallways of school; headphones in, world tuned out, a secret for only you; parties and milestones and romance and breakups and war and sex and death. To understand rock 'n' roll is to understand ourselves as individuals and as a part of a larger society.

Punk rock is both an aberration of and a conformity to rock 'n' roll. A music that is often characterized as an oddity, an attack, or a monstrous deviation from all that made rock great, punk still works within the conventional social and political structure that made rock so powerful and meaningful. Punk is seemingly discordant—loud, riotous, hard, aggressive, assertive. It took rock and set it on fire, slashed and burned it, and then took a sledgehammer to it for good measure. But punk also rebuilt rock 'n' roll; it paid homage and its respects to the gravestone it laid; it was the truculent, eye-rolling asshole teenager to the dinosaur, disapproving parent of rock 'n' roll but it couldn't and didn't outrun its DNA. Punk embodied the youth that rock 'n' roll had aged out of: personal alienation, anger, exigency, radicalism, with a healthy dose of paradoxical apathy and political activism.

Nowhere are these contradictions and consistencies more evident than in the Washington, DC, hardcore punk scene. This book aims to delineate, describe, explore, and examine hardcore in Washington, DC, during its zenith of both impact and innovation, 1978–83. During these indispensably creative and influential years in DC music, hardcore punk was not only simply born—a mutated sonic stepchild of rock 'n' roll, British and American punk—but also evolved into an uncompromising and resounding paradigm of and for a specific segment of DC youth. Through the revelatory music of DC hardcore, a new formulation of sound, and a new articulation of youth, arose: one that was angry, loud, fast, and minimalistic. With a total of only ten albums among all five bands over a five-year period, DC hardcore cemented a small yet significant subculture and scene. More specifically, this book considers two major components inherent in any genre of popular music: aesthetics and the social politics that stem from those aesthetics. We will consider the way music communicates, its structure—facets like timbre, melody, rhythm, pitch, volume, dissonance—and simultaneously dissect how these features communicate messages of social and cultural politics, expressly representations of race, class, and gender.

In this way, attending to sound is attending to self. This book looks at DC hardcore as a challenge to and a scaffolding for how the performance of music is also a performance of self, constructing distinctive, frequently complicated and contradictory representations of race, gender, and class. Essential to this evaluation of aesthetics and the consequential cultural politics is an assessment of the unique sociohistorical circumstances of place; that is, how the particulars of DC as a city—including racial and socioeconomic histories and demographics, political predilections both locally and nationally, the musical milieu, and individual upbringing—worked to (re)contextualize and (re)imagine the meanings created by and from sound.

Introducing DC Hardcore

Subsequent chapters will more fully trace the history of hardcore in DC, but this introductory section offers a brief synopsis—a musical intro, if you will—of the bands of Washington, DC, hardcore, of their music and sound, their chronology, and the band members themselves. It should be noted that this book is intentionally limited in its scope and span; indeed, the ensuing chapters focus nearly monolithically on the (largely white and male) music and bands between the years of 1978 and 1983,[2] when the DC hardcore scene was first born until it transformed into a different kind of musical genre. I also make no claims of providing an exhaustive list or analysis of DC hardcore bands during these years. During those formative years of DC hardcore, there were heaping handfuls of hardcore bands that formed. The Do-It-Yourself (DIY) ethos of punk, along with the minimalistic nature of music making, allowed for a proliferation of amateur musicians and inexpert bands. That was, in part, the point of the entire movement. But through the glut of garage-and-basement-based bands, a few became emblematic of DC and hardcore. I argue that the bands within these pages are the most prominent, powerful, and persuasive people, sounds, and representations of DC hardcore, offering a lens into how their music worked as political action: Bad Brains, Teen Idles, Minor Threat, State of Alert (S.O.A), Government Issue (GI), and Faith.[3] In part, these bands were so significant to the scene because of the people in them. Ian MacKaye, who cofounded Dischord Records and came to be one of the most influential punk musicians in the country, was in Teen Idles and Minor Threat, while his brother was the front man for Faith.

3

Henry Garfield was the lead singer for S.O.A, the short-lived DC hardcore band that led to his notorious gig as the lead singer for California-based Black Flag (and now, actor, poet and activist).

Besides the unique and geographically specific hardcore sound these DC bands all shared, they also had the DIY spirit that exemplifies hardcore. Coming from the suburbs of Maryland and Virginia and the racially and economically diverse neighborhoods of Washington, DC, these bands were inspired to pick up instruments, sing into microphones, and write lyrics—often without any formal musical education. What they did have was passion, angst, feelings of alienation and isolation, both personally and politically, that found articulation through sound. These bands are also notable for the music they produced and the albums they created and released—genre-twisting, innovative, and unimaginably assertive sounds that re-envisioned punk rock. And, in developing these songs, these albums, and performing where they could whenever they could, DC hardcore bands also found they weren't alone. A small, fiercely dedicated, and equally discontented audience related to the music and its message. Soon, DC had an entire hardcore punk scene.

Let's meet the bands.

BAD BRAINS

Composed of lead singer HR, brother and drummer Earl Hudson, bassist Darryl Jenifer and guitarist Dr. Know, Bad Brains emerged from Washington, DC, in 1978, creating a sound and music that "defined the essence of hardcore."[4] Jenifer lived in Southeast DC, a predominately African American district, and in high school befriended neighbor Sid McCray, who eventually introduced Jenifer to British punk rock via the Sex Pistols and the Damned. Paul Hudson (who would later change his name to HR) and his younger brother, Earl Hudson, were products of a military family, moving all over the world until settling into a Maryland suburb directly across from Southeast DC. After graduating from high school and flunking out of a premed major in college, Paul picked up work as a security guard—as well as a destructive heroin habit. With his son's birth in 1977 and a lack of direction in his professional life except for his love of music, Paul was inspired by his father's copy of Napoleon Hill's *Think and Grow Rich*, a Great Depression–era self-help book that touted a concept known as Positive Mental Attitude—PMA. Harnessing PMA to his musical aspirations, Paul formed a jazz fusion band with friend Gary Miller (soon to be known as Dr. Know), brother Earl, and Jenifer. Modeled on their musical hero Chick Corea's *Return to Forever*, one disastrous basement show, including a stage-fright-stricken Jenifer who refused to play, and a cascade of boos and beer bottles raining down on the band, ended the short-lived jazz fusion band. With the assistance of McCray, the band absorbed the sounds and styles of punk rock, connecting to the sense of rebellion, of belligerency, and of shock and awe that punk embraced.[5]

Starting as what could only be called a punk cover band, playing the Sex Pistols, the Damned, and the Saints, among others, Bad Brains began performing their own material in live shows across the area—the Atlantis (later to become the 9:30 Club), the Bayou, and Madam's Organ, to name a few—and quickly amassed a reputation for mind-numbing speed, flawless technical skill, and nearly interminable power and dynamism. In 1979 they released their first recorded music on a Limp Records DC punk compilation, *30 Seconds over DC*, with their song "Don't Bother Me."

The premier hardcore band in DC, Bad Brains played anywhere in the city that would have them, causing mayhem wherever they went. They were often banned at venues, leading to their eventual hardcore classic "Banned in DC." As they refined their sound and their rowdy, musically explosive shows became legendary, Bad Brains took their act on the road, hitting the burgeoning hardcore scene in New York and attempting a tour in England, which was quickly aborted after an incident with British customs. The group finally recorded their first full-length album in New York during three months in 1981, releasing *Bad Brains* in 1982 as a cassette tape. With cover art featuring the Capitol with a bolt of lightning striking and shattering its dome, the album became the definitive sound of hardcore punk, music that was "monstrously tight and musical and exhilarating and inspirational."[6] As Adam Yauch of the Beastie Boys claims in the linear notes of the tape, *Bad Brains* is "the best punk/hardcore album of all time."

That album, however, proved to be not just the pinnacle of Bad Brains' hardcore career, it was also their only one. By 1982, the band had fully dedicated themselves to the Rastafarian lifestyle, a religion and way of life HR and some of the other band members had been dabbling in during the previous years. They abandoned hardcore in favor of full-time reggae and isolated themselves musically and socially, adopting a patois, a hatred of Babylon (a white-controlled, decaying modern civilization), homophobic views, and an eventual dissolution of their commitment to DC, moving full-time to New York City. Their influence, however, continued well past their punk demise, propelling an entirely new generation of DC hardcore bands.

THE TEEN IDLES AND MINOR THREAT

Before there was Minor Threat there was the Teen Idles and before the Teen Idles there was the Slinkees. Galvanized by a Bad Brains, Cramps, and Urban Verbs show, Wilson High School students Ian MacKaye and Jeff Nelson abandoned their long hair and their focus on skateboarding for punk, forming the fleeting punk-inspired band the Slinkees. Adding fellow classmates Mark Sullivan and Geordie Grindle, the teens picked up instruments for the first time in their lives, playing covers of "Louie Louie" and originals like "I Drink Milk" and "Conservative Rock." When singer Sullivan left for college, the band re-formed as the Teen Idles, this time with MacKaye's friend and local punk Nathan Strejcek on vocals, despite the fact that he had never sung before. They performed their first show in Strejcek's basement at the end of 1979.

The Teen Idles emulated the style of their musical heroes Bad Brains, who had befriended the young band members and even had taken to borrowing their equipment and utilizing their practice space. As Nelson explained, "Bad Brains influenced us incredibly with their speed and frenzied delivery. We went from sounding like the Sex Pistols to playing every song as fast and hard as we could."[7] After the boys graduated from high school, they took a bus to California to play two shows in Los Angeles and San Francisco. The trip cemented the alienation and marginalization they were already experiencing in DC; thrown out of MacKaye's uncle's house in LA, beaten up at the Greyhound station, turned away from Disneyland after the security guard called them "punk faggots," the trip also had a positive effect, coalescing a sense of hardcore identity, particularly in its fashion (Doc Martens or work boots, chains and spurs, and bondage straps sewed onto their pants) and an inclination toward violence as a mechanism of self-defense.

This estrangement was also developing in the DC scene, with older punks, minus Bad Brains, mockingly labeling them "Georgetown punks" or "teeny-punks" and criticizing their lack of musical aptitude as a laughable novelty. But the band persevered, ultimately adopting the disparaging "Georgetown punks" as a rallying cry, putting out their eight-track *Minor Disturbance* EP in 1981 on the MacKaye- and Nelson-formed record label Dischord, funded by each band member contributing the $150 they had made on the tour for the production of the album. Yet even before the EP was released, the band dissolved, with Grindle quitting, Strejcek forming Youth Brigade, and MacKaye and Nelson remaining and reconstructing anew, creating perhaps the most famous and influential hardcore band of all time, DC or elsewhere—Minor Threat.

MacKaye, who had been dissatisfied with Strejcek's domination of writing and singing, took over as lead singer, Nelson continued on drums, and Lyle Preslar on guitar and Brian Baker on bass were added. Playing regularly at venues around DC and still modeling their sound on their friends and musical inspiration, Bad Brains, Minor Threat "blew away" crowds playing what *Washington Post* writer (and punk aficionado) Howard Wuelfing called "extremely fast but with extreme precision."[8]

In 1981 the band put out two landmark albums on their Dischord label, *Minor Threat* and *In My Eyes*, "one of the greatest punk records of all time,"[9] with MacKaye "hiss[ing] out the lyrics like they're meant to kill."[10] With those two albums, Minor Threat initiated (unintentionally, according to MacKaye) the straightedge hardcore phenomenon, a no-drinking, drug-free, promiscuous-sex-avoidant movement. After a brief breakup when Preslar went to college at Northwestern, Minor Threat reunited in 1982 when Preslar dropped out of school. During this reunion, they went on tour with fellow DC hardcore bands, moved into the now famous Dischord house in Arlington, Virginia, a sort of DC hardcore punk community house where many teen punks lived outside their parents' homes for the first time, while at the same time dealing with scene-based accusations of selling out. By 1983 Minor Threat had begun to morph, in part as a result of Baker's demand to switch from bass to guitar and the addition of Steve Hansgen on bass. The band released *Out of Step* in

1983, the biggest Dischord release yet, but the chemistry of the band had been irreparably damaged. Minor Threat's demise in 1983 signaled the corresponding passing of this particular type of hardcore in DC.

STATE OF ALERT (S.O.A)

S.O.A was extremely short-lived, starting in October 1980 and disbanded by July 1981, known perhaps less for their music and more for their front man Henry Garfield[11] and the violent eruptions that occurred during their performances. Garfield and MacKaye were childhood friends, high school classmates, skateboarders, and, in the late 1970s, huge punk enthusiasts. While MacKaye formed the Teen Idles, Garfield, who "couldn't play an instrument but . . . could damn well carry the cabinets and amps"[12] became their de facto roadie, going to California with the band and recording every live show on his stepfather's tape deck.

By the time the Teen Idles had disbanded and reformulated as Minor Threat, taking with them the Exhorts singer Lyle Preslar, Garfield had decided his lack of musical training shouldn't be a barrier to being in a punk band and filled Preslar's role, renaming the band State of Alert. S.O.A started playing in October 1980, with hardcore's signature bellicose, uncompromising sound; the music was rudimentary but radical, particularly Garfield himself, who became renowned for his provocative, aggressive singing and performance style. The band also included Michael Hampton on guitar, Wendel Blow on bass, and Simon Jacobsen (1980–81) and then Ivor Hanson (1981) on drums. Performing only nine shows in their incarnation, S.O.A was technically sloppy but emotionally brutal; their music was messy and intense, and their shows were known to be among the most violent at the time.

Dischord released their nihilistic 1981 EP *No Policy*, an album about, according to Garfield, "anti-everything I didn't like . . . it was all about no fun, fear, oppression. My message was 'Kill the World.'"[13] The album was stripped down, even slipshod, but its energy, DIY-ethos and sound, as one music blogger noted, "beats your goddamn face in." The band never had the opportunity to record another album, however. After jumping on stage at a hardcore show in New York, singing along with friend HR and even sitting in as a guest singer for his favorite Black Flag song "Clocked In," the California-based vocalist Dez Cadena called Garfield in DC and asked him to audition for the band (Cadena wanted to play second guitar rather than sing). Garfield nailed it and, after S.O.A's final, violence-filled performance in Philadelphia, he left DC—and his last name—and headed for Los Angeles as Henry Rollins.

GOVERNMENT ISSUE (GI)

The longest-running—and with the most line-up changes, more than ten in all—DC hardcore band, together in one form or another from 1980 to 1989, GI began at the Unheard Music Festival at dc space at 7th and E Streets NW, a two-day punk-style music festival organized by *Washington Post's* Howard Wuelfing. That evening was the first time the band had ever played together—and it showed. John Stabb, GI's singer and only perpetual member, bounced up and down, screaming out mostly incomprehensible lyrics, while the rest of the newly formed band, all classmates of Stabb from the private all-boys school St. Anselm's Abbey in Northeast DC, played sloppily along.

Starting in 1980, Stabb was on vocals, with John Barry on guitar, Brian Gay on bass and Marc Alberstadt on drums; by the fall of 1981, Brian Baker (of Minor Threat) had taken over on bass but quickly changed to guitar as Tom Lyle started on bass; the lineup changed again in the spring of 1982, as Baker went back to Minor Threat, Lyle moved to guitar, and Mitch Parker became the bassist; Parker was replaced by Rob Moss in the summer of 1983.

One of the top hardcore bands in DC, GI melded punk with near-circus-like showmanship and, with its ever-revolving door, acted as an incubator for nearly all DC hardcore musicians. Stimulated by the sounds of S.O.A, Minor Threat, and Bad Brains, GI took a similar hardcore approach, with an utter lack of musical experience, a hard-driving, aggressive tempo, and many songs under the one-minute mark. But unlike many of the other DC hardcore bands, GI tended toward overtly political lyrics in their first two years, writing "Hey Ronnie," a 1981 diatribe against the newly elected president, and "No Rights," about the police's abuses of punk teenagers. By 1982, though, Stabb's lyrics were "more on a gut level in the vein of Black Flag . . . music is an intense therapy session for me";[14] their sound began to transform as well, incorporating more melodies and structure.

During the band's zenith, and hardcore's height, GI was, according to Dave Smalley of Dag Nasty, "one of the best bands in the history of American Hardcore," releasing *Legless Bull* in 1981 (on MacKaye and Nelson's Dischord label), *Make an Effort* in '82 and *Boycott Stabb* in '83 before succumbing to a more mainstream heavy rock sound. According to guitarist Tom Lyle, who joined in 1982, the band was never monogamous with the hardcore punk identity: "We weren't going to march lock-step either musically, lyrically, or anything else like any other band on the DC scene, or anywhere else."[15] After leaving the Dischord label, GI went on to release eight other albums on different labels, straying from the traditional hardcore sound into more psychedelic, hard rock, and heavy metal sonic territory.

FAITH

Faith formed in the summer of 1981, picking up the pieces of hardcore bands' past: from S.O.A came Michael Hampton on guitar and Ivor Hanson on drums, along with Chris Bald on bass and Ian MacKaye's brother, Alec, on vocals. Before the formation of Faith, vocalist Alec MacKaye and guitarist Eddie Janney played together in the Untouchables, putting out the singles "Nic Fit," "Rat Patrol," and "I Hate You" on Dischord's 1981 hardcore DC punk compilation *Flex Your Head*, before storming the stage at the 9:30 club (after being rejected by the club's owner) and borrowing Minor Threat's instruments for their farewell performance of "If the Kids Are United." Soon after, in November 1981, Alec and Eddie added Hampton, bassist Bald, and drummer Hanson and reorganized as Faith, playing their first show at HB Woodlawn High School and quickly making an impact on the hardcore scene. Sonic Youth guitarist Thurston Moore cites Faith as "the most potent distillation" of DC hardcore, with their "refined minimalism. . . . it wasn't just about the trash and the speed and the sound. . . . it was this raw style of songwriting."[16] The band put out just two releases—a split LP with fellow DC hardcore band Void, 1982's *Faith/Void*, and 1983's big-brother-Ian-produced *Subject to Change*—shifting, in a subtle but significant way, the sound of hardcore; their music combined the conventional hardcore ideal of speed and strength with more subtle nuances of metal and melody.

This sonic swing was due, in part, to the use of two guitarists. Though Alec asserts this arrangement was to integrate more complex guitar ideas, to avoid guitar malfunctions at live shows, and to get a fuller sound, the effect was a more melodic, softer hardcore sound. Instead of hardcore's patented wanton, whirlwind chord changes, the guitars are polyrhythmic, with more complex guitar work, and, in an almost treasonous move, there are even some guitar solos.

Alec's singing style had also changed. While in the Untouchables, his grueling, demanding shout-singing style often caused him "to pass out or hyperventilate"[17] but his vocals in the Faith were well-defined and lucid. As the Hold Steady's lead singer Craig Finn notes, in Faith's brand of hardcore, "musicality often trumps their rage," music that is "angry and dangerous without being cartoonish."[18] Their lyrics still tended toward the nihilistic (with tracks like "No Choice," "More of the Same," and "Limitations"), and the songs were still less refined and more visceral, but MacKaye's darker, more evocative singing style marked him as "a gravel-throated chronicler of turmoil and tedium."[19]

Much like DC's other hardcore bands, Faith was ephemeral, staying together for less than two years; before *Subject to Change* was even released, the band had dissolved as a result of internal personality clashes, with all the band members dispersing and eventually sprouting into some of the most influential and important new posthardcore bands in DC.

The Road Map: Chapter Outline

The remainder of the book will take a brief walk down punk's musical memory lane to the late 1970s and early 1980s, exploring the sonic history of Washington, DC, and then taking a deep dive into DC hardcore, looking at the ways in which DC-based hardcore punk rock creates, challenges, and replicates sociopolitical meanings, positions, and understandings through both an analysis of sound and the scene itself, including the people, the fashions, the dancing, the performances, and the places of DC hardcore.

Chapter 1 briefly and broadly contextualizes the city of Washington, DC, musically, culturally, and politically. The chapter presents a streamlined overview of the sociopolitical history of DC, starting with its creation in the 1700s, up until the birth of hardcore in the late 1970s and early 1980s, charting the shifting political landscape and mapping the changing and often dramatic racial and socioeconomic demographic differences in certain neighborhoods of the District. Then the chapter dips its toes into the musical history of Washington, DC, as a city, looking at both its broader cultural narrative and the specific kinds of music and types of bands that preceded the creation of hardcore punk.

The remainder of the book consists of two sections—the music of DC hardcore and the scene of DC hardcore. In the first section, the chapters focus on the sounds of hardcore, rather than the cultural scene that arose from the genre. This includes close readings of lyrics, analyses of sound, and the relationship of these two musical facets to sociopolitical acts by analyzing every major album released by Bad Brains, Teen Idles and Minor Threat, S.O.A, GI, and Faith between 1978 and 1983. Each chapter uses one of these bands as the main paradigm for understanding race, class, and gender respectively, but we'll also look at how these bands overlap, contradict, and complicate these political constructions of sound.

More specifically, chapter 2 focuses on the musical aesthetics of race, using Bad Brains and their seminal 1982 release of the same name as an exemplar of how DC hardcore creates and simultaneously deconstructs conventional representations of a black DC identity. The chapter scaffolds Bad Brains' music within the black musical tradition of blues and jazz, as well as the cultural and musical positioning of the electric guitar. This binary of blackness is then contrasted with and complicated by the whiteness of the music of Minor Threat and S.O.A.

In chapter 3, the music of Teen Idles and Minor Threat is used as the paradigm for sonic socioeconomic stratification, and their music is analyzed through class-based sound aesthetics and choices: instruments, composition, lyrics, vocals, and recording. Along with their DC hardcore brethren, the music of these bands is explored for the ways in which they parallel, heighten, or obfuscate the performance of class, grounded within the parameters of the DC scene.

In the final chapter in the first section, S.O.A, GI, and Faith will be the center of attention, with the emphasis on the ways in which these three bands' music constructs—and at times complicates—conventional representations of (white, privileged) masculinity. The chapter looks at the texture, timbre, volume, and lyrical content of DC hardcore bands through the lenses of hegemonic masculinity: anger and aggression, emphatic sexuality, and the privilege of power and control.

The second section explores DC hardcore through the corporeal and sociocultural, political, and economic dimensions that are integral to the music and the scene. Its chapters intersect with, complicate, and expand on the meanings created in the music of the bands in section I. It includes an analysis and discussion of cultural artifacts (photographs, flyers, etc.) of and from the scene, as well as commentary and memories from participants in the scene, culled from newspapers, magazines, liner notes, and interviews conducted with Ian MacKaye at the kitchen table of the Dischord house, in addition to members of the scene themselves—fans and musicians alike.

Chapter 5 considers the role of cultural production in the DC scene, including the Do-It-Yourself (DIY) ethos in recording and performance, the creation and subsequent power of Dischord records, and the ways in which issues of class, race, and gender infuse what, how, and why DC punks produce music and its accompanying artifacts. In chapter 6, I survey the emergence of straightedge within the DC hardcore scene, tracing its classed, raced, and gendered underpinnings in and as a hardcore ethos. Straightedge is discussed not just as a sound or an identity, but also as a subcultural political movement. Chapter 7 centers on the body in the DC hardcore scene. It includes the way intersectionality and corporeality is imbued in hardcore punks' fashion, hairstyles, and use of violence in dance and performance, as well as the ways in which these facets of the scene are grounded in the specific sociohistorical context of Washington, DC, in the late '70s and '80s.

Finally, the transformation of the social, cultural, and musical landscape of DC hardcore is considered in the concluding chapter, investigating how and why the sound of hardcore changed after 1983. Covering four key DC posthardcore bands—Rites of Spring, Marginal Man, Beefeater, and Embrace—the chapter tracks the modifications and adjustments in sound within the context of the previous chapters' political lenses: race, class, and gender. These sonic changes are linked to the social, political, and personal changes occurring at the same time, ultimately signifying the demise of DC hardcore.

1

DC Rising

*The (Musical) Life and Times
of Washington, DC*

There is a distinctive relationship between music and the city from which it comes. Detroit and Motown, Nashville and country, New York and hip-hop—music and the places from which they emerge interact, influence, and transform one another. Cities are contested spaces where elites and formidable interest groups struggle to shape representation, manipulate images, and wrestle for the financial and cultural power that comes with such control. And contained within these spaces are particular places, a built environment that, in part, creates, limits, and complicates opportunities for individuals economically, socially, politically, and—important for the purposes of this chapter—culturally. Contemporary geographers and cultural studies scholars have both explored the ways in which place and space act as one (re)presentation of a society's ethos, as a site in which and on which power is reproduced, negotiated, and challenged. As Murray Forman describes in his work on hip-hop, place and space act as "social conflicts involv[ing] engagement of fluctuating intensities . . . and scales as various transformative strategies are deployed in the attempt to extend control and domination over the social landscape."[1]

Music is one such space. It is a space of social conflict and of power struggles, and it is a space that is created, transformed, and in turn, helps (re)create place itself. As Sara Cohen argues in her 1991 seminal music ethnography of Liverpool, music and place are forms of, and inform, material and social relationships. The local bands in her study were an outcome of their "social practices, processes, and interactions in musical creation and performance 'on the ground'" but likewise cannot be understood without being "situated at a particular point in time within the particular socio-economic, political, and cultural conditions of one British city environment."[2] In part, this mutually constitutive relationship of music and place is grounded in the physicality of place and constrained by what Barry Shank describes as "the institutional and discursive structures that constrain and enable their [musicians'] performances," including the metaphysical history and culture of the space and place as music "map[s] out a relation to this history."[3] As Shank detailed in *Dissonant Identities*, the punk scene of Austin, Texas, was as much a product and influence of the music clubs in which bands performed as it was the identity of Austin as a liberal bastion in a conservative stronghold. The scene's do-it-yourself credo aligned with Texas's long-standing love of bootstrapping and individual entrepreneurship, but its practical evolution as a music scene stemmed from college students gathering at Inner Sanctum Records and bands playing at the dilapidated Raul's, a Mexican bar-turned-music-venue.

Another intersection of musical space and place is the development of a collective, place-based identity. Although place acts as a catalyst for the production of music—and vice versa—both also construct identity markers for the habitants within that particular place. Connecting individuals to one another, and communities to constructions of place, music works as "symbolic anchors in regions, as signs of community, belonging, and a shared past."[4] For example, in Cohen's study, the long and nuanced history of Liverpool music (including, of course, its most famous residents, the Beatles) was critical in creating a regional identity for bands—even of different genres—in the 1980s. In the same way, Shank explored the ways in which Austin's musical memory—from singing cowboys to hillbilly and honky-tonk to more modern country music—allowed for and encouraged new music-based identities like punk. And the music contributing to these identities reflected the places themselves, "figur[ing] prominently as organizing concepts delineating a vast range of imaginary or actual social practices that are represented in narrative or lyric form and that display identifiable local, regional, and national aesthetic inflections."[5] In this way, place and identity are not independent of one another, nor is the relationship linear; the function of place and identity within the production of music is a dialectic, neither determinative nor exclusive.

This relationship between music and cities is then linked not just to the development of sound itself, but perhaps more interesting is the way in which sounds' social and individual meanings are created and received. Sound, music—really, any form of communication—is only viable insofar as it can be "read" and comprehended by others. This is, of course, the extremely streamlined and simplified version of semiotics: words (also sounds, symbols, colors, clothes, etc.) only have meaning, or only have very specific *kinds* of meaning, given the context of time, place, and culturally-agreed-upon connotations. Think of the word *bitch*. With a denotation that has its roots in canine genitalia dating back to the first millennium, its twenty-first-century meaning is entirely contingent on who is saying it, to whom one is saying it, and where, when, and why one is saying it. Girlfriends saying "bitch, please" to one another during a mani-pedi in Miami conjures a different meaning than a political leader describing a colleague as a bitch on the floor of Parliament. And all this, of course, is different from the meanings created by the 1980s vernacular "bitchin' Camaro" or even a 1960s surfer commenting on the "bitchin' waves." In other words, meanings are made by time and place. And so is music. As music theorist Theodore Gracyk states, "as a specifically musical gesture, a guitar riff or a melody or a dissonant voice is strangely mute. It represents nothing [at] all. Its capacity to mean anything, to convey one meaning rather than another or to support one ideology rather than another, rests on its relationship to previous music."[6] How this is done by and in DC hardcore will be explored in subsequent chapters, but suffice to say in chapter 1, we should see cities as places and spaces that at once help create and are created by music, and also as places and spaces in which music is consumed—on record players in living rooms as teenagers, in basements of buildings as college students, in outdoor amphitheaters in parks with your children—and meanings about that music are made.

It is the particularities *of* those spaces and places that help inform an understanding of the music itself and thus its meaning(s). Both cities, and the music that comes from them, "encompass the physical city and its material features, including architectural edifices, the above- and below-ground crossroads, and the public and private space within a delineated geographic boundary, as well as the symbolic city, which is to say the representational expressions of urban cultures, experiences, and identities," including their "imbalances, hierarchically structured divisions, competition, and contradictions."[7] In this way, music and place and space are inextricable from how music is understood, how its "communicative structures cohere," and how it is "made sensible and bestowed with values and meanings in social terms."[8] The experience of music depends on place and space.

The Washington, DC, hardcore scene was no exception. Hardcore punks actively engaged "with the social, political, and economic realms that [underlay]"[9] their city, and their music and their scene worked to help define spatial relations between Washington, DC, as a region, as part of the larger country, and as a part of their own identity. DC's distinctive qualities all contributed both to the ways in which music was created and to the ways in which it was consumed. Understanding this relationship includes asking how social conditions—including racial and socioeconomic composition, prevailing political positions, cultural expectations, and spatial and geographic realities—in Washington, DC, from 1978 to 1983 could alter, influence, form, and help construct both the sound of hardcore punk and its concurrent sociopolitical meanings. This includes the musics of DC's spaces and places—and the ways in which music- and place-based identities were formed, survived, or lost. As the preceding paragraphs imply, it was the unique intersection of DC's sociopolitical, economic, and spatial histories, along with its soundscapes and cultural production landscapes, that provided the foundation for one of the city's most unique and symbolic musical sounds: hardcore punk.

A Very Short History of DC

The Potomac region—long before it was designated as the District of Columbia or crowned as the nation's capital—was first settled in the early 1600s, primarily by groups from three disparate cultures. First there was the indigenous population, who settled around what would later be the delineation of DC proper, as well as along the waterways in later-day Maryland and Virginia, subsisting on an agrarian model of hunting, farming, and fishing. As much of the history of the United States bears out, the second group—English colonial settlers primarily moving north from Jamestown, Virginia—entered the Potomac region and eventually attacked and nearly eradicated this native population, occupying the land for themselves, their families, and the tobacco farms that would come to be an economic demigod for the area. The third group was likewise a product of the historical US narrative of colonization, enslavement, and white domination, and one that foretold the divisions that would come to epitomize the racial divide in DC in the 1970s and 1980s—slaves from West Africa. Although some black people arrived as laborers and servants in the early second decade of 1600 and worked in the tobacco fields, by the 1660s these individuals were nearly unilaterally enslaved by their English bosses, joined by literal boatloads of already enslaved Africans shipped to the Potomac region.

More than a century later, the seeds of revolution had been sown and opposition to English rule had reached a fever pitch in many of the colonies, among them the northern Virginia towns of Fairfax and Alexandria, the former of which formed the country's first militia unit with George Washington as its commander. The thirteen original colonies were pronounced free by the time the war had ended in 1783, and, after the collapse of the Articles of Confederation, the newly united nation ratified its Constitution. As a part of this new document, Congress was given the power to establish a federal capital, including its location, oversight of its planning, and the assignation of a formal government. By 1790, the Potomac region and the ten-mile-square radius that had been cobbled together from parcels of Virginia and Maryland had become as a federal district "Columbia" and as a city district "Washington." A decade later, Washington had officially become the federal capital.

The first few decades of the new century were characterized by fights over home rule and representation;[10] the slow but steady construction of federal buildings such as the White House, the Capitol, and Marine Barracks; canals to increase trade along the Potomac River; and neighborhoods such as Navy Yard and Capitol Hill, all in defiance of the War of 1812, which saw the destruction of government buildings, including the White House. These years were also punctuated by a growing black population, the majority of whom were free blacks enticed to the city by the availability of work; this population was in stark contrast to the discriminatory and racist black code laws passed by DC, as well as the city's positioning as a center for slave trading. Juxtaposed with this free and enslaved black population were the so-called Washington elite, the white, upper-class political officials that both lived and worked in the city. Not to be forgotten were the middle-class Washingtonians, also white, who owned restaurants, shops, and saloons and worked as clerks or bookkeepers, in addition to the white laboring class, who worked as fishermen, craftsmen, and servicemen for those middle-class proprietors. As the power of the federal government grew between the 1820s and the 1860s, so too did federal-related commerce (primarily in the form of construction of federal buildings), as well as the neighborhoods that began to flourish in the city. More than ten thousand people were inhabiting southwest Washington by 1860, and new neighborhoods like Foggy Bottom, Anacostia, and Judiciary Square attracted individuals from all social classes and ethnic backgrounds.

The Civil War radically altered not only the trajectory and sociopolitical landscape of the United States but also the citizens of the capital city itself. The war's first battle in Bull Run, just thirty miles away from the capital, foretold the vast changes that would occur in the city. DC became the center of the national war effort and simultaneously became a beacon of modernization because of that effort; as floods of people came to the city in the form of soldiers, relief workers, and refugees from the war, city services—including sanitation, education, transportation, health care, and fire and police protection—were shored up through the allocation of funds and the hiring of new employees.

By the end of the war, with the fall of Richmond, the surrender of Robert E. Lee, and a cumulative death toll of roughly six hundred twenty thousand, which included the assassination of President Abraham Lincoln as a reaction to the Union victory, Washington, DC, had suffered physical, emotional, and economic damages that were slow in healing. Reconstruction ushered in a new era of the federal government, expanding its role and powers in a way that had a massive impact on the city itself. Intervening in civic matters such as black voting rights, education, and public works projects, the federal government sought to lead by example on the issue of black civil rights (and the Republican party hoped to gain the everlasting loyalty of newly enfranchised blacks), while simultaneously taking away the city's ability to home-rule in 1874. At the same time, new leaders in the black community emerged from the city, including Frederick Douglass, embracing DC's slowly shifting tides of economic, social, and political opportunity. The city itself—and its place as not just a political but also a cultural, social, and economic center—was also expanding with the construction of W. W. Corcoran's Gallery of Art in 1871, the Center Market in 1872, a new railroad station 1873, and the resumption of construction on the Washington Monument in 1880.

The turn of the century brought with it the "City Beautiful" movement in Washington, DC, promoting the city as a shining beacon of the nation, replete with better parks, new monuments and bridges, and marble-laden buildings. Simultaneously, neighborhoods within the city limits were growing and changing, each with their own unique persona and inhabitants. Capitol Hill housed middle-class blacks and whites in unpretentious abodes, and Southwest boasted smaller rowhouses for the laborers. Northwest, on the other hand, developed into an upper-class enclave, with Dupont and Logan Circles, Kalorama, and streets around Connecticut and Massachusetts Avenues featuring mansions. Both inside and just outside the District, suburbs were beginning to pop up in neighborhoods like Mount Pleasant, Le Droit Park, Chevy Chase, and Brookland, as well as across the line in Maryland and Virginia. This rapidly expanding housing market aligned with the growth of government jobs, and, as a result, a growth in the private sector as more occupants needed more services. Alongside that, Washington, DC, became a publishing center, with nearly seventy-five newspapers active in 1905, including the *Washington Post* and the black-centered *Washington Bee*.

World War I brought a temporary influx of new federal employees to the city in order to manage the war effort, prompting housing, food, and transportation shortages. Other changes were also occurring in the District. The women's suffrage movement picketed the White House and finally received President Wilson's endorsement as the Nineteenth Amendment was passed in 1920; after World War I, the racial tensions always brewing in the city reached a boiling point, with daily discrimination and segregation compounding a loss of civil rights in the previous years, leading to a five-day race riot in DC.

The racial tensions did not, of course, end with the end of the riots. Throughout the next four decades, Washington, DC, emerged as a city split in two. One city was the pristine, white testament to the nation's capital, epitomized by the building of the Lincoln Memorial in 1922, the Mall in 1933, the Supreme Court in 1935, and the National Gallery of Art in 1942. The other city was the residential, private, and often shoddier face of DC, as the population doubled in the 1930s requiring nearly one-third of all of the city's land used for housing. This dual-faced city was also dichotomized by race, with black and white occupants firmly ensconced in separate neighborhoods. Blacks primarily lived in Northwest, with other strong communities in Foggy Bottom and Southwest, while new housing was chiefly built for whites who resided in Burleith and neighborhoods near American University. Gentrification was already afoot in Georgetown, with white homeowners pushing out working-class and black renters, and suburban sprawl had spilled in Virginia via Arlington and into Maryland through Takoma Park, Silver Spring, and Bethesda, all white havens of different income levels.

In the 1940s and 1950s, as national campaigns against discrimination and segregation began making their way into the public consciousness and the public justice system, Washington, DC, not only followed suit but also set the precedent for these sociocultural and legal battles. The National Committee on Segregation in the Nation's Capital included a bevy of legal, academic, and political superstars and fought for economic, residential, political, and social justice, publishing a blistering 1948 report named *Segregation in Washington* to illustrate the everyday realities and sociopolitical and economic implications of segregation. Another group, the Coordinating Committee for the Enforcement of the DC Anti-Discrimination Laws, took legal action up to the Supreme Court, which ruled in 1953 that the city's civil rights acts from 1872 and 1873 were still valid, thereby ending segregation of public services (at least officially, and not including public schools). The fight over public schools, however, also centered in DC, with the Strayer Report, a Congressionally authorized study of public-school systems that unsurprisingly found that black schools had fewer buildings, less money, and fewer teachers than white schools, correlating to lower test scores for black students. Adding to DC's racial legal woes, Howard law school professor James Nabrit sued the DC Board of Education for turning away black students to a newly constructed junior high school, which, on appeal to the Supreme Court, was joined with the famed *Brown v. Board of Education* case from Topeka, Kansas. The reaction by the DC Board of Education was swift, integrating the school system immediately in September of 1954.

DC in the Mid-20th Century

The two decades preceding the birth of hardcore in Washington, DC, saw a continuation of the struggles the city had endured since its establishment as the nation's capital. As the seat of the world's superpower, DC was at the center of a network of programs, agencies, and administrations that included thousands of US and foreign dignitaries and politicians, not to mention private companies, organizations, and associations created to sway and influence those dignitaries and politicians. At the same time, DC was perpetually growing and changing with the demographics, neighborhoods, and overarching built environment shifting to reflect the influxes of new immigrants, new federal employees, new institutions, and gentrification programs that abounded within the city and its outlying metropolitan areas. The following sections provide a short and admittedly streamlined picture of what Washington, DC, looked like in the mid-twentieth century, a social, political, and economic milieu that, in conjunction with the cultural landscape, provided fertile ground for the DC hardcore scene that sprouted up and ultimately thrived for a few glorious years in the sun.

THE SOCIOPOLITICAL LANDSCAPE

The 1960s and early 1970s in Washington, DC, were punctuated by civil-rights campaigns such as the March on Washington, the Student Nonviolent Coordinating Committee (SNCC), and the Poor People's Campaign, violence in the form of riots after the assassination of Martin Luther King Jr., the seemingly endless war in Vietnam, a rotating cast of presidents from Kennedy to Johnson to Nixon to Carter, and a fight to reclaim self-governance for the city including the Twenty-Third Amendment in 1961—which gave DC residents the ability to vote for president and vice president—the 1967 appointment by President Johnson of the first mayor of DC, Walter Washington, and the Home Rule Act of 1973 that formed a city council and allowed residents to choose their own mayor, who, in 1978, was Marion Barry, formerly founding student chair of SNCC.

By 1978, the second year of Jimmy Carter's presidency and arguably the birth of the DC hardcore scene, the US economy was plummeting: inflation was sky-high, the cost of living had increased dramatically, prices on everyday items were out of control, there was an oil embargo and ensuing energy crisis, and government attempts to battle these economic dangers failed on a grand and public scale. Attitudes toward debt and consumption had also shifted, with the advent and wide dissemination of credit cards, devaluation of savings funds, and continual near-idolization of conspicuous consumption. At the same time, international market competition had an upsurge, slowly prying loose the chokehold the United States had had in the business and manufacturing world. The political environment of the country was equally polluted. Carter had already entered office encumbered by an endemic distrust of government; after the disasters of the Vietnam War and Watergate, the public had lost faith in both the moral compass of their elected officials and their ability to solve any of the nation's most pressing problems. As Carter dubbed it, a "malaise" had beset the country, a condition diagnosed by "a crisis of confidence . . . that strikes at the very soul and spirit of our national will,"[11] only exacerbated by his administration's powerlessness to resolve the economic and energy crises. Trust in government, and its adjacent institutions—the media, the military, and even professionals such as doctors and lawyers—was at an all-time low: down from 80 percent in the 1950s to 33 percent in 1976.[12]

This portrait of government, and by extension the city of Washington, DC, which had become an easy metaphor of that government, was painted with the patina of incompetence, overreach, and micromanagement—a depiction that set the stage for a simmering antiliberalism and the 1980 election of Ronald Reagan to the presidency. Campaigning on a softened version of conservative extremism, Reagan played to antielitism and a promise of a tax revolution, shoring up all at once class and racial resentments in addition to social and cultural disparities. Intellectuals (also known as bureaucrats) were portrayed as affirmative-action-loving, middle-class-hating Democrats, and the big-tax government was splattered with allegations of taking "our" money to fund "them"—social welfare programs that disproportionately benefited people of color. After the years of women's liberation and changing social mores, Reagan's brand of conservatism promised a return to family values, abjuring the immorality and wantonness of expanded sexual and gender roles, as well as its implications for the government. The former California governor's election, however, seemed not as much an unambiguous adoption of the neoconservative ideology but more of a referendum on the country's feelings toward the government.

Yet the nostalgic, near-obsessive romanticization and glorification of Reagan that so often occurs on the right in contemporary society was nowhere to be seen in the first years of his presidency. By 1982, two years into his first term, a recession loomed large as the manufacturing industry neared insolvency, unemployment rocketed, and the economy continued to wither. And after cutting a panoply of social-welfare programs, drug abusers and mentally ill patients were kicked out of institutions, causing a surge in homelessness; all this reflected in Reagan's approval rating, which had nose-dived to a meager 35 percent.[13]

PLACE, CLASS, AND RACE: A CITY DIVIDED

Despite the larger national trends and overarching political undercurrents in the late 1970s and early 1980s, the city of DC did not act as a direct reflection of the bigger partisan or demographic topography. Undoubtedly influenced by the prevailing political winds, particularly with the government-centric workforce populating the city, Washington was also a unique and dichotomous microcosm of the race- and class-based contradictions and contrasts occurring in the rest of the country.

The end of World War II had seen an explosion of urban growth in the city, cementing the changing residential demographics of DC and altering the residential landscape. A postwar economic boom not only brought more jobs in both the public and private sector, but also an explosion of construction, with any remaining space in the city filled with apartments and houses. The population of DC had doubled between 1940 and 1950, and then doubled once again between 1950 and 1970. This new construction frenzy spilled over to the immediate suburbs of Virginia and Maryland, trying to meet the growing housing needs of a growing population with the help of federal policies that created the Interstate Highway program and connected the suburbs to the city in what was come to be called the Beltway, as well as subsided home loans through the Federal Housing Administration and the Veterans Administration.

Such federal housing policies in the 1950s and 1960s were, however, explicitly and definitively limited to white citizens, upholding the spatial segregation already happening in the city and foreshadowing its endurance in the suburbs in a phenomenon known as "white flight." The racial composition of the District and the suburbs also fluctuated greatly; in 1950 there were a little over five hundred thousand whites and only about two hundred eighty thousand blacks living in the city, but by 1970 those numbers had almost inversely switched (209,272 whites and 537,712 blacks), a trend that was sustained until 1980 (with fewer than one hundred seventy-two thousand whites and almost four hundred fifty thousand blacks).[14] Nearly all the expansion in the suburbs was from the settlement of white families from other places in the country, and most of the African American newcomers, with strong roots in Virginia and the Carolinas, inhabited DC. Moreover, the US Immigration Act of 1965, which eliminated a national-origin quota system, as well as the Refugee Act of 1980, which offered political asylum to a larger number of individuals from communist countries, greatly added to the diverse ethnicity of the city's inhabitants. This racially divided geography also applied in the city itself, which saw segregation in housing and neighborhoods based primarily on race and secondarily on class. Urban renewal programs in the 1960s and 1970s attempted to "clean" the streets of the District, targeting Southwest neighborhoods that were primarily black and using the tool of eminent domain to bulldoze more than five hundred acres, six thousand homes, and fifteen hundred businesses, leaving about twenty-three thousand DC residents, most of whom were black, displaced and without reasonable recompence.[15]

Throughout the 1960s and '70s, DC's residents, marked clearly by their minority race status, still suffered from substantial income and socioeconomic disparities. In part, the inequities were a vestige of more than a century of racist political and economic policies, including the disenfranchisement of black DC residents, tax policies that unfairly targeted blacks, restrictions on employment opportunities and sectors, and restrictive racial covenants for housing and loans. These economic inequalities were exacerbated by the race riots of 1968. Sparked by the assassination of Martin Luther King Jr. and culminating in looting, violence, the destruction of many black neighborhoods and the use of federal troops to quell the uprising, the city suffered during nearly a decade of economic and social recovery. With more than eight hundred fires, twelve deaths, and more than a thousand more injured, a number of consequences beyond the fiscal surfaced, including the rapid protraction of self-selected segregation and the flight of middle-class African Americans from the once-flourishing U Street and Cardozo neighborhood.[16] As a consequence of the rapidly shifting city demographics, the distinction between races and classes became both conflated and more pronounced. The glistening white purity of the White House and its inhabitants stood in clear and ugly contrast with the poverty in which refugees, immigrants, and minorities were living only blocks away.

By the 1970s, another wave of gentrification occurred in DC, principally as a consequence of young professionals rejecting the suburbs and being enticed to the cities. Indeed, at the end of the decade, nearly 15 percent of apartments in the city had already been—or were going to be—converted into condominiums. And despite the political and legal action taken by DC residents for whom displacement loomed large, as well as the victories they won through the city council such as rent control, first rights to purchase, and a cessation of condo conversions, the city was unequivocally divided spatially along race and class lines.

ANACOSTIA   Bisected by the river, Anacostia was historically the neglected stepchild of the city, developing as a neighborhood known in the late 1970s as both a cohesive and strong community for blacks and, simultaneously and somewhat contradictorily, as a "symbol of urban decay and danger."[17] Like the racial demography of many DC neighborhoods, Anacostia's population originally consisted mainly of whites, who made up a whopping 82 percent of its population in 1950. By the time the era of civil rights had dawned, and after the 1968 riots in DC, blacks in Anacostia had become the majority. In part because of white flight to the suburbs and in part because of the gentrification of other neighborhoods under the veneer of urban renewal, the Southeast continued to be abandoned. In 1970 the vacancy rate was 4.5 percent in Anacostia, in contrast to the DC-wide rate of just 2.8 percent; meanwhile, 75 percent of zoning was for apartments in Anacostia, in contrast with the rest of the city, where zoning laws required at least 80 percent of housing to be for single family dwellings.[18] In fact, a 1970 DC Department of Urban Renewal report found that such zoning laws created a "captive real estate market" that restricted "the movement of the black population into the suburbs" and was "discriminatory in a geographic sense because of its denial and/or discouragement of adequate home ownership opportunities in one part of the city."[19] When a townhouse development went up in Anacostia in 1975, it was the first development of single-family dwellings to be built in twenty-five years.

In addition to the racialized and classed spatial discrimination in Anacostia, city services were scarce and inadequate: public schools were crumbling and overloaded, mass transportation was scanty, and public spaces were woefully missing. Anacostia had no health-care facilities, compelling residents to cross the river to DC General Hospital; at the same time, more than 83 percent of Anacostia schools were over stipulated volume, and despite the need for mass transit in a neighborhood whose topography made bus routes unfeasible, Metro tried—and failed—to bypass Anacostia completely. A 1972 challenge by the Anacostia Economic Development Corporation saved the Metro stop, but it was the last to be built, circumventing the nearly hundred sixty thousand people who would benefit from the transportation.

CAPITOL HILL, ADAMS MORGAN, AND GENTRIFICATION   As previously mentioned, waving the banner of "restoration" the historically poor and black areas of Washington became targets of upper- and middle-class gentrification in the late 1960s and into the 1970s and '80s. Most of these neighborhoods had been decaying, with real estate stagnating and houses that had been "run down by overcrowding and the combined neglect of tenants, landlords and cautious bankers."[20] Buying up inexpensive properties in Capitol Hill, Foggy Bottom, Mount Pleasant, Logan Circle, and Adams Morgan, the demographics of these neighborhoods became clear quickly: white, well-off individuals. In some cases, these people were hoping for a real estate boom, attempting to restore and flip these houses, selling them to the increasing influx of back-to-the-city whites; others were simply interested in the multiracial character of the neighborhoods, as well as their suitability for commuting.[21] Either way, the end was the same—the displacement of poor and often black and Latino families who were exiled by rising rent and mortgage prices.

GEORGETOWN   Georgetown, arguably the birthplace of the DC punk rock scene, had, in the late 1970s and early 1980s, the same restoration and gentrification attitude as other historical neighborhoods. In 1791 Scottish settlers laid out a tract in Georgetown called New Scotland in what was then Maryland. Georgetown (or George Town, as it was first known) was meant as a lynchpin in not just the north-to-south trading route in the colonies but also as an international trade center. Centered on the waterfront, Georgetown was conceived as, first and foremost, a port.

By 1800, Georgetown was incorporated into Washington, and the census counted three thousand residents in Georgetown. The 1800s continued prosperously for the (white, upper-class) few, with mansions still standing today built in the first decade of the new century, including Dumbarton Oaks and Tudor Place, as well as the establishment of what would become Georgetown University, which gave out its first degrees in 1817. After the Civil War, Georgetown's African American population thrived, as newly freed slaves migrated to the neighborhood and the area with its waterfront flourished. However, the next decade saw flooding from the Potomac River that damaged the C&O Canal and, with it, the Canal Company, the major source of the economy. Georgetown suffered economically for the next couple of decades, even earning a reputation as one of the worst slums in the cities with abandoned and dilapidated houses lining the streets.

One of the first major waves of gentrification that would later engulf the city—and still continues into the second decade of the twenty-first century—began in Georgetown in the 1920s. The working-class populations of blacks and Irish who rented rooms and lived in alley housing were slowly pushed out by the influx of new federal workers after World War I and courtesy of the New Deal, who bought up properties to renovate and live in and established all-white homeowners' associations to maintain neighborhood control. Such a power play was aided by the Supreme Court decision in *Corrigan v. Buckley*, which upheld racial covenants, making black home ownership nearly impossible. Two decades later, Georgetown legally acquired the status of a historic district, which served to fortify its exclusive nature, driving up both property taxes and housing prices.

Georgetown became the seat of the new bourgeoisie, where there was "a disproportionately high incidence of 'money and brains' and 'bohemian mix' neighborhoods."[22] Georgetown was the symbol of gentrification in DC and in the 1970s finally reached its exalted rank in "the 'influence industry," with its emphasis on the iconography of prestige and image,"[23] when the waterfront was secured by a national park and a rapid development of high-end boutiques took over the main streets of the neighborhood. Transforming to fit its moneyed population, Georgetown was marked by changes in businesses and shops, housing prices and real estate, adamantly fighting every attempt to bring a Metro stop and its accompanying (unwanted, less-moneyed) passengers to the neighborhood. Signified within these developments was of course not simply the built environment itself, but the connotations that accompanied such expansion. Georgetown was a site of "spectacle and display,"[24] where "implicated in [a] purchase, be it of gourmet ice cream, a nouvelle cuisine meal, or a dance lesson, is the status of being at that shop in that neighborhood and buying that particular brand."[25]

Despite the pageantry of this particular neighborhood, Georgetown was in no way representative of the rest of the city, where enclaves of poor, racially, economically, and politically marginalized communities were housed in areas next to upscale shopping centers and decadent government buildings. The predominantly white, upper-class citizenry of Georgetown was often seen to have "an atmosphere of lingering Jim Crow . . . especially among older residents and the wealthier older guard."[26] Georgetown was the privileged, elite, and white corollary to the predominantly black, disempowered underclass that bordered it. The area was an emblem of what DC wanted to be or projected itself to be—powerful, influential, rich—more than a true representation of what it was.

A Very Short History of DC Music

Despite its storied history and metaphoric prestige as the nation's capital, Washington, DC, as a city did not have a musical identity in any cohesive sense until the late 1970s, when hardcore punk became (part of) that definition.[27] Chicago was home to the blues; Nashville had country; New Orleans claimed jazz; and San Francisco birthed acid rock. But DC was different. Although it laid claim as the birthplace of many a famous and diverse musician (including Duke Ellington, Marvin Gaye, Tim Buckley, Shirley Horn, Eva Cassidy, and Al Jolson) and boasted some of the most popular music venues in the 1970s and 1980s (the Bayou, the Cellar Door, the Warner Theater, and the Crazy Horse, just to name a few), the city had not produced a homegrown, consistent genre of music.

JAZZ IN DC

In part, DC can be understood both contemporaneously and historically as a breeding ground for jazz musicians, with its institutional benefactors like the Smithsonian, the Kennedy Center, the Duke Ellington School of Music, Howard University, and the Library of Congress, and acting as a platform to "nurture players who often set out for New York, Nashville, Chicago, and Los Angeles to leave their marks."[28] The District did, however, have a thriving, African American–based musical community centered on jazz in the U Street area during the 1920s and '30s. As racial tensions steadily increased during these decades, U Street became a primarily black neighborhood, blossoming with African American–owned businesses like supper clubs, restaurants, and the aforementioned jazz clubs, and the neighborhood symbolized the influence and magnitude of the black community in DC, as well as in the jazz scene.

Nicknamed the "Black Broadway" by jazz singer Pearl Bailey, U Street was lined with jazz clubs like Bohemian Caverns, Republic Gardens, Lincoln Colonnade, the Jungle Inn, and True Reformers Hall. Often these clubs, halls, and stages were filled not by Washingtonian musicians, per se, but by traveling musicians and artists that filled the seats. For instance, Billie Holiday sang "Strange Fruit" at Howard University in the spring of 1940 and had a three-week residency at Club Bali in 1949, where she broke the club record for number of shows. Club Bali was also where legends like Louis Armstrong, Sarah Vaughan, and Lester Young played. And as ragtime descended in popularity, Jelly Roll Morton became a resident of DC in 1935, playing and managing at the Jungle Inn, the first integrated club on U Street.

Of course, any history of DC jazz, even one this brief, must include DC native and local hero Duke Ellington. Born to two piano-playing parents and raised in the northwest corridor of DC, Ellington began slipping into Frank's Holiday Poolroom through an alley across the way from Howard University, at fourteen years old, absorbing the music and techniques of ragtime pianists Cliff Jackson, Claude Hopkins, Eubie Blake, and Doc Perry, among others. His education at Dunbar High School, a segregated black secondary school known for its high academic standards, was essential in formulating Ellington's musical knowledge. One teacher, Henry Lee Grant, gave Ellington private lessons to teach him harmony, while another, Doc Perry, taught him to read sheet music. It was in DC that Ellington began writing his first songs and formed his first dance band, Duke's Serenaders, who played their first gig at True Reformers Hall, just a couple of blocks down from Ellington's childhood home. Between 1917 and 1923, Ellington played gigs and in local clubs and cafés around DC, including the Howard Theatre, and even performed at embassy parties and private social balls both in the city and in Virginia, playing for segregated audiences in a time when to do so was extremely rare. Despite Ellington's financial and cultural success, the DC jazz scene ultimately proved too small for Ellington, who left the city to pursue his career in Harlem in 1923, landing his famous gig at the Cotton Club four years later. Ellington later named his band the Washingtonians in honor of his hometown, and despite his success in New York, frequently returned to play in DC throughout the next few decades until his death in 1979.

By the 1940s, the jazz scene in DC had slowly begun to change. The integration of jazz began in earnest thanks in part the Ertegun brothers, Ahmet and Nesuhi, who came to the city as sons of the Turkish ambassador to the United States. (Ahmet later went on to cocreate Atlantic Records with Herb Abramson.) Although "whites had long gone to U Street and the Howard Theatre to hear Great Black Music,"[29] no concentrated effort to market integrated music events had occurred until the Erteguns. As Nesuhi later recalled in an interview with the *Washington Post*, "Jazz was our weapon for social action."[30] Inspired by their success, Benjamin Caldwell, the owner of Club Bali, opened a new space in 1947, Music Hall, at Ninth and V Streets NW and with it a nondiscriminatory policy for both musicians and audiences, launching one of the first music spaces with mixed-race crowds and bands. Just a year later, a popular disk jockey at radio station WWDC, Willis Conover, also contributed to the integration of DC jazz, holding the first of many mixed-race jazz concerts at venues such as the All Souls Unitarian Church, the National Press Club, and the newly opened Music Hall.

Jazz even started to make its way into the *other* DC—the federal government—to mixed effect. Despite the Eisenhower administration's development of the Jazz Ambassadors program in the 1950s, a State Department creation that was meant to use jazz as a tool of the Cold War by sending jazz musicians to Iraq, Greece, the Soviet Union, and Egypt to spread its cultural message, the program was met with resistance by the racists inhabiting the legislative branch, including senators from the Deep South. The potent symbol of jazz as an American music, as *the* American music, not only was clearly fraught with problems of appropriation and discrimination but was also resisted by large swaths of both congressmen and American people who feared it was a "plot to mongrelize America," according to the White Citizens Council of Alabama.[31] Jazz was not fully accepted into the centralized DC mainstream, or as Huddy "Leadbelly" Ledbetter put it, "this bourgeoise town," until 1962, when for the first time in history, jazz was played in the White House with the Paul Winter Jazz Sextet playing during a children's program in the East Wing. That same year, Howard University began a jazz studies program, and two years later Washingtonians voted for president for the first time since 1800. Yet it was not until 1987 that Congress, under a bill sponsored by John Coyers of Detroit, Michigan, voted to preserve jazz as "a national treasure." Under HR 57, Conyers defined jazz as "a unifying force, bridging cultural, religious, ethnic, and age differences in our diverse society," and a recognition of "the African American experience." The bill of the same name also spurred HR-57, a jazz club and preservation center in DC, which opened in 1993.

BLUEGRASS IN DC

While rarely a feature of DC's musical history, bluegrass was also a crucial aspect of the local music scene, first gaining a foothold in the capital after World War II, when Appalachians from West Virginia and other southern and mountain regions came to the city for jobs, bringing with them their musical talents and preferences. Radio stations took notice, with a handful in Virginia and Maryland—WKCW in Warrenton, WARL in Arlington, WGAY in Silver Spring, and WDON in Wheaton—dedicating large chunks of hours to bluegrass programming. By the 1950s, DC had a blossoming bluegrass scene of its own, with genre-shaping bands and virtuoso talents in the form of Buzz Busby and the Bayou Boys, the Country Gentleman, and Seldom Scene.

By the 1960s bluegrass in DC had found its home at a local bar-turned-music-hall in South Arlington, Virginia: The Birchmere. While the owner Gary Oeleze had no affinity for bluegrass, nor any intention of turning the restaurant he purchased into a music venue, he needed the customer revenue at night, saw the burgeoning bluegrass scene, and wanted to give the musicians a place to play that respected the genre. Oeleze attempted to legitimize bluegrass as a music, putting up signs asking the audience to remain quiet during the performances and enforcing the rule by throwing out a dozen patrons in one night alone. The Birchmere became the home for not only local bluegrass acts but any bluegrass bands traveling up and down the East Coast.

The '60s also saw the first bluegrass festivals (the original in Fincastle, Virginia, located just a short drive away from DC) and featuring talent from DC, Baltimore, and Kentucky. Around the same time, in the middle of the decade, WAMU—the local FM station in DC—began bluegrass programming, sometimes having up to forty hours a week of just bluegrass.[32] Both these events are credited with bringing bluegrass more into the mainstream, particularly in DC, where President Jimmy Carter invited Bill Monroe and the Seldom Scene to perform at the White House in 1980. Indeed, the 1970s and 1980s saw a revitalization of bluegrass, with weekly bookings of bluegrass acts in clubs and music halls (in addition to the Birchmere, the Red Fox Inn at Bethesda, Maryland, was a popular venue), as well as the First Annual Indoor Bluegrass Spectacular on March 11, 1979, at the Capital Centre, hosting more than ten thousand fans of bluegrass. Acts like Patent Pending, the Johnson Mountain Boys, and Eddie and Martha Adcock grew from the tight-knit DC scene and are said to have served as inspiration for the US Navy's launching of its own DC-based bluegrass band, Country Current. Indeed, by 1983, the *Washington Post* touted that "Washington is the acknowledged capital of bluegrass."[33]

DC'S OTHER MUSICAL CULTURE

The primary focus of the city's musical ambitions was not, however, entrenched in the jazz-soaked, segregated streets of the U Street area or the country-inflected sound of bluegrass but instead was built both on the assumption of "high" culture's superiority and DC elite's fears of cultural mediocrity. Like much of the history of DC as a place, its musical history is premised on institutions thought to represent the (white) majesty, standing, and power of the city, as well as the hand and financial backing of government.

The United States Marine Band was established by Congress in 1798 and was frequently invited to the White House to play patriotic hymns, originally composed marches, and the national anthem. Since that time, a bevy of high-brow musical institutions have been chartered and funded (at least in part) by the federal government, including the National Symphony Orchestra in 1931, after failing to survive earlier in the decade. Playing to white audiences in Constitution Hall, and outdoor concerts on the Watergate barge starting in the summer of 1935, the National Symphony was often joined by Marine and Army bands, as well as other city's orchestras. Around the same time, concerts and recitals were held at the Phillips Gallery near Dupont Circle and, after two endowments in the 1930s, chamber music concerts began to take place at the Library of Congress. Despite these federally funded shows and concerts, as DC historian Keith Melder notes, "The capital could not claim to be a center of show business or the performing arts."[34]

Disappointments did not prevent the city from trying. The Washington National Opera was established in 1956 by music critic (formerly of the *Washington Star*) Day Thorpe, along with Paul Callaway as its first music director, the former choirmaster and organist of the National Cathedral. With ten thousand dollars of seed money from patrons Gregory and Peggy Smith, the National Opera first put on Mozart's *Abduction from the Seraglio* in 1957 at George Washington University's Lisner Auditorium. By 1958, Washington, DC, was accruing some acclaim from such influential publications as *Newsweek*, which proclaimed it "The Sparkle on the Potomac," and the *New York Times*, which declared the National Opera to be "The Capital Revival." However, lack of steady funds and of a formerly conceived company meant that each production of the Washington National Opera was done individually, and to various degrees of success throughout the 1960s. With the concurrent creation of the John F. Kennedy Center for Performing Arts in 1971, the National Opera finally found its permanent home.

It should be noted that during these decades, and regardless of certain publications' often-tepid accolades, DC was still regarded as an abyss of

proper "culture." A 1962 *London Times* writer described DC as "culturally
. . . among the underdeveloped capitals of this world,"[35] and President
Kennedy himself lamented to the Trustees and Advisory Committee of
the National Cultural Center in 1961 that "Washington lacks great assets
which London, Paris, Rome, and even Moscow have in being centers not
only of government but also of national cultural activities."[36] It is perhaps
ironic then, that it was the Kennedy Center, nestled on the banks of the
Potomac near the Lincoln Memorial, that ten years later loomed largely
as an emblem of both DC's political pedigree and its cultural aspirations.
Rooted in the 1958 passage of the National Cultural Center Act, the Kennedy Center was designated in 1963 to carry out the artistic mandate of
the legislation, particularly as it applied to classical and contemporary
performances, as well as an educational center. Nearly $23 million dol-
lars later, in a private-public partnership that continues today, the Kennedy Center opened with a gala in 1971, punctuated by the opening of
a world premiere by composer and conductor Leonard Bernstein, with
a performance of a requiem mass honoring President Kennedy. Finally,
DC's cultural scene had arrived. At least according, once again, to conventional cultural institutions. The *New York Times* lauded the Kennedy
Center after its opening, crowing, "The capital of this nation finally strode
into the cultural age tonight with the spectacular opening of the $70 mil-
lion [Kennedy Center,] . . . a gigantic marble temple to music, dance, and
drama on the Potomac's edge."[37]

It seems, once again, that only a specific *type* of music was understood
as culture, and only a certain *genre* of sound was classified as worthy of
congressional funds and acknowledgment. Indeed, the *New York Times*
superciliously declared in their 1980 Arts and Leisure section that "Washington today is a changed city—no longer a cultural backwater but a
metropolis where the arts are thriving"[38] citing the Washington Opera
and the National Symphony Orchestra as evidence. Not only did this
writer unsurprisingly devalue any other forms of music in DC before
these groups, including the jazz scene of the '20s and '30s, as "cultural
backwater[s]," along with the racial and economic implications connoted
in such a label, but he also reified one particular form of music as "real"
arts, music that, once again, suggests certain socioeconomic and racial
standing. The association between conventionally high-class music and

culture has a long history in the city: local citizen J. Hillary Taylor pleaded with Congress in a 1948 letter to the editor to fund "this magnificent cultural goal" of a classical music conservatory;[39] another DC resident suggested that "Washington, DC [was] a pool of intellectual and cultural stagnation" in his 1953 letter;[40] and *Washington Post* columnist Judith Martin bemoaned the fact that "concert halls are filled with lower-level culture types who are there to spin little day-dreams into music, rather than to take in sound in its purest form"[41] in 1973.

Even the music that qualified as high culture still found itself embroiled in the racial politics of the city. When famous black contralto Marian Anderson was invited in 1939 to sing in Washington, DC, the Daughters of the American Revolution (DAR) refused to allow her to perform at Constitution Hall, citing a clause in their rental contract that precluded blacks from playing in the hall. It was not until the formation of a "Marian Anderson Citizens Committee," along with the public resignation of DAR membership by First Lady Eleanor Roosevelt, that the secretary of the interior finally authorized permission for the concert to be held outside at the Lincoln Memorial. Throughout the early to mid-twentieth century, and even creeping into the latter half of the century, the cultural elites and the general public accepted Theodor Adorno's dichotomy between "serious" and "popular music," categorizing any musical culture in Washington, DC, as necessarily high culture—classical, chamber, and opera—and ignoring the rest (jazz, bluegrass) unless it was culturally and politically expedient.

GO-GO

Although this book is limited in its scope to the DC hardcore scene, it would be shamefully remiss and intellectually misleading if there were no discussion of the other musical innovation that was emerging from the streets and schools of DC at the same time: go-go. The musical and spatial history of go-go parallels that of DC hardcore and bespeaks a tale of two cities: one divided by race and class, one part visible, the other hidden. In a city still stymied in persistent prejudice, go-go epitomized the other, less visible side of DC—black, disenfranchised, ignored, but still optimistic, living for the groove.

Go-go materialized from the southeast corridor of DC—Anacostia— and the musical annals of its fellow brethren: funk, soul, and even hip-hop.

Beginning in the DC-based funk and soul-inspired bands, go-go was born fully grown in the person of Chuck Brown, the "Godfather of Go-Go," by the mid-1970s. As with punk, two noteworthy spaces became integral to the creation of go-go—schools, the bastion of youth culture, and the local clubs, the materialization of that culture. The public schools in Southeast DC served a dual function: They worked as a physical place where future members of the go-go scene could meet and bond. And they operated as an educational foundation for musicians, teaching black youth the basics of horns and percussion that became so primary to the music of go-go. High schools such as Ballou, Woodson, Coolidge, and Cardozo, while named for prominent figures in the political world of the other (powerful and white) DC, were in the 1970s still for all intents segregated, with nearly 90 percent of the students being African American and poverty-stricken. Despite problems of overcrowding, a lack of funds and disproportionate concern for "white" schools versus those in Southeast, these neighborhood high schools brought together members of the community, allowing young black students to relate. School offered a way to formulate and maintain relationships, some of which were the kernel for bands themselves. All the members of Experience Unlimited, a prominent go-go band, attended Ballou High School in Southeast, where they were "accustomed to hard work and perseverance,"[42] a work ethic that translated into their music later on. Schools also served as physical spaces for the performance of go-go; as one former Southeast student recalls, "I remember going to see my very first go-go band in 1978 . . . performing outside in an old school yard. From that moment on, I was hooked."[43] More than just the sociological inspiration and physical proximity Southeast schools offered, the DC public school system was central to emphasizing the importance of music. Marching band was a central aspect to the high school experience in Southeast, with citywide competitive events that not only made music a prominent place of pride for young African Americans but also taught them how to read standard musical notations for saxophone and trumpet players and play the drums for such future go-go percussionists as Trouble Funk's T-Bone and Junk Yard's Heavy One.[44] The heart of go-go came from these students—from the streets and poverty that forced them into these schools together, to the introduction of music that offered self-respect, and finally to the clubs where go-go exploded in Southeast DC.

Go-go was an underground music, not played on many radio stations and rarely venturing outside the confines of DC. Yet within the District, go-go popped up all over—at high schools (such as Oxen Hill and Potomac), at clubs (like Atlas Disco and Black Hole), and at recreation centers and restaurants—all of which had the common denominator of being either owned or patronized by nearly 100 percent African Americans.[45] Reclaiming or reusing urban public space was one key component of go-go. By playing outside the mainstream venues (as both a choice and an economic and physical reality) and performing shows in heavily lower socioeconomic, urban settings, go-go obscured the lines between performer and spectator.

Much as hardcore did for its scene, the music of go-go itself acted as a metaphor for this particular part of the city, at once constructing a collective identity for Southeast and offering a voice to the oft-marginalized citizens of the city. However, unlike punk songs, the songs of go-go were not laced with overtly political references, and the musical structure was not tied so intimately to feelings of rebellion and anger. Indeed, the emphasis in go-go was not on lyrics, which are often obscured by the noise level and prominence of the instrumentals, but on the groove—the sound and complementary body motion that sound inspires. What lyrics there are refer either to communal issues (e.g., Backyard's "My Block," which discusses the ills of urban life), or the groove itself, (e.g., Chuck Brown's "I Feel like Bustin' Loose" or Junk Yard's "Let the Beat Go On"). The lack of emphasis on lyrics lends itself to an underscoring of the music itself as the focus of participation, community, and identity; go-go's music functions as a unifying force, creating and maintaining community bonds in its structure and presentation.

The ritualized nature of a go-go show, along with its entrenchment in distinct places of performance, are also essential to the construction of a raced and placed identity. A Southeast identity, a black identity, is deeply rooted in the specific, local experience, which can be expressed as a go-go identity. Such an identity is necessarily contingent on exclusion in two ways: The African American, DC go-go identity is marked by its ability to give blacks a voice in a city that has traditionally marginalized and disenfranchised them, making self-identification a product of oppression and abandonment. Second, and perhaps more interesting, it is the way in which the go-go raced and placed identity is about erecting boundaries to exclude the outside world. That is, go-go became not just a product of exclusion but a tool to propagate it. As go-go producer James Avery says, "This is not just a tourist city. We live here! Our music is about that. We're really the people about the street, the people who *really* live in Washington."[46] Go-go historians Kip Lornell and Charles C. Stephenson Jr. agree, contending that "the distinctive sound of go-go provides aural evidence of blackness . . . if you understand go-go—if you get it—you're marked as both an African American and a Washingtonian."[47]

FIRST-WAVE PUNK IN DC

Although the avant-garde, proto-punk, and first-wave punk scene had, by 1976, centered itself in New York in the form of Patti Smith, Television, the New York Dolls, and the Ramones (among many, many others), its influence was slowly spreading, leaching outward and down toward the District of Columbia. Despite the fact that no punk bands had ever played in DC, and at the time the self-styled alternative radio station WHFS played less commercially viable music only at night, punk's sound found its way into the city. In part, this infiltration was thanks to Georgetown University, a Jesuit institution that was staunchly conservative but also highly prestigious and moneyed, which also boasted WGTB, a student-run radio station. The radio station, which was accused by Vice President Spiro Agnew of being "the voice of Third World communism . . . in academia,"[48] served as almost the lone voice of dissent within the tight-laced community of the university, allowing students to air not only rebellious political views but also some of the new music coming from New York's budding proto-punk scene.

A handful of punk-inspired bands sprouted in the two years before punk transformed into hardcore, playing at the few bars that would permit them, self-producing tracks in their basements, bonding together against a mainstream that rejected them, and forming the kernel of the first DC punk scene. In the summer of 1976, Overkill was saluted as the city's first punk band, with lead singer Barney Jones scaring away patrons at the soon-to-be punk-band-friendly local bar, the Keg, with his aggressive heckling of the audience and use of strange props and the band playing loud, antagonistic garage rock covers. One of the longest-running DC punk bands was the Kim Kane–led Slickee Boys. Before even playing a live show, the band recorded an EP, *Hot and Cool*, including one original song ("Manganese Android Puppies," a psychedelic-garage-rock-sounding mash-up that would have sounded at home on a later-year Jefferson Airplane album) and four covers: the Hangmen's "What a Boy Can't Be," the Yardbirds' "Psycho Daisies," an instrumental version of the theme from "Exodus," and Vince Taylor's "Brand New Cadillac." Channeling the punk DIY spirit, Kane formed his own label with a friend and put out the album on vinyl himself. Two years later, on a local label run by Rockville native and resident record-store owner of Yesterday and Today, Skip Groff, the band recorded "Mersey Mersey Me," an explosive 45 with the straightforward punk-propelled drive of "Put a Bullet thru the Jukebox," with a rant that declares "Disco sucks!/ It makes me want to puke." If not strictly a first-wave punk album in the Ramones/Dictators/Suicide strain, the Slickee Boys' pop-punk-acid-rock sound, DIY sensibilities, and provocative onstage antics made them one of DC's premier punk bands.

Other pre-'78 DC bands sought their musical muses from around the edges of punk's sound. The Look, featuring New York transplant Howard Wuelfing (who, as mentioned earlier, later wrote for the *Washington Post* on the hardcore scene) and Georgetown University Foreign Service student Robert Goldstein, combined the art-rock sounds of Roxy Music with the trash rock energy of Richard Hell and the Dictators. And American University students Keith Campbell and Roddy Frantz founded the Controls, playing a Patti Smith type of poetry-chanting, guitar-slashing, visceral punk. One of perhaps the oddest of the DC punk-style bands was White Boy, the brainchild of thirty-six-year-old James Kowalski, who dubbed himself "Mr. Ott" and enlisted his teenage son (named "Jake Whipp") and played a Suicide- and Cramps-inspired kind of punk-progressive heavy metal, with songs like "I Could Puke." According to *New Musical Express*, their 1977 DIY EP "made Iggy Pop sound like a church warden."[49] As DC residents took up guitars, formed bands, and embraced the DIY spirit, the kernels of punk took root.

Hardcore Is Born

It was in DC in the late 1970s and early 1980s that the boys who would be hardcore kings began their ascent, dragging alongside them the perhaps invisible but still tangible musical, social, historical, and political narratives of their city. Although its backstory may have started long before, the seedlings of the hardcore scene began to sprout in earnest in 1977. This was the year of the Atlantis—the soon-to-be space of punk shows that evolved into the powerhouse musical venue the 9:30 Club still rocking today—and the opening of Skip Groff's record store, Yesterday and Today, in a strip mall in Rockville, Maryland. Groff's store offered past and future punks employment and also a meeting place. Equally important was Groff's in-house studio, Inner Ear, and the founding of his label, Limp Records. But these mythic beginnings were also occurring in the most innocuous of places—at Woodrow Wilson High School in Northwest DC, where skater Ian MacKaye befriended Jeff Nelson in a tenth-grade German class; in Glover Park, where MacKaye's family took in Henry Garfield after his mother kicked him out; in the living room of Sid McCray, who shared his newly bought Sex Pistols and Damned albums with Anacostia native and African American Daryl Jenifer. The list of places and people that spurred the scene would be staggering, the coincidences and intersections and serendipitous encounters, engagements, and relationships even more so. Suffice it to say, these crevices—the gaps between people and places and spaces and ideas—are what came together, against most odds, to create the now-legendary hardcore scene in DC.

PART I

The Music of DC Hardcore

2

The Racial Aesthetics
of DC Hardcore

It is impossible to talk about DC hardcore without talking about Bad Brains, the near-indisputable kings of the scene who blazed the ferocious, powerful, and deafening trail for every DC hardcore band (not to mention hardcore bands around the country, and even grunge, metal, hard rock, hip-hop, pop, and R&B bands throughout the decades).[1] And Bad Brains cannot be talked about without mentioning race. Of course, their being black in the Chocolate City in the 1970s and early 1980s, or in the case of the Hudson brothers, right outside the city, was not unusual—it was the norm. Being black in the punk scene, however, was not quite as typical. It was downright aberrant, some might say. The same might be said of their music: succinct eruptions that nearly invariably clocked in under two minutes and thirty seconds, peppered by the seemingly impossible velocity of Dr. Know's guitar, the powerful demolition of Hudson's drums, the ominous drubbing of Darryl Jenifer's bass, and the permutation of squeals, shrieks, and maniacal rage that was HR's vocals. As Kenny Inouye, hardcore fan and future guitarist for DC band Marginal Man, explains, "Everything was so different about it—the sound, the way they played, the speed, the guitar tones. That just opened up a whole new door."[2]

This chapter uses Bad Brains, and their 1982 eponymous debut, as an exemplar of the complicated and often conflicting ways in which race is (de/re)constructed in DC hardcore, not solely because they were almost the only representation of black sound in a nationwide hardcore scene, but also because they defined and inspired what DC hardcore was. With an album of fifteen tracks in total, three of which are fairly straight-ahead reggae ("Jah Calling," "Leaving Babylon," and "I Luv I Jah"), the remaining thirteen are the authoritative and pioneering chaos that would come to be called hardcore. Their album, and its legacy both within and outside the DC scene, provides a framework in which to understand the ways in which their (white) successors reconstructed and reappropriated a complex history of racialized sound. This chapter, in part, attempts to trace what Kevin Fellezs calls in his work on jazz fusion the "continual process of transformational musical practices," including the "interaction and exchange between tradition and innovation [that] redraw musical borderlines, creating a 'new tradition' that rests atop the sedimented interchanges of the past, awaiting its own transformation."[3]

The Power of Noise: Hardcore as Jazz

Despite contentions of black essentialism, jazz (and blues) are considered a fundamental facet of black American identity. This collective construction of blackness was particularly potent through the retrospective lens of the '60s and '70s black aesthetic cultural movement, which attempted to incorporate and highlight overt political sentiments into the artistic sphere in an effort to reshape the representation of and struggle for a collective racial consciousness. Jazz, like the blues, has its origins in slavery, blending the African-inflected musical influences of additive syncopation, riffs, improvisation, and the chorus principle of the slaves with the European American musical forms of proportional syncopation, and harmony and the European-based chorded instruments introduced by white masters. With its combination of a rhythm section (drums, bass, piano, banjo) and melody instruments (trumpet, clarinet, trombone), jazz was often understood as a more lighthearted and joyful music, with its (recorded, at least) birth frequently accredited to the freed blacks of New Orleans in the early 1920s. The initial evolution of jazz—from classic to ragtime to swing and big band—was marked by the innovations, transformations, and traditions of African Americans, as well as the eventual acceptance and, in many cases, imitation and appropriation of, the genre by white musicians. In fact, the development of later jazz styles, from bebop to cool jazz to hard bop and finally free jazz, can in large part be attributed to the homogenization of early jazz sounds, primarily by radio-friendly white (and black) musicians.

What both blues and jazz share, undoubtedly, is the potential for and promise of cultural resistance for African Americans. As musical manifestations of historically contingent realities for African Americans, it is no wonder that blues and jazz became a symbol of black identity. In very tangible ways, these two genres of music were built around, and tell the story of, oppression, struggle, defiance, and, ultimately, liberation. And although such an identity never was, and could never be, monolithic, nor without its contradictions and inconsistencies, jazz and blues operated as what Langston Hughes described as "express[ion] [of] our dark-skinned selves without fear or shame."[4]

The members of Bad Brains, as African Americans, were not only conscious of jazz and blues' musical history, but also in many ways were connected to and engaged with the implications and associations of their complex, culturally negotiated racialized musical identity. Significantly, the high school–era members of what would become Bad Brains were not only fans of jazz in general, but also of jazz fusion specifically. As high school students, the band members gathered in a friend's basement every Tuesday and Thursday to "just kick it—Return to Forever and John McLaughlin. We didn't have the chops, we just used to sit around and emulate them guys."[5] Jenifer recalls bringing in jazz fusion albums to school, eschewing contemporary rock because jazz was "about the chops and the riffs,"[6] the instrumental dexterity and complexity of the music. Even before they formed as the punk outfit Bad Brains, HR (Paul Hudson), Darryl Jenifer, Earl Hudson, and Dr. Know were Mind Power, a jazz fusion band in the style of Weather Report and Mahavishnu Orchestra. Jazz fusion was perhaps as controversial to the black musical community as punk was to the white musical community; it was seen as not quite jazz and not quite rock and thus sat in a racial and cultural schism. Despite the national appropriation of jazz as a uniquely and proudly American sound, its roots firmly stood in the narrative of marginalized black communities. Yet (white) rock 'n' roll, particularly within the late 1960s and early 1970s, was slowly usurping the American music mantle and the cultural and social capital that accompanied it. As Fellezs argues, "fusion articulates the ill-fitting intercultural mergings occurring at the breaches of cultures, mergings that have become increasingly central to individuals' mobile sense of belonging among competing sets of loyalties."[7] Fusion sat at the crossroads of jazz and rock, of whiteness and blackness, a position Fellezs describes as a crucial in-betweenness. It was music without a genre, which functioned within the cracks between genres.

This positioning of jazz fusion reflects the syncretic and complicated environment that the members of Bad Brains were in during high school—musically, racially, and personally. Perhaps more significant, I argue, like those jazz fusion musicians, Bad Brains helped create the DC hardcore sound *because* of their in-betweenness. This in-betweenness was first a function of "being both inside and outside genre categories, disturbing assumptions about musical traditions, including the ways in which membership (legitimacy), mastery (authority), and musical value are ordered."[8] Bad Brains do this through their in-betweenness of not (black) jazz and not (white-washed) rock, and even more so, not (white) American or British punk creating, like the jazz fusion bands they admired and ultimately musically abandoned, an "informal, even feral set of musical practices and aesthetics."[9] Theirs was a new sound, unmoored from conventional (black) jazz, popular (white) rock 'n' roll, and also (polycultural) jazz fusion. Dissolving Mind Power, after one gig and an unsuccessful two months, HR explained, "All the while we was jazz, we wanted to innovate; we wanted to be part of something new and different and real."[10] As a result, the band reimagined rock, jazz, and punk, forming Bad Brains in this liminal space, a hardcore band whose music, in its distinctive sound, still represented the raced identity of jazz, in addition to the whiteness of contemporary rock 'n' roll.

Despite their refusal to stay within the parameters of traditional jazz, which, according to Dr. Know, had gone "*pffft,*" the reconstitution of the outfit now known as Bad Brains incorporated perhaps *the* trademark of the traditional jazz genre—at least the one that distinguished and differentiated it as an exclusive African American form of music: technical prowess. In creating their brand of hardcore, what music journalist Mark Coleman called "a crucial music for crucial times," Bad Brains highlighted their in-betweenness: undermining the (white) punk idealization of musical amateurship and sloppiness in adopting the (black) jazz model of technical dexterity. As Jenifer himself noted, "Bad Brains took the musicianship of Jazz and grafted it onto the I-don't-give-a-fuck rough-and-ruggedness of Punk Rock."[11] This musicianship that Jenifer refers to is not, however, one grounded in Dixieland or swing or even jazz fusion, it was from what jazz scholar Scott DeVeaux terms the evolution and revolution of bebop.[12]

As DeVeaux explains, in one way bebop is simply the continuation of the jazz tradition, an evolution of musical style still cocooned within what some consider the crucial characteristics of the genre. But bebop is also historically and culturally constructed as a revolution, a way black jazz musicians used their exceptional musical skills to rebel against the homogenization and mainstreaming of their music into conventional white culture. As swing continued to serve as a popular backdrop to dance music, with an integrated audience and musicians in swing bands, many African American jazz musicians saw a sort of musical appropriation of their genre. What once performed as a marker of race and identity, and as an almost-proud acknowledgment of marginalization, soon was diluted by the incorporation of the white middle class and the assignation of jazz as "a mark of U.S. national identity."[13] In a conscious effort to demarcate themselves both as black men and black musicians, a small group of jazzmen transformed the popular style of jazz, creating what would be known as bebop. Although some white musicians played it, "the bebop revolution was distinctly African-American—a movement with a firm base in the musicians' community of Harlem."[14] Gone was danceability—bebop was to be listened to, not danced to. Rather than emphasizing the beat, rhythm defined bebop, in addition to advanced harmonic hearing and great technical technique. Virtuoso players such as Charlie Parker, Dizzy Gillespie, Bud Powell, and Thelonious Monk saw themselves as an elite group of musicians, intentionally using their musical expertise to exclude music critics and those musicians who weren't talented enough to play bebop. In bebop, "the more difficult it was, all the better,"[15] and musicians were known to reharmonize standards on the fly, forcing musicians to prove their musical chops and weeding out those whom they deemed less skilled. Indeed, the characteristics of bebop—the irregularly accented fast pulse, the frantic rhythmic sound and asymmetric phrasing, and its hot tone—were a line of delimitation for those "as a matter of *taste* and cultural *stance* were unable to identify with the new assertion of 'blackness.'"[16]

Bad Brains' aesthetic reformulation of punk rock as hardcore paralleled and performed a reclamation of black musical identity through musical technique in bebop, including the "fascination with technical virtuosity and harmonic complexity, fueled by an engaging combination of restless curiosity."[17] In its relatively short musical life, punk—in its British predecessors and US contemporaries—was grounded in the antithesis of musical expertise, much less virtuosity. Simplicity and mere proficiency in instrumental ability were the musical calling cards of punk's past. Perhaps not coincidentally, the racial makeup of these punk bands was, almost exclusively, white. Bad Brains, then, as black musicians in a white genre, asserted their "blackness," their in-betweenness, their racialized musical identity, by surrogating for the bebop musical tradition—by playing the loudest, the fastest, and the most complex punk yet to arrive on the scene. Their musical evolution and revolution were a way to "relocalize musical approaches in order to achieve uniquely individual voices"[18] by "questioning conventional mappings of identity as articulated through musical genre formation, performance practices, and the bodies who perform them."[19]

Nowhere are Bad Brains' musical chops more explosively on display than on their first single, "Pay to Cum." Frequently recognized as *the* song that jump-started the hardcore sound, "Pay to Cum" interprets and transmutes jazz into punk into hardcore with its fast tempo, instrumental dexterity, and seemingly discordant sound. Clocked at a mere one minute and twenty-five seconds, the song is so fast "you had to double-check your turntable speed."[20] HR spits out lyrics at a pace that makes it seem as if the words trip over one another, fusing the lines into an almost undecipherable blur of speed, punctuated only by a slightly more enunciated shout of the final word at the end of the verse. Tellingly, it takes HR only four seconds to sing the first verse, a nearly improbable task with the lines "I make decision with precision/Lost inside this manned collision/Just to see that what is to be/Perfectly my fantasy." The breakneck vocals repeat in the remaining three verses but are contrasted interestingly with the relatively slower and noticeable reverbed articulation of the song's two bridges. Appearing after the first two verses, the bridge's lyrics are sung at half time—"And all in time/With just our minds/We soon will find/ What's left behind"—while the bass, guitar, and drums remain at full speed, offering a juxtaposition of tempos and highlighting HR's vocal abilities within the verses.

Yet the vocals seem almost secondary to the velocity of the rhythm section of "Pay to Cum." The song opens with the "free-fire guitar rage"[21] of Dr. Know's blasting guitar, a mere two-second guitar introduction that detonates four riffs within that short span. In this seemingly impossibly fast song, each instrument moves from riff to new riff every few seconds. Hudson's drums erupt soon after the song begins, a torrential combustion of pounding thumps and crashing cymbals. As the punk zine *New Yorker* claims, "the sheer stamina behind the rhythm section of bassist Darryl Jenifer and drummer Earl Hudson pulls listeners in like a riptide [and] guitarist Dr. Know floods the senses with chortled leads." Bad Brains' pure power to play with that sort of speed showed their capabilities as accomplished musicians, rather than as amateur punks noodling away in their garage with three chords.

Speed was complementary to precision and technique. And one way Bad Brains highlighted their musical aptitude was their variation of chord progressions. Dr. Know's guitar goes from E to B to G to D to A and then back to E in "Pay to Cum," while Jenifer's bass hits G to D to A to E. Although these chords do not necessarily indicate the kind of overt musical complexity often found in jazz, or even other rock music of the day, the range was not only unusual for the heretofore minimalism of punk rock but also in conjunction with their mind-blowing speed and tight play, which was nearly impossible to replicate. As Dr. Know acknowledges, "we wanted to be known as the fastest band in the world. . . . At the same time, we didn't want to be doing the same three-chord routine . . . we had something to prove musically."[22] And they were recognized for it. As Greg Hetson of the Los Angeles band Circle Jerks famously said of Bad Brains in 1981, "They'll blow you away. They are the best band on the East Coast, possibly the whole USA, possibly the world."

The Body and the Throat: Bad Brains as Blues

There may seem to be a less obvious and uninterrupted line between Bad Brains' brand of punk and blues than there is with jazz, but the corollaries between the two genres of music are nevertheless palpable and meaningful. Like jazz, the development of blues as a genre of music was undeniably linked to both African Americans and to the institution of slavery. In the fields, devoid of agency and, in many cases, literacy, blues became a form of communication and identification, reflecting the realities of the everyday and constructing an imagined community with fellow slaves. Adopted from their African musical heritage, the blues were eventually characterized by an AAB twelve-bar standard structure, employing a call-and-response form, and most typically improvising lyrics about sorrow and commiseration. As W. E. B. Dubois claims, blues were "the authentic expression of African-American experience,"[23] encapsulating not just blacks' African origins, but also the material and psychological results of US slavery and subsequent diffusion into and experiences in post–Civil War urban centers.

In part, the association of the blues with black emotiveness is intertwined with not just the history of African Americans but more specifically the bodily construction of blackness as a derivative of that history. With its origins within slavery, the blues were labeled, both by those involved in the black aesthetic movement and by those critics and historians of music, as a manifestation and outcome of the collective black experience. Despite the whiffs of racial essentialism, this categorization by itself is not problematic. However, the sociocultural value of the blues, its meaning to the development of R&B, and later, rock 'n' roll, tend to center on the race-based dichotomy of mind versus body. Without the formal musical training of European-centered music, the blues and those who participated in the creation of it often incorporated spontaneous, highly improvised performances, with tempos, beats, and tunes created around emotions, rather than technical compositions. Situated within the realities of the blues' foundations, black music—and the blues especially—was consequently labeled primitive in its expressiveness, too "natural" and "basic," as differentiated from the deliberate and cerebral (and therefore superior) white-created music.[24]

This racially constructed musical emotiveness was epitomized by the vocals of blues singers. The analogous relationship between voice and emotion is grounded in the idea that "the basic mode of expression lies in . . . the effects of the human larynx," with vocals allowing for the manifestation of amorphous feelings that "communicate reactions to the world in the form of description, analysis [and] evaluation."[25] That is, the sound of the voice has been noted—by listeners from music critics to fans to social psychologists—as endowed with the ability to capture emotion, which is linked to an explicit social set of life experiences. More specifically, our basic emotions (sadness, anger, pleasure, disgust, joy) have a parallel vocal acoustic, and the musical performances that parallel those tend to create similar sentiments. Vocals as carrier signals, however, do not imply a stable or unified perception of meaning, particularly when it comes to indicators such as race, class, gender, and sexuality. Instead, "racialized meanings and associations commonly assigned to vocal color are *not inherent* to the voice" but are instead a product of socialization and cultural construction of difference.[26]

The singing style of the blues, then, tends to embody an understanding of blackness linked not to biologically based difference in timbre or texture, but instead to the oppression and tyranny of slavery. The emotion expressed by singers of the blues was inextricably tied to the collective memories of sorrow and agony tied to slavery and centuries of oppression and marginalization, which imagined vocal styling as a direct manifestation of a specific social and historical context. Indeed, the blues are exemplified by what music historians label "an expressive sensuality" that directly reflects the "frustration, hurt, and anger that blues singers and their audiences feel."[27] What's more, such an association becomes the quintessential feature of blackness. As music historian Simon Frith has argued, "The essence of black music performance is the expression of the performers' feelings, and the possibilities of such expression depend on the music's vocal qualities."[28]

For country blues singers, this is embodied by the "agonized screams" of Elmore James, the way that Howlin' Wolf "sang with his damn soul," and the "moaning and trembling" of Muddy Waters.[29] These vocalists, like Blind Lemon Jefferson, who shouted his melodies, harken back to the roots of slavery in the form of field shouts and hollers, as well as the expressiveness of spirituals, in combination with the lack of any formal vocal training. By the mid- to late 1930s, as the blues made its way to cities, the primary vocal style of the urban blues was shouting, led by men like Joe Turner, Jimmy Rushing, and "Hot Lips" Page. In this way, blues singers disregarded the Western standards of vocals—with its emphasis on pitch and the standardization of vibrato and timbre—in their very inclusion and accentuation of emotions as the benchmark for singing. It is important to note, however, that the aforementioned vocal stylings were the purview almost exclusively of *men* who sang the blues. Although women were an integral part of the blues—both in African American circles and in the music of the more integrated mainstream—singers like Mamie Smith, Ida Cox, Bessie Smith, and Ethel Waters performed the blues in the more traditional smooth and polished style. In this way, the blues emotiveness is not only associated with blackness, but with black masculinity.

HR, listed on *Bad Brains* not as the singer, but as the "throat," embodies the blues tradition of emotional vocal evocation. Like the so-called "shouters" of blues and R&B before him, with a style of which there was no white equivalent in practice or use, HR's singing merely estimated pitch and was typically composed of a hard and hoarse sound. Paralleling the construction of a black masculine music known for its physicality, primitiveness, and feeling, HR asserts his racialized roots in his performance of hardcore punk vocals, more specifically within his constant tension between singing and screaming. The first song on Bad Brains' 1982 album "Sailin' On" immediately depicts HR's ability to balance fury, yearning, and sadness through the manipulation of his voice. A song about heartbreak, a somewhat typical trope in blues, though more unusual in the realm of punk rock, HR sings the first few lines clearly, elongating the final word of each line as if to emphasize the words and the simultaneous feelings of rejection, but with a clarity of enunciation not often found in punk singing generally, nor Bad Brains specifically: "You don't want me anymore/So I walked right out that door/I play the game right from the start." The last line of the first verse, however, builds swiftly, with HR spitting in rapid-fire staccato ("I trust you, you use me, now my life's all—") until he reaches the final two words of the line, screeching "torn apart." The quick rat-a-tat of his rasping vocals evoke the pressing sentiments of accusation, of the fast and pounding charges of heartbreak and betrayal, until HR's pain can't be contained anymore and, "morph[ing] from sweetly soulful crooner to fiery banshee wailer,"[30] he explodes, screaming "torn apart" and conjuring up the metaphor of his own vocal cords being shredded like his heart.

After a straightforward chorus sung almost cheerily ("So I'm sailing, yeah I'm sailing on/I'm moving, yeah I'm moving on/Sail on, sail on, sail on, sail on"), the façade of matter-of-factness is ripped away by a gutwrenching screech at the end of the line. It's as if HR has vocally detonated after the seeming peace of sailing away from this woman, and the juxtaposition of these relatively calm vocals with the almost maniacal shriek acts to reinforce and underscore the mercurial nature of love. This vocal contradiction continues with the second verse, when HR's biting vocals are matched at the end of every line with his band, acting as backup singers, crooning "oh-oh" in classic doo-wop style. The aggression of the lead singer's voice, and its overt performance of the pain that accompanies any lost love, is paired with the connotation of sweet sentimentality that infuses the doo-wop harmonies. Not only does this serve as an enactment of the complexities of feelings (and, of course, love) but it also reinforces HR's bond to the racialized musics of his past.

HR's inventive and emotive use of his voice enacts not just the emotions of personal heartbreak and suffering but also reactions to the complex and often incongruous demands placed on a black man in a white world and on a black band in a white genre. "I," the tenth song on their 1982 release, sees HR's vocals once again acting as an aural signifier of confusion and pain, despite the almost indecipherable lyrics he is spewing. Sung in a lower octave than the rest of the song, HR seems to physically expel the first few lines of the first verse. And although the words are hard to understand, even upon multiple listenings, his voice mirrors the sentiment: "Not as much but with such intensity/I'd like to be what they would not want me to be/I like to cram their chivalry inside their guts."

The words seem to be crammed down the listener's throat by HR, who pushes the sounds out from his lower register until, in the final line of the first verse, his voice goes into a higher range as he squeals, "I'd like to leave it all behind with the rest of the nuts." The inability to fully understand the lyrics without the assistance of liner notes only serves to reinforce the physicality of the sound; much like the construction of blackness in blues, it's the body that is valued over the mind. HR himself notes in a 1982 *New York Rocker* interview, it's "very tribalistic, very physical, going back to the original basics. It's almost uncivilized."[31]

This primal nature is underlined by the chorus that directly follows. Made up of merely one word—*I*—the chorus is half-sung, half-shouted in a discordant nasal tone that suggests testimonial, blame, and perplexed bewilderment all at once. Many a music critic has noted HR's ever-changing vocal texture, "alternately soul-deep or bile-encrusted wailing, spitting, and sneering,"[32] but what they fail to note is how these qualities are often *not* separate, not juxtaposed line by line—as the case is with "Sailin' On"—but how these two seemingly incompatible characteristics often occur in his voice at the same time.

While the *I* is expressed in the simultaneous soulful and self-tortured texture of HR's voice, the bridge offers a more accusatory sound when singing about the corollary "you." As HR pants out, "I guess it's too bad/I guess it's too bad" the three remaining band members answer in strong unison "for you"; this call-and-response continues for two lines, with Dr. Know, Hudson, and Jenifer representing the collective condemnation of the "you," barking out their answer with a low and resolute tone. But such charges turn inward again at the end of the song, when *I* is once again shrieked—and held for five seconds—without any response. HR's *I* is unanswered but for his own "oh," which is drawn out in a near-yodeling effect, redolent of wailing fervor of a preacher delivering a sermon. It is this testimonial—this assertion of self, muddled and confused with both soul and bile—that is reminiscent of the blues and its musical brethren in gospel. HR's vocals are, as *Rolling Stone* dubbed them, "the expression of the church of music," and his simultaneous rage and desire—delivered in the form of yelps, melodies, cries, grunts, and chants—link him to both the style and the history of this uniquely African American music.

It should be noted here that even though HR is an exceptionally emotive vocalist, his vocal stylings are not so different from those of other hardcore singers of the same time. This is true within the DC scene—Ian MacKaye, Henry Garfield, and John Stabb, for instance—but also at other local hardcore scenes in the late 1970s and early 1980s, including L.A.'s

Keith Morris (Circle Jerks) and Darby Crash (Germs) and San Francisco's Jello Biafra (Dead Kennedys) and Ricky Williams (Flipper). However, two major caveats should be added. First, the implications of sound cannot be extricated from "the bodies that perform them."[33] HR's vocals emerge from a black body and contained within that historically and culturally marked space are the always-already present musically and politically contingent signifieds. Such connotations cannot issue from white bodies. As subsequent chapters will explore, the privilege of the white body speaks more to assertions of class-based and gender-based power and hegemony. Besides, in the case of DC hardcore, and the later New York scene, HR and Bad Brains were the prototype for hardcore sound both vocally and musically. Their racialized sounds were also reproduced by white musicians, once again altering the meanings of those sounds.

The blues, and Bad Brains' form of punk, were not and cannot be so straightforwardly defined as merely a function of vocals and lyrics. Yes, singing style and lyrical content were essential components in the evolution of the genre and its representation of African Americans' cultural and social positioning, but it was the sound of the music itself that was fundamental in the marginalization and subsequent social location of blacks. The sound of the blues, and later R&B, including the unrelenting rhythms, raw energy, and indelicate lyrical content, was correlated with blackness and deemed inappropriate for conventional white audiences. It was the threat—racial, sexual, and, consequently, political—of R&B's sound, its noise, that stood as an assertion of self for African Americans and portended the demise of traditional white mainstream values of prudence, conservatism, and domination. As Buddy Guy remembered in *Guitar World* magazine, "they'd always tell me to turn that amplifier down, don't play that, that's *noise*. And I'd say, man, this is my blood, this is *me*."[34] Certainly, the control of sound, the management of the codes that music symbolizes, are essential in promulgating the established norms of society. Just as the homogenized pop sounds of Tin Pan Alley epitomized the white American ideal (despite the somewhat ironic fact that the most prolific and popular Tin Pan Alley musician was Jewish American Ira Berlin, writing and performing at a time when Jews were not seen as white) and country music personified the white working class, white artists such as Pat Boone, Perry Como, and the McGuire sisters figuratively bleached the societally menacing sounds and lyrics of African American rhythm and blues. R&B, and its accompanying electrified guitars and strong drum backbeat, embodied aggression, resistance, and uncontrollability.

Punk rock in general, and Bad Brains specifically, represent what *Washington Post* arts critic Paul Richard in 1980 called "abrasive, primitive" music that to many could barely be designated as music at all.[35] The band's distorted guitars, the loud volume, and the screamed vocals led institutional authorities like Prince George's County chief liquor inspector Jerry Kromash to assert in the *Washington Post* that "this type of music draws undesirables" to the extent that area citizens were "afraid to cross the street to go to their cars" when a punk show was in town.[36] Much in the way R&B was thought to sexualize youth, punk's noise was thought to incite violence. Indeed, Bad Brains shows were often broken up by the police, who agreed with another *Washington Post* critic that Bad Brains' "anarchic, aggressive, juvenile, jarring"[37] noise threatened the peace. Like R&B, punk was accused of appealing to the most primitive of elements, bringing out crudeness, barbarism, and vulgarity. Such complaints were grounded in the sounds of the music itself—the "impotent rage" described by *Psychology Today* writers in a 1977 article about punk music was expressed in the frenzied buzz-saw guitars, driving drums, and howling raw vocals; these sounds indicated a menace, based not solely on race, but also on age and sociocultural ostracism.

Noise acts as a disruption of communication; it interrupts, masks, and covers a message, simultaneously serving as a warning of an actual threat or injury—think about a fire alarm, a home invasion alarm, or an ambulance siren. And volume, the sheer loudness of sound, is often the main characteristic of these offensive noises. Analogously, Bad Brains act as both a disrupter of the typical flow of communication, particularly as a musical form—with its off-the-charts volume and screamed vocals that eschew enunciation for passion and obfuscate immediate and explicit comprehension of lyrics—and the threat of physical harm—implicit in the loudness and the distorted, minimalist, repetitive, and sometimes atonal sounds of the guitar, bass, and drums. Their music evoked what the *Washington Post's* Harry Sumrall characterized in a 1979 article as "strident militancy, anger and physical and musical grossness"[38] that refused to be ignored in its uncompromising noise. Yet this energy, this so-called violence, was the epitome of those who played punk, just as R&B's noise represented African American bluesmen. Henry Garfield remembers his first Bad Brains show as "scary and incredible. . . . HR had me pinned to the floor and was screaming in my face. It was one of the biggest moments in my life."[39]

The Unbearable Whiteness of Being

It is crucial to recognize that Bad Brains' subversion, their power to disrupt, is at least in part conferred on them because of their blackness. That is, because "racialized ideologies support generic categorizations because race [is] a fundamental fulcrum"[40] on which specific types of music are established, Bad Brains as black bodies performing racialized in-between forms of blues and jazz in a white-dominated punk and rock milieu present a different set of possibilities—and constraints—than do other (white) hardcore bands. This is particularly true as is revealed in the relationship, both musically and physically, between Bad Brains and their direct (white) descendants, Minor Threat. Ian MacKaye and Jeff Nelson, both of Teen Idles and, later, Minor Threat, found their place within the burgeoning hardcore punk scene, first as fans of Bad Brains and later as friends of Bad Brains. It was this friendship, between the fledging punk band Teen Idles (and afterward Minor Threat) and the relatively elder statesmen Bad Brains, that greatly influenced the playing style and emotive aesthetics of the former two.

The tutorship and influence of Bad Brains on Teen Idles and Minor Threat is well documented. After Bad Brains had returned from New York broke, Teen Idles invited the band to use their equipment and practice space; their musical power was an instant inspiration. Guitarist Brian Baker notes that the band's influence was "absolutely enormous,"[41] particularly on the somewhat antithetical hardcore aesthetic of technical prowess. As MacKaye recalls, "Here we are making this racket and complaining how shitty our equipment is, and then they would pick up our very same shit and play this amazing music. It was like another world."[42] As musical descendants of Bad Brains, Teen Idles and Minor Threat continued the African American tradition of musical exceptionalism in the face of white musical appropriation. Indeed, that bebop-inspired technical exclusivity that Bad Brains sustained and recreated in punk rock acted as a template for their all-white disciples. The technical skills of Minor Threat were, according to *Washington Post* music critic Howard Wuelfing, "A quantum leap. . . . I was blown away to see that they could play with such speed and not have the structure of the song melt underneath. The difference . . . was Bad Brains. They set the example of how to play extremely fast but with extreme precision."[43] Nelson agrees, noting how the band "influenced us incredibly with their speed and frenzied delivery."[44]

It would be somewhat outlandish to argue that Minor Threat was somehow embodying the black musical traditions of blues and jazz. Positing that "extramusical concerns are fundamental to teasing out meaning from sounding,"[45] Minor Threat was simply carrying on the (white) rock tradition of technical dexterity. Or, more specifically, they were carrying on the invisibility of whiteness wherein their music "protect[ed], legitimate[d], and secure[d] white privilege" and "collective white identities [were] produced and white identities normalized."[46] Whiteness has historically been grounded within the genres of specific forms of musical craftsmanship, and blackness has stood in contrast to, or at least parallel to, those genres. In this way, the whiteness of Teen Idles and Minor Threat and their hardcore punk was, as scholar Richard Dyer describes, normalized and assumed.

More than just the music, Teen Idles and Minor Threat connected to the feelings of ostracism and marginalization that impelled the African American music of the blues. MacKaye recounts how being a punk in the sociocultural context of Washington, DC, "meant you were a magnet for getting shit. You saw how people acted. You kind of understood what it was like to be a black in America, to be just judged by the way you looked."[47] Just as Bad Brains channeled prejudice, and the accompanying anger and frustration, into their hardcore punk in the musical tradition of the blues, so too did Teen Idles and Minor Threat. Says MacKaye, "For me it's a total emotional outlet. I think the function of music is . . . the blues."[48] To be black was to be consigned to a lower social status; the same was true, if to a significantly lesser extent, of being punk. The black "blues" of punk offered Teen Idles and Minor Threat a vehicle to express that pain.

Of course, it is undeniable that the whiteness of the band members offered a form of privilege not granted to their Bad Brains colleagues. Although their status as punks conferred a considerable psychological, and sometimes physical, burden on the band members, their skin color still allowed for the privilege of invisibility. Clearly, we are unable to gauge what affect the band's race had on the reception and influence of their music; however, just as plainly, we must consider the historical freedom granted to whites, particularly within the field of music—to criticize, to challenge, to evoke passion rather than fear. Whiteness also acted as permission, or at least conventionality, to enter an already-white punk scene.

This whiteness, including the privilege, power, and centeredness accompanying it, also provoked one of Minor Threat's most controversial songs, "Guilty of Being White," released on their 1982 *In My Eyes*. The lyrics seek to distance the white band members from the racist, oppressive, and horrific tragedies of our past and also decry what MacKaye sees as reverse racism that he was experiencing at his high school: "I'm sorry/ For something I didn't do/Lynched somebody/But I don't know who/ You blame me for slavery/A hundred years before I was born. . . . I'm a convict/GUILTY/Of a racist crime/GUILTY/I've only served/GUILTY/19 years of my time." On the one hand, Minor Threat (and the national punk scene more generally) construct themselves as a deliberate Other, an explicit ally of racial solidarity and an enthusiast of institutional annihilation. And as punks, their whiteness was, to a certain extent, caveated by self-construction as a punk, as an Other. They initially sought to mark themselves as different. One the other hand, despite their allyship and their self-Othering, they were still white and still received what DuBois termed the public and psychological wage of whiteness—social and material privileges that accompany their ownership in the dominant race.[49]

MacKaye has strenuously argued he wrote "Guilty of Being White" as an antiracist song,[50] a reflection of his direct experience:

> I live in Washington DC, which is 75% black. My junior high was 90% black, my high school was 80% black, and throughout my entire life, I've been brought up in this whole thing where the white man was shit because of slavery. So I got to class and we do history and for 3/4 of the year

slavery is all we hear about. . . . I mean, I'm white, fine. A hundred years ago, I was not alive . . . so whatever happened a hundred years ago, I am not responsible for. . . . People have to get off the guilt wagon. And I'm just saying I'm guilty of being white—it's my one big crime.[51]

What MacKaye's point ignores is the cultural and practical privileges that white bodies possess, as well as the historical, structural racism engrained in US institutions. It also ignores the recentering of whiteness that occurs with this song, wherein the trauma and suffering of black bodies is sidelined by individual feelings that speak to the "relational, contextual, and situational ways in which privilege can be at the same time a taken-for-granted entitlement, [and] a desired social status, a perceived source of victimization."[52]

Clearly, difference cannot be elided by music. And, in fact, racial difference permits a different form of music. While Bad Brains do construct their racial identity by the composition and sound of their music, their lyrical content strays from any overt critique or assessment of race relations. The reason could be, in part, their already outsider position as black men within a nearly exclusively white punk scene. Minor Threat's whiteness both within and outside the larger DC punk scene facilitated their ability, their privilege, not only to discuss race, but also to sing about it in a way that was outside the typical sociopolitical realm.

Instrument(s) of Race: The (Re) Racing of Punk

The role of race in DC hardcore becomes even more muddied and complicated when we take into consideration the racialized history of rock 'n' roll and its superstar, the electric guitar. As noted before, music acts as interpreted sound, and that interpretation, as with the shared comprehension of language or any other system of signs, is constructed in and by society at large. Any analysis of sound, including, of course, this book, has its foundation not in some inherent or biological reaction to specific sounds, but instead in what music theorist Susan McClary describes as the "conferring of social meaning" wherein groups of people "agree collectively that their signs serve as valid currency."[53] Rather than a reflection of society, music constructs society, infusing sounds with socially constructed meanings and readings. The same is true for instruments, including the electric guitar.

Within the social milieu that determines and constructs the understandings of race-based aesthetics of instruments and their sounds, the electric guitar was first connected to African Americans. Its signification of blackness came from two separate elements of society: the historical relationship between the instrument itself and African Americans (the acoustic guitar) and the culturally constructed meaning (specifically, black hypersexuality and the threat of violence) derived from its electrified sound. The acoustic guitar, and its musical comrade, the banjo, was integral to the music of African slaves and, consequently, was central to the establishment of the blues, in large part because its flexible tuning was critical for "the non-tempered, microtonal melodic language" of the blues.[54] As the country blues sound made its way into the urban centers, blossoming into city blues and its progeny, R&B and jazz, the electric guitar rose in instrumental celebrity along with its players—Charlie Christian, Muddy Waters, and Chuck Berry, to name just a few—whose playing had adapted to the advancements in amplification technology.

Yet it was at this juncture that the historical narrative of African Americans and the guitar collided with the cultural construct of blackness in America. Although the electric guitar and its accompanying slide techniques offered the bending and distorting of traditional Euro-American notes toward a more traditional African sound, the prominent association of this type of playing by African Americans was as threatening; this alteration of sound, particularly through the means of amplification and volume, was associated with the construction of blackness—one based on excess and criminality. The sound of the blues-based rock guitar—distorted, rough, loud—came to stand for blacks themselves, at least to mainstream (white) culture. In a nation where blacks were deemed a threat, both politically and sexually, the electric guitar epitomized that menace.

The cultural discourse of blackness as a threat, and the electric guitar as a symbol of that racialized and sexualized threat, was personified by the epitome of the next generation of black guitarists—Jimi Hendrix. Licking, playing, flicking, manipulating his ax, Hendrix's guitar became a part of his body or, as music scholar Steve Waksman calls it, a "technophallus."

Acting within the already pronounced construction of black male hyper-sexuality, Hendrix linked his explosive sonic innovations with his sexual performance, often squatting down with his guitar jutting from his groin, and at times arching back, coaxing timbral distortion and jolting notes, the guitar's neck bulging from his legs.

Bad Brains' use, manipulation, and sound of guitars in their 1982 album acts to ground them within the framework of black rock 'n' roll, carrying with it the complicit sexual and violent threat. In the most fundamental sense, the electrified, warped loudness of the band's guitar served as a link to the instrument's racialized past and its relationship to rock itself. As music theorist Albin Zak III argues, "the symbolism attached to sounds in rock is a source of identity for artists, styles, and audiences. . . . Sounds carry with them entire stylistic legacies."[55] The electric guitar's function and metaphor in black musical history ally Bad Brains' black selves (and the concurrent identity of musical innovators and dangers to traditional cultural norms)—whether intentionally or not—to the white world of punk.

At the same time, the guitars of *Bad Brains* did more than simply fortify the racial and musical connection to the electric guitar; sonically, they reimagined the cultural meaning of that sound, recoupling the instrument to the danger and menace still culturally associated with blackness. The reassertion of the signified of the electric guitar as black, threatening, and violent was a reaction to rock's whitewashing of the electric guitar as signifier. As our cultural narrative has borne out time and time again, the most threatening elements of society tend to be first appropriated, then diluted, and ultimately popularized by the mainstream, neutering the risk to hegemony. This trajectory proved accurate with mythos of the electric guitar. Once an emblem of black masculinity and sexuality, and with it the connotations of danger and aggression, the electric guitar was, in the '60s and '70s, converted to a symbol in the white man's purview, in both an attempt to assume the sexual power of that symbol and to transform its power into a sign of technical (white) mastery. Like the blues players of the 1950s and the rock 'n' rollers of the early 1960s, Bad Brains used the electric guitar and bass to create sounds that ran contrary to conventional musical norms, conveying with them the aggression and simmering threat of political and sexual violence much of society feared from African Americans.

64

Take the opening notes of the fourth song off of their album, "The Regulator," where lurking danger is personified by the low and ominous bass line. The insistent repetition of G to D to A to E acts functionally as an introduction to the song but representationally as a warning. The metaphors are nearly boundless—the lull before the storm, the slow drumbeat toward war, the writing on the wall—all analogous to the steady yet portentous cultural milieu of sounds predicting what dangers lay ahead. The bass line pulsates for only five seconds until the electric guitar attacks, slashing in over the bass line, one power chord at a time, with vibrating distortion, signaling the storm that is upon the listener. After this four-chord burst, the electric guitar joins the bass line for nearly the rest of the song (from 0:10 to 1:00), and in doing so reiterates and reinforces the menacing augury with its parallel wailing. Indeed, the bass and guitar resonate like the titular regulator—a watchdog of sound, a sonic control of violence—until the guitar, the song, the band, cannot be contained anymore: at the one-minute mark of the song, Dr. Know's guitar erupts in a frenzied onslaught of noise, abandoning the measured cadence of a warning into a fully realized conflagration of sound. The bass and guitar in the song stand in for the cultural threat of blackness. Restraint dissolves into chaos. In the social construction of race, blacks are ultimately resigned to their primitive or bodily impulses, whether that be violent tendencies (fears of a cultural coup shouldered since slavery) or sexual propensities. "The Regulator" embodies this anxiety sonically, at first representing merely the looming threat implied by their race, but eventually actualizing their brutal potential with ferocious intensity and speed.

This juxtaposition of moderation and madness is a hallmark of the album's sound; the materialization of the guitar's antagonism and its accompanying intimations of danger remains central, but always contrasted with the constraint of tempo. The dizzying, unrelenting guitar riffs of "Banned in DC" are interrupted halfway through the song by a breakdown—the slowing of tempo (at times to almost half time of the original) and the establishment of a new groove, which seems to soften the guitar assault of the song's first minute but nevertheless contains undertones of contained bellicosity in its jagged bass line and piercing guitar solo (not to mention HR's agonizing vocals). "Right Brigade," with its military-inflected guitar introduction, followed by the raucous unrelenting brashness of lightning-quick guitar riffs, is also injected with and fragmented by a breakdown in the middle of the song, trading guitar speed for guitar solo and emphasizing repetition of phrasing over velocity. As an interesting note, Bad Brains is the first, and almost the only hardcore band at the time, to employ this breakdown technique,[56] which evidences the duality of race and sound within the band. The guitar behaves as both a signifier of the traditional, though sonically reconstituted, threat posed by blacks (politically, socially, sexually, musically) and as the actualization of that violent promise. Placid opening bass lines and innocuous guitar phrasing, brief breakdowns that revert to more conventional tempos, all act as a tease, a possibility of docility. Yet such sonic submissiveness is continually toppled by the searing, juddering, and conventionally dissonant sounds of Dr. Know's volatile guitar, reminding the listener that there is nothing safe about being black in a punk world, much less a twentieth-century America.

Once again, however, the racial implications of Bad Brains' sound are not nearly so straightforward. As previously alluded to, the guitar as a sexualized and violent symbol of blackness was convoluted and ultimately reconstructed by the onslaught of white blues–based rockers in the form of British Invasion bands and the ensuing rock spin-offs of the white-dominated progressive rock of the 1970s, changing from a sign of black sexual prowess and aggression to a symbol of white-dominant technical expertise. Legions of white British bands were influenced by the bluesy R&B styles of African Americans, which included not only the emulation of black guitarists of the '50s and '60s, but also the contemporary symbol of both black sexuality and musical virtuosity in Hendrix. In this way, white rockers were able to reproduce or assume a particular kind of blackness, mainly one that co-opted the race-based sexuality and aggression constructed into the electrified sound. And although both the blues and R&B guitarists and the white British guitarists were accomplished musically, the bifurcation between the generations and races tended to be cast in the conventional racially biased binary of emotion versus intellect that grounds white privilege and often white supremacy. The primal nature of the electric guitar's sound was linked to the emotiveness (sexual and otherwise) of African Americans, whereas the technological and technique-driven advances of the guitar and its sound were attributed as

a white contribution. Regardless of the historically, culturally, and sonically tethered association of African American music and the electric
guitar, contemporaneously the instrument is understood as the domain
of white male virtuosos.

Rather than sexuality and the threat of noise as the defining characteristic of the (black) electric guitar sound, soloing and technical skills, leading
to the heroization of guitar players, became the identifiable (white) sound
of the electric guitar. So while the cult of guitar gods was a direct result of
the white, blues-based guitar virtuosos like Eric Clapton, Jimmy Page, and
Duane Allman attempting to emulate the performance and skills of such
black guitarist idols as Jimi Hendrix, B. B. King, and Charlie Christian,
the musical identity of the electric guitar was reworked to deemphasize
black sexuality and accentuate white technical ability. Eric Clapton himself attributed this new focus on guitar skills and long, intense solos on
the deviation from traditional black blues guitar. After constructing his
career around B. B. King riffs, he said, "my whole attitude has changed.
. . . I'm no longer trying to play anything but like a white man."[57] The
subsequent musical march toward progressive rock, with bands such as
Yes, Genesis, and Emerson, Lake and Palmer, saw the complete absence
of so-called black sounds. This shortage was, to a large extent, intentional.
It was as if "black musicians are now implicitly regarded as precursors
who, having taught the white men all they know, must gradually recede
into the distance as white progressive music, the simple lessons learned,
advances irresistibly into the future."[58] With the focus on ornate orchestration, progressive rock idolizes the technical aspects of musicianship over
all else and, with that, seemingly reconstructs the culturally and racially
understood sounds of the electric guitar.

Despite this change in the sociocultural narrative of the electric guitar,
the guitar solo was integral to Bad Brains' guitar performances in their
1982 album, functioning as a seeming contradiction to both the punk
and black representation of the electric guitar. Certainly, punk originated in large part from hostility toward the progressive and art rock
ethos that tried to elevate music to what they saw as a high-brow standard, including its near-ubiquitous emphasis on soloing; regardless of this
genre-espousing disdain, and its connections to a deliberate and (outwardly) racially divergent type of guitar focus, Bad Brains frequently and

consistently incorporate guitar solos in their songs. Of the eleven hardcore punk songs on *Bad Brains*, seven of them feature guitar solos. When one includes the reggae songs, the number of guitar solo songs still sits at an incredible 50 percent. The length of the solos vary—eleven seconds each in "Sailin' On" (0:55–1:06) and "Don't Need It" (0:44–0:55), fifteen and seventeen seconds respectively in "I" (1:21–1:36) and "Big Takeover" (2:13–2:30), nearly thirty seconds during "Banned in DC" (1:27–1:53), and over two guitar solos in "Supertouch/Shitfit" (0:40–0:51 and 2:00–2:13), and, finally, a nine-second and then twenty-seven-second solo in "Right Brigade" (0:45–0:54 and 1:41–2:08). And if "Attitude," "The Regulator," and "Fearless Vampire Killers" don't contain guitar solos, per se, the use and prominence of the guitar are still accentuated. What's more, most, if not all, of Dr. Know's guitar solos sound similar to those found in early heavy metal and '70s hard rock. The shredding guitars of "Right Brigade" would be just as at home in the trenches of Deep Purple's "Smoke on the Water" or Van Halen's "Eruption" solos. That is, the sound of the guitar solo in Bad Brains is in no way uniquely punk; perhaps because of the lack of other accompanying instruments, the *Bad Brains* solos tend to mimic the noise of contemporary rock rather than stand in defiance of it.

It should also be noted that, while not a frequent occurrence in hardcore, other bands in local scenes did incorporate guitar solos. Agent Orange (Orange County, CA), the Adolescents (Orange County, CA), Black Flag (Los Angeles), Minutemen (Los Angeles), Circle Jerks (Los Angeles), and Agnostic Front (New York) all have guitar solos in songs that were contemporaneous with Bad Brains. And it should also be said that a smattering of guitar solos can be found in abundance in proto- and first-wave punk (the Ramones, the Dictators, Television, New York Dolls, the Voidoids, the Clash, Dead Kennedys, the Sex Pistols, to name just a few), as well as in hardcore post–Bad Brains, beginning in 1985 as the influence of metal and thrash crept into the hardcore sound (the Misfits, Leeway, Total Chaos, Anti-Flag). Of course, every single one of these bands and their members were white, and their whiteness—the normality of their whiteness and the naturalization of this whiteness—makes a guitar solo in the age of progressive rock not an act of subversion or assertion, but instead a nearly unremarkable fact. And although the location of said (white) guitar solos within the hardcore genre *is* within itself remarkable, the whiteness of the guitar solo simultaneously reinforces the whiteness of guitar solos musically and culturally.

In this context, Bad Brains' guitar solo glorifications can be understood as a complex reaction to the racialized understanding of rock and of the electric guitar. In one way, Bad Brains was bolstering, or at least reestablishing, technical virtuosity as a mainstay of black musicians in the vein of jazz greats Charlie Parker, Ornette Coleman, Miles Davis, and Thelonious Monk. That Dr. Know's "flawlessly tight . . . guitar playing was light years beyond his peers"[59] was a reflection of the band's attempts to reinscribe the boundaries of racially represented musical skills, particularly in the matter of guitar expertise. Rather than ceding the guitar solo to white rock musicians, Dr. Know asserts his musical talent and dexterity through elaborate and repeated solos, serving as both a contemporary challenge to the glut of white guitarists and as a reminder of the guitar's racialized history and representation. At the same time, the album's featuring of multiple guitar solos acts as a confrontation of the white-dominated genre of punk, a way of circumscribing their black selves and isolating them from the white punk ranks. If (most) punks despised guitar solos, then Bad Brains' embrace of them could signify their Otherness within this nearly all-white musical landscape. Solos act as a way to intentionally mark (racial) difference.

3

The Sounds of Stratification

Socioeconomic Class and DC Hardcore

In the 1980 US Census, 15.3 percent of civilian DC families were living under the poverty line, 1,007 of them white families and 18,992 black. The DC poverty rate contrasts with that in the greater DC metropolitan area, including Maryland and Virginia, where only 6.2 percent of families were living under the poverty line. Of those employed in DC, nearly 44,000 were private or salaried-waged, and approximately 40,000 were federal workers. The census also showed that nearly 39,000 students were enrolled in high school in the District in 1980, 35,000 in public school and 3,600 in private school.

Smack in the middle of those socioeconomic statistics were the teen-aged boys of Teen Idles, later to be Minor Threat, perhaps the most recognized and celebrated hardcore band from DC and, with it, Ian MacKaye, its uneasy if not reluctant flagbearer and herald. As teenagers from Northwest Washington, Teen Idles (MacKaye, Jeff Nelson, Nathan Strajcek, and Georgie Grindle) and Minor Threat (MacKaye, Nelson, Brian Baker, and Lyle Preslar) lived relatively comfortably within the white middle- to upper-middle-class echelon. Jeff Nelson grew up primarily overseas as a son of a State Department worker and went to Woodrow Wilson High school. MacKaye, whom Henry Garfield of State of Alert later described as "bored by their lives in middle-class white DC,"[1] had grandparents who wrote for magazines and parents who also were writers and were active in the civil-rights movement. Nelson and MacKaye, along with Garfield, watched (and sometimes made) homemade pipe bombs explode for fun when they weren't skateboarding or listening to hard rock and punk. And Lyle Preslar and Brian Baker (the latter of whom MacKaye once referred to as a "snotty little fucker")[2] both attended the elite Georgetown Day School. These relatively privileged teenagers quickly went from skateboarding outsiders to hardcore gurus, exploding into one of the most influential punk bands of the early 1980s. Influenced by friends and local hardcore innovators, Bad Brains, Teen Idles, and Minor Threat drew on and amplified their ferocious, frantic sound and technical prowess, becoming the standard-bearers for hardcore punk with four of their albums, *Minor Disturbance* (1980), *Minor Threat* (1981), *In My Eyes* (1981), and *Out of Step* (1983).

Music as Class Stratification and Punk's Classed Status

Taste, that indescribable, often-changing, slippery, and exclusive concept that Pierre Bourdieu characterizes as "one of the most vital stakes in the struggles fought in the field of the dominant class and the field of cultural production."[3] For years, academics have understood taste as a socially constructed criterion, one that offers both a way to categorize, assess, and offer consistency to one's sense of self and, at the same time, serves as a symbolic delineation of social boundaries. Taste makes you cool or unhip, powerful or insignificant, bourgeois or elite, in the know or clueless. But taste is also always linked to a preference for specific cultural goods: what you buy, what you wear, what you consume. In this way, not only is taste constantly grounded in a consumption-based framework but it also reproduces the larger social structure already in place. Such structures are built by, and ultimately constrained by, certain segments of society, frequently based on differences such as race, gender, and, for the purposes of this particular chapter, class.

Within the realm of cultural production, within the consumption choices available, philosopher Pierre Bourdieu declared that "nothing more clearly affirms one's 'class,' nothing more infallibly classifies, than taste in music."[4] Bourdieu's reasoning depends, in part, on his conception of musical culture as metonymy for spirituality, a symbol of the soul in its interiority, separate from the material vulgarity of the physical. In the same theoretical vein, Bourdieu argues that musical preference denotes a separation between the practicality and necessities of everyday life and the privilege of understanding and appreciating aesthetics—primary factors indicative of class division. That is, a person reared in relative wealth, unencumbered by the functional needs of everyday survival, retains the freedom to nurture a taste for the purely aesthetic or ornamental; artistic merit is a feasible and reasonable goal of the affluent rather than consumption of cultural goods that are pragmatic or functional. Differentiation in musical taste allows one to reaffirm one's status in the hierarchy of social order and, at the same time, perpetuate the hegemony associated with the dominant preference. Musical preference, then, is an indicator of class because of its association with a specified set of cultural knowledge (implying with that an analogous set of economic, social, and educational knowledge) and an assertion of status because of that class.

Think about the classed and social implications of jazz, opera, or classical music as opposed to country, bluegrass, or blues; each has a (culturally constructed and power-driven) connotation of who listens: who can listen, who wants to listen, who "understands" enough to listen. And each connotation is classed (and raced, and often gendered). However, it is also important to note that the connotations, these cultural statuses, are not static and immutable. Instead, as historian Lawrence Levine argues, cultural hierarchies have always been "subject to modifications and transformations," dependent on the specifics of historical, social, and economic contexts, not the least of which includes "ethnic, class, and regional distinctions."[5] That is, the classed and cultural connotations of jazz in the 1940s was quite different from what it was in the 1960s, just as opera's relationship to class and culture was markedly different in the 1860s from what it was in all of the twentieth and twenty-first centuries. Despite the historically contingent nature of music's cultural status—and the relatively more contemporary onset of the postmodern theoretical framework and with it the move toward an obliteration of the dichotomy between high and low culture and its associated assignation of social status—music still serves as a prominent site of struggle for self and class definition.

Punk's place in the sociocultural hierarchy was likewise conditioned on the specific historical, social, and musical moment in which it arose. And in the 1970s, its positioning was clearly juxtaposed with rock's newest favorite child, progressive rock, and its aging grandparent, rock 'n' roll. The elder statesmen of rock 'n' roll, manifest in the Rolling Stones, the Who, the Beatles, and their generation, had long been declared dead or at least in a medically induced coma, as *Melody Maker* announced in 1976, "Millionaire rock stars are no longer part of the brotherly rock fraternity that helped create them in the first place."[6] Progressive rock, on the other hand, was firmly within the canon of so-called high art, with a focus on meter and rhythm, harmony, and formal shape, as well as its near-worship of musical expertise through its reverence for and obsession with lengthy musical solos. Despite the fact that there were best-selling progressive rock records in the 1970s, the construction of the genre was conspicuously viewed as separate from commercial pop music, both by the musicians themselves and their fans. The view of progressive rock as art rock positioned the music as a privileged place, and this partitioning of commercial success from artistry (even if it was only theoretical, rather than actual) advanced a specific politics of aesthetics, moving toward the modernistic canons of classical music, where the "demand [for] an investment of cultural capital . . . reinforces social distinctions and class barriers by encoding messages that alienate, confuse, or bore less-educated viewers."[7] That is to say, inextricably linked to this politics of aesthetics and progressive rock's intentional construction as art were explicit class-based political and social complexities.

If, then, progressive rock reflected "the culture of middle-class rock—pretentious and genteel, obsessed with bourgeois notions of art and the accumulation of expertise and equipment"[8]—and rock of the '60s pointed to a conspicuous consumption ethos that was now associated with the millionaires of arena tours, punk was the revolutionary. And part of this sonic revolution was grounded in class. Punk was intentionally "the culture of working-class . . . banal, simple-minded."[9] Punk's roots—in both American proto-punk and Britain's initial formulation of punk rock—explicitly attempted to enact an aesthetic of the working class, at once reinforcing the stratification of musical taste as class status and challenging the boundaries of what music could and should sound like. The Velvet Underground, whose members came from the comfortable middle to upper-middle class, rejected the sound aesthetic analogous to their up-bringing, favoring the "raunchy and devastating," basking in the fact that their music was "totally inaccessible,"[10] or, in the words of Iggy Pop, "How could anybody make a record that sounds like such a piece of shit? . . . This just sounds like trash!"[11] This rejection of middle-class values in-cluded the definition of "real" or "good" music as harmonious, melodic, and traditional. Iggy Pop and the Stooges used blenders, washboards, hammers, and oil drums as instruments, not only creating an atonal and highly abrasive sound that seemed to echo the working-class spirit and economic realities of their hometown of Detroit, but also incorporating some of the actual tools of the blue-collar worker. The Ramones didn't know how to tune a guitar or put a drum kit together, and their short bursts of songs like "Beat the Brat" and "I Don't Wanna Walk Around with You" were in reaction to their disdain for and alienation from the middle-class neighborhood they inhabited.

Influenced by the sounds and class consciousness of proto-punkers, England's punk rock even more unambiguously took on the mantle of class, its chaotic noise, loud volume, and amateurish musical abilities acting as an articulation of the frustrations of the working-class youth caught in the flood of unemployment and inflation. The Sex Pistols rev-eled in punk's aesthetic and revolutionary possibilities of shocking the upper class, with lyrics declaring, "I am an antichrist/I am an anarchist. . . . Your future dream/Is a shopping scheme," simultaneously assailing the sanctity of religion, government, and consumerism in a five-minute song, and deriding the Queen of England as "ain't no human being." Like its American predecessor, British punk's sound sought to signify populism in its "abrasive vocal and instrumental encounter with musical forms,"[12] valuing volume over virtuosity and denigrating the concept of musical legitimacy embraced by progressive rock and even rock 'n' roll proper. By eschewing formal musical training and the corresponding class-based appreciation of traditional tonality and harmony in its devotion to an aes-thetic of dissonant noise, early punk laid the groundwork for how class, and its corresponding cultural depiction and taste, inspired, infused, and confused hardcore's sound.

74

The Sound of Hardcore Punk
as a Performance of Class

Hardcore was punk. But it was also a rebellion against punk. Or at least parts of what punk had become in its few short years in the spotlight. Just as the history of music has proved over and over again, the culturally constructed status of genre is continuously in flux. Jazz, once stigmatized, became the appropriated emblem of American musical ingenuity. Rock 'n' roll, before its prognosticated untimely death in the glut of money and disconnection from mainstream youth in the 1970s, was a terrifying din of wild (black, sexualized, male) youth. And punk, if still clinging to its iconoclastic badge of honor, had also begun to reek of mainstream respectability. The Ramones were being produced by Phil Spector and charting on Billboard. The Sex Pistols had broken up and Johnny Rotten's new band, Public Image Ltd., had charted on the UK's Top Ten. The Clash had signed with CBS Records for a staggering one hundred thousand pounds, charting in the UK and becoming a best seller in the United States. No matter its roots, punk rock had lost its (marginalized) edge. Enter hardcore.

Hardcore more generally, and DC hardcore more specifically, reclaimed the musical mantle of ostracism from British and American punk. It scoffed at the cultural ascent of "mainstream punk" and rejoiced in questionable musical pedigree. One of its classed musical embraces was their choice of instruments. Musical instruments act as a tool of and symbol for social control, establishing an emblematic and exclusive relationship between strata of class (and race, as discussed in the previous chapter) and echelons of instruments. To some extent, class-based instrumental categories have to do with pragmatic financial means—can a person afford to buy a piano? A clarinet? A saxophone? But perhaps even more interesting, sonic classifications are often defined by the culturally constructed relationship between sound and class. Instruments that produce delicate, polished, soft sounds are associated with refinement, gracefulness, and civility: strings (violas, violins, lutes, and harps) and woodwinds (flute, oboe, and clarinet) are foremost in this category. Even within the category of traditional symphonic instruments—which, because of their already monied and socially exclusive nature[13] seem to value the upper class over the others—there is a sliding scale of class-based status.

Prestige is often assigned to specific categories of instruments based on timbre; those with a higher-pitched sound indicate a feminine, cultured connotation, whereas instruments that produce a lower sound imply a gruffer, lower class. In this way, the flute suggests a higher status than the saxophone, though both are woodwinds, and the French horn intimates a higher class than the trombone.[14] The guitar, however, has been near-continuously associated with the lower class. Its "sharp, rough timbre of plucked strings"[15] is reminiscent of traveling gypsies, ranchers, and African Americans: those people without a large income or the traditional patina of sophistication. Playing guitar symbolized a certain roughness and vulgarity, making it a perfect symbol for class rebellion in the 1960s and '70s.

DC hardcore bands, whether intentionally or not, participated in this cultural hierarchy of instruments, playing instruments that were sonically associated with the uncouthness and primitiveness of the lower class: the jagged, strident sound of the electric guitar, the rumbling, menacing resonance of the bass, and the booming, undomesticated din of drums. These instruments, and their accompanying sound, carried with them a legacy of marginalization and exclusion from the idealized mainstream culture (with a capital C), and DC hardcore simultaneously internalized these culturally prescribed socio-musical relationships and rejected these binary assignments.

It must be said that this instrumental performance of class was not limited to DC hardcore. L.A. and Orange County's scene, which was a sort of simultaneous invention of hardcore as it was happening in DC (think Isaac Newton and Gottfried Wilhelm Leibniz for calculus or Charles Darwin and Alfred Russel Wallace for evolution), was chock-full of hardcore bands committed to the classed implications of guitar, bass, and drums: Middle Class, Adolescents, TSOL, Black Flag, Youth Brigade, just to name a few. And the so-called southern California hardcore sound, along with the monumental influence of Bad Brains and the DC hardcore sound, infiltrated the up-and-coming hardcore scenes across the nation. Hardcore as a sound become defined by this instrumental austerity. Boston hardcore (SSD, Gang Green, Negative FX), New York hardcore (Agnostic Front, Warzone, Cro-Mags), Chicago hardcore (Articles of Faith), Detroit hardcore (Necros), Phoenix hardcore (Meat Puppets), Vancouver hardcore (D.O.A.), Austin hardcore (Dicks, MDC), and pockets of other cities and towns across the country all pledged allegiance to this instrumental minimalism.[16]

The class-based implications of hardcore may have been national, but they were also local. Who was playing these instruments, how these instruments were being played, where they were being played, when they were being played—all these elements are crucial in better understanding how sound wields particular power in particular times, places, and spaces. And such particulars were indeed unique when we are talking about Teen Idles and Minor Threat in Washington, DC. For the members of Teen Idles and Minor Threat, the adoption of these culturally constructed lower-class instruments was not a product of necessity or hardship but instead was a deliberate rejection of the cultural implications of instruments the band members were privileged to both learn and listen to. As MacKaye admits, "Music was never a choice for me. The instruments and the approach—that I will say is a choice."[17] MacKaye's mother played the piano and he received lessons when he was a child; drummer Nelson played the tympani in the school orchestra, an instrument typically associated with the elitism of classical music; even bassist-guitarist Baker's first instrument was an acoustic guitar, with its softer sounds of string plucking, rather than the harsh distortion of amplification, connecting to the Renaissance-era lute guitar, Baroque court music, and the folk songs of the Romantic period, as well as to the classical guitar, used in orchestration and classical music. Members' upbringing grounded in the realm of upper-class instruments was consciously renounced. Instead, the members of this band, and the whole of DC hardcore, used culturally demoted instruments—guitar, bass, and drums—and the unrefined, abrasive sounds that attended them. Doing so was a classed statement. "By conferring aesthetic status on objects or ways of representing them that are excluded by the dominant aesthetic of the time,"[18] the bands deployed a potent middle finger in the face of not just the bourgeois, but also their own relatively privileged background.

But the use of downwardly classed instruments can be fully understood only in context and in conjunction with the composition of the music they made. If the guitar, bass, and drums were the form, Teen Idles and Minor Threat songs were the content—and their content continued the assertion of a lower class-based musical identity. The least overt but perhaps most consistent way Teen Idles and Minor Threat created classed music was the composition of the songs themselves. Incorporating the punk rock credo of "three-chord democracy," the bands used the same guitar chords—in the same order—nearly uniformly. Teen Idles' *Minor Disturbance* has six songs on it, all of which have the same chord progression: E/B/G/D/A/E; Minor Threat's *Minor Threat* is virtually identical, with seven of the eight songs using the exact same progression;[19] and every single one of the eight songs in *Out of Step* also follows suit. The only small deviation comes in *In My Eyes*, where two of the four songs cut the chord progression in half (G/D/A/E) and the other two use the elongated version.

The effect of this repetition and simplicity was a populist statement. By streamlining the way a person can create music, Teen Idles and Minor Threat demystified the musical creation process and, to a certain extent, purged the sanctity of the musician as an all-powerful creator of truth. If any teenage kid with a guitar and nominal knowledge of music can make music, there can be no cult of the star, no ossified distance between fan and performer. The four albums mentioned in the previous paragraph could be played by anyone who learned their basic chord progressions; twenty-five songs, all within the grasp of nearly everybody of any class. The reproducibility flew in the face of the complex, intentionally exclusionary music of the social elite—classical music was not so easily or straightforwardly recreated nor was punk's rock contemporary, progressive rock. But Teen Idles' and Minor Threat's musically political statement—E/B/G/D/A/E—spoke of egalitarianism and communalism. Not only did one not have to have the cultural capital to learn socially privileged instruments, but also only needed to learn one five basic guitar chords to create music.

Even more so, the *way* Teen Idles and Minor Threat played these basic chords (and the equally rudimentary bass chords and drum patterns) proclaimed how their music depicted a working-class, amateur identity. Unlike the conventionally constructed definition of musical talent, which included artistry as technical prowess, the bands' brand of punk happily elevated passion over expertise. Musical education was analogous with the cerebral highbrow form of culture, whereas the band esteemed the so-called philistine value of natural artlessness or emotional candor.

As MacKaye admitted to punk zine *maxiumumrocknroll*, "I'm a brutally emotional music person. . . . I refuse to take lessons because I'm scared that the way I play will become warped if I learn the technical aspects and will take away my personal approach and my totally emotional way of playing."[20] This intentional emphasis on feeling rather than procedural skill was, in part, a reaction to the professionalization of music and the band members' parallel feelings of musical ineptitude. Preslar remembers his "really awful"[21] guitar playing as a kid, and MacKaye almost gave up on music because all he saw were professionals doing it. Yet these deficiencies were transformed into badges of pride in the space that hardcore provided. A lack of education, typically a sign of a lower-class identity, was metamorphosed into cultural rebellion; unprofessional playing, or playing with emotion rather than with culturally mandated talent, was a mindful restructuring of musical value. As the Teen Idles sing in "Get Up and Go," "You keep talking about talent/Talent?/What do you know?/Instead of studying theory/We're going to get up and go!" The band's "limited ability,"[22] which HR of Bad Brains characterized as "very enthusiastic"[23] but not technically skilled when they first began, was a refusal to be held to a class-based musical standard and a symbol of identification with those who were marginalized by mainstream cultural paradigms.

This identification was not necessarily generalized or nationalized, but instead specific to the often marginalized substratum of DC. Teen Idles' and Minor Threat's music, their sound, signified the building frustration and overlooked disconnect between the upper-class façade of DC and the disparate reality of those less privileged. Repetition and monotony in the bands' music act as a symbol of the sameness and ennui of working-class tedium. The aforementioned duplication of the same chord progression contributes its part; the recurrence of E/B/G/D/A/E operates as routine and ritual—not only the accessibility of basic chords as classlessness but also the repetition as the slog of everyday life. Indeed, more than 70 percent of people employed in DC in 1979 worked blue-collar jobs: in manufacturing, transportation and public utilities, retail trade, repair services, and nondurable goods.[24] The day-in, day-out sequence of wage-earning work is reflected and represented in the streamlined automation of the chords in Minor Threat and Teen Idles' songs. In this way, the commonplace is elevated. These songs refute their cataloging of standardization as low-brow;[25] they rebuff cultural expectations of and fondness for shiny, brass-driven pop music or lovelorn power ballads; and they deny the record industry's classification of complexity as art.[26] The bands used unvaried standardization and mechanization as a prized aesthetic of the working person. Just as their Detroit proto-punk predecessors, the MC5 and the Stooges, used discordant repetition and standardization of sound to at once repudiate and reappropriate the ideology of mechanization of a Fordist society, the music of Teen Idles and Minor Threat embraced the burdens of the working class and, at the same time, used sonic metaphors to disrupt and upset mainstream society. Consistency—even monotony—of (musical and labor) routine provides a comfort, a security, and an understated strength.

This musical reminder of the realism of the everyday is essential to the sound of Teen Idles and Minor Threat and stood in musical opposition to the gloss and polish of mainstream music and concurrent political opposition to the values that sort of music embodied: luxury, pretense, romance, and a sunniness bordering on denial of material problems. Their opposition, their creation of a binary, allowed for the classed parallels of Teen Idles' and Minor Threat's music. As Simon Frith explained, "the real/unreal distinction depended on a series of musical connotations—ugly versus pretty, harsh versus soothing, energy versus art, the 'raw' . . . versus the 'cooked.'"[27] The music's rawness, and its associated binary of working-classdom, is achieved in a number of ways. First is the minimalism of sound previously discussed in this chapter: not only do Teen Idles' and Minor Threat's songs rely on just three instruments,[28] but also their songs nearly exclusively use a simple verse-and-refrain structure. The structure is an aural declaration of restraint; if intros, bridges, and codas were musically illustrative of the excess of the upper class, then a basic verse-chorus-verse-chorus arrangement typified working-class austerity. Second, the bands' raw "realism" continued in the punk tradition of brief, powerful bursts of songs. Trimming the fat of decadence, the bands' minimalism of lyrics and sound serve as a class statement against excess. On Teen Idles' *Minor Disturbance,* no song is longer than one minute and thirty seconds (and the shortest clocks in at forty-four seconds); Minor Threat's self-titled EP is a total of nine minutes and twenty seconds, and the two longest songs are a minute and forty-two seconds, with the shortest at forty-six seconds.

Although songs on *In My Eyes* and *Out of Step* are longer ("In My Eyes" is two minutes and fifty-nine seconds and the latter has three songs over three minutes: "Betray," "Look Back and Laugh," and "Cashing In"), the vast majority of these four albums are still notable for their persistent brevity. The succinctness of the songs manifests the repudiation of glut and to the ideals of asceticism and frugality. As MacKaye explains, "I will say what is exactly on my mind and do it in 32 seconds."[29]

How the music was produced also relates to the bands' focus on realism. Their albums eschew repeated takes, track mixing, and studio manipulation in general in favor of the authentic, unprocessed sounds of the instruments, their voices, and the reality of recording. The instruments are clearly separate in their recordings—you can hear each one individually and can spatially locate them. For instance, in "Filler," the guitar is clearly placed on the left and the bass and drums are on the right, and a thin texture is also evident in "Straight Edge," where the horizontal structure of the instruments' setup reflects more that of a live performance than that of a studio recording. The studio itself—Inner Ear—was a homemade getup of local engineer Don Zientara, including a reel-to-reel four-track recorder and a mixing board set up on the porch with its power cords running down to the basement. The sound of the albums reflects this shoestring setup; you can hear the verbal cues and studio chatter on a number of tracks: MacKaye mumbles "play it faster" over the opening riff of "Minor Threat" and assures the listener "that's a promise" with a laugh at the end of the song; you can hear the guitar being tuned at the start of "Steppin' Stone"; the beginning of "12XU" has MacKaye saying "This goes out to everybody. Ready?" and he asks "is that good enough?" answering himself "I think so" at the end of "Stumped." The inclusion of these unremarkable asides, typically absent in studio recording, highlights the work, the reality, of creating music. Rather than expunging the traces of band members as fallible mortals needing to tune their instruments, requiring more than one take, or chatting among themselves and with the producer, these additions make the tracks uglier (as a binary to the pretty polish of pop songs) by stressing, and therefore elevating, the place of the producer instead of simply the product.

Then there is the noise. The cacophonous noise of the songs brings attention to its cause. The noise bewilders and grates, intentionally so, lifting the humdrum of musical routine to a chaotic and feverish extreme. Noise captures your attention; it startles you, pulls you from the predictability of your surroundings, and makes you eager to seek out the source. Noise is raced (as discussed in chapter 2) and is classed—it organizes and categorizes. A considerable part of this emotive noise was the vocal delivery of both Strejcek (with Teen Idles) and MacKaye (with Minor Threat). Both vocalists had no previous experience singing and employed the punk vocal tradition of shouting, rather than harmonic singing. The effect is more of an emotional appeal than anything else, in part because the volume and speed of the shouting tends to obscure any easy comprehension of the lyrics. On songs like Teen Idles' "Getting in My Way," the only recognizable lyrics are often punctuated at the end of a sentence, when the titular *way* is rhymed with *stay*, *day*, and *gray*. What *is* easily decipherable is the urgency, fury, and ruggedness of Strejcek's voice, which is only strengthened by the distortion of the microphones and authentic recording process. Strejcek seems to be throwing out lyrics like challenges—quick, harsh deliveries that taunt the listener, even without the full understanding of what he's saying. The discordance, the vocalization itself, is as important, if not more so, as the words that are being spit out.

MacKaye takes the vocal intensity and dissonance to another level, using his voice as a weapon to inflict feelings of pain, frustration, and sheer primitiveness. In "Filler," he howls out the first line "What happened to you?" drawing out the last word over three seconds, before flinging out the last word of the chorus ("filler") in a fully enunciated two-syllable punch of a yelp. This vocal style was a signature of MacKaye, who "spouted his lyrics like a frantic drill sergeant, halfway between a holler and a bark."[30] In "Seeing Red," the chorus is yelled with such resolve and exigency that MacKaye's voice sounds nearly hoarse; when he expels the line "Red/I'm seeing red" the listener can almost visualize the strain on his throat and envision the snapping of his vocal chords. His guttural roughness demands attention and invokes alarm—in the connotative tone and texture of his voice but also in the tangible bodily harm it could cause. And when MacKaye roars, "You built that wall up around you/And now you can't see out/And you can't hear my words/No matter how loud I shout" in

"Screaming at a Wall," his jarring, strident yelps embody the lyrics he is singing; his earsplitting shouts are a plea to listen and the volume of the sound, the intensity and texture of his voice, are the aural demand for the listener's attention.

Even more striking is MacKaye's juxtaposition of the spoken word and yelling, highlighting and commenting on the conventional civilized/primitive and concomitant high-class/low-class dichotomies. "In My Eyes" opens with MacKaye speaking in a cartoonish, buoyant deep voice, intoning "You tell me you like the taste," which is immediately followed by the unforgiving scream of "You just need an excuse," with each word skewered and enunciated separately, every bellowed syllable an accusation. This pattern repeats in the rest of the first verse:

> You tell me it calms your nerves (*spoken*)/You just think it looks cool
>   (*screamed*)
> You tell me you want to be different (*spoken*)/You just change for the
>   same (*screamed*)
> You tell me it's only natural (*spoken*)/You just need the proof (*screamed*)

The last line of the first verse ends in a half-scream, half-spoken exhortation, without any musical accompaniment: "Did you fucking get it?" The contrast between the caricatured civility of the spoken word, which is linked to markedly facetious logic and mainstream justification (I like the taste, it calms my nerves, it's natural), and the primeval screaming, which is linked to the act of truth-telling, of a nakedness of the emperor-has-no-clothes sort, is not only evident, it's meant to be shocking. The niceties of a proper society, including a way of speaking and of thinking, are revealed as ridiculous next to rude reality. If yelling is low-brow, it's also shown to be more authentic and truthful; the relationship between values and aesthetics (beauty truth, truth beauty) is inverted and subverted. This vocal tactic is used a number of times in Minor Threat songs, with the calm spoken word as a symbol for "polite society," which is continuously set against the seething wails of unrefined plebeians: the voice of political correctness in "Guilty of Being White," a declaration of human sameness in "Straight Edge," and as the "humanity" in "Out of Step (with the World)." In a truly postmodernist bent, Minor Threat blurs the sonic high/low boundaries of singing versus yelling, paralleling and ultimately exposing the false binary of vulgar/sophisticated, primitive/ advanced aesthetics.

The not-so-subtle middle finger to polite and civilized society included the liberal and joyful use of profanity in their songs, a socially constructed low-brow form of communication. Considered obscene and by some even blasphemous swearing, particularly publicly, has a strong historical and cultural association with social class. The word *vulgar* literally means "common," and most often profanity emerged from lower-class transliterations of words.[31] The list of expletives in the songs of Teen Idles and Minor Threat is fairly extensive—fuck, shit, crap, pissed off, asshole—second only to the number of songs in which these swearwords appear. In *Minor Disturbance*, expletives are found in "Fleeting Fury," "Teen Idles," and "Fiorucci Nightmare," and in the three Minor Threat albums they appear in "Filler," "I Don't Wanna Hear It" (sample lyric: "I don't wanna hear it/Know that you're full of shit/ Shut your fucking mouth/I don't care what you say"), "Small Man Big Mouth," "Minor Threat," "In My Eyes," "Out of Step," "Betray," "It Follows," "Think Again," "Look Back and Laugh," "Sob Story," and "No Reason." To a certain extent, of course, the depth and breadth of these words is merely a reflection of the anger and frustration the band members were feeling; but more significant and more complicated is what that anger is directed at and how it's directed. The repeated use of profanity, particularly in the recorded, public forum of music, is a literal and figurative "fuck you" to conventional, upper-class linguistic and social values, which cherish public propriety, verbal cleverness, and adherence to their constructed version of proper behaviors and look down on open displays of anger, coarse language, and an ignorance or outright eschewal of what is deemed common decency.

This attack on conventional (read: upper-class) values was metaphorically tied in a bow and then stomped on by the bands' use of tempo, volume, and timbre. Their atonal attack of noise produces not only a feeling of speed and energy but also a sense of an unbounded assault on conformity itself. For instance, the forty-four-second offensive that is the opening track of Teen Idles' *Minor Disturbance* begins with a sneering guitar riff played with furious disarray, and, as the hammering drums kick in a few seconds later, Strejcek's voice blasts indecipherably through; this guitar-bass-and-drum strike reprises over and over again, with the same riffs played repeatedly, evoking a feeling of being thrashed continually. The onslaught continues in the next track, "Sneakers," where a menacing drum roll is succeeded by ominously strummed bass power chords that conjure a heavy-metal dark sound before the tempo picks up and a shredding guitar solo intercedes a minute into the song. Each of the remaining songs on the album, "Get Up and Go," "Deadhead," "Fleeting Fury," "Fiorucci Nightmare," and "Getting in My Way," use the same combination of nonstop speed, a rhythmic blitz in the form of crashing drums, and the repetitive, abrasive riffs of piercing electric guitar and a booming bass, and impenetrable lyrical shouting that produced, as MacKaye called it in punk zine *Touch and Go*, "total noise— not like bullshit noise—but songs with a really rough edge."[32]

Minor Threat was similarly inclined. Their riffs are sinewy—powerful, muscular, and lean—with a nonstop barrage of velocity, volume, and aggression; their sound is jagged and distorted, like a serrated blade trudging through bone. Nelson's drums are a violent sledgehammer, at one turn a brutal military-style death march and at another a tornado of crashing cymbals and improbable speed. Each song is a visceral eruption, a blur of sound that, compiled into an entire album, is an uninhibited and concerted assault of unbroken noise, an aural confrontation that, even to MacKaye, "at first it didn't sound like music to me. It was such a shock to my ear."[33]

And that was the point. This weird, jarring noise that was called hardcore was, in part, an answer to the conservative, traditional cultural mores of DC's prim and proper cultural and economic ladder-climbing society. Musical virtuosity and harmonic melodies were for a different population of the city—the elite. The city that Minor Threat and Teen Idles sang about, the *way* that these bands sang about the city, established a narrative that evoked anger, danger, and pain. Their frenzied feel and sound of disorder and turmoil, the noise of hardcore, served as a proclamation against the regulations, intellectualism, and claims to propriety—the patina of cultured refinement—that were the hallmark of DC's cultural milieu. They did so intentionally; as DC punk authors Mark Andersen and Mark Jenkins contend, "the songs raged, but not blindly or inarticulately."[34] The form and sound of their music, the noise of Minor Threat and Teen Idles, was designed specifically as a threat, as a warning, as a representation of the way they felt about the state of culture in their city.

THE PARADOX OF CLASS AND CLASS-PASSING

Although the inception of Teen Idles and Minor Threat certainly arose from an emotional compulsion, and their sound consistently incorporated a minimalist, noise-centered aesthetic, the early deficiencies in the bands' practical musical skill quickly dissolved in a drive for and emphasis on precision and prowess. Minor Threat's lineup, particularly, transformed the amateur spirit into a more rigorous musical attitude. As guitarist Baker notes, the reason was in part the influence of their heroes and mentors, Bad Brains, who "were incredible musicians. . . . They taught us that just because it's punk rock, it doesn't mean you have to play shitty. They were really, really accomplished musicians."[35] As the previous chapter has made clear, Bad Brains took pride in their musical virtuosity, and their technical talent was always-already linked to a racialized musical history. At the same time, the intersection of race and class is nearly impossible to extricate, particularly in the United States, where the American Dream is sold beneath the narrative of a classless, socially mobile, rags-to-riches veneer. And according to this narrative, our history is replete with the conflation of race and class, focusing on the former while ignoring the latter. Still, race is also always infused with class; whiteness in our country signals middle- and upper-classdom, and people of color signal lower socioeconomic status. Thus, when Bad Brains models musical brilliance, it is assigned (even by me, in the previous chapter) to a framework of race rather than class. But their musical chops should also be seen intersectionally, as a way to perform at once race and transcend the connotation of class that is linked to their blackness.

Following in Bad Brains' footsteps, the development of Minor Threat into accomplished musicians ignores (the privilege of) whiteness in lieu of the classed connotations of such musicianship. Drummer Nelson, who, like MacKaye, had been one of the only two members who belonged to both Teen Idles and Minor Threat, was revered for his speed and skill. He "played like a machine—with his wiry arms moving at a blur, they looked like piston rods on a locomotive; his stamina was mind-boggling,"[36] and, according to Baker, was viewed as the best drummer in the city. Guitarist Preslar played six-string bar chords "lightning-fast with incredible precision . . . playing full-position bar chords at that speed"[37] with a "strength, speed and accuracy that are extremely difficult to duplicate"[38] and "set the standard for all hardcore to come."[39] Baker, who was first a bassist and later switched to electric guitar, had been a child prodigy, jamming with Carlos Santana at age twelve on stage at a show in Detroit. Known as a gutsy and dynamic guitar player, Baker's bass playing was characterized as "downright pummeling,"[40] and his rhythms produced a robust and vigorous sound. Together with vocals from MacKaye, Minor Threat's music was lauded for its "speed, power, and precision of a jackhammer . . . with flat-out sprints that had the band playing as fast as they humanly could."[41]

These public accolades—albeit primarily within the confines of the punk scene—were mounting for the DC hardcore musicians: L.A.-based punk fanzine *Flipside*'s readers voted Minor Threat "band of the year," their show with the Dead Kennedys "the best gig" of all of 1982,[42] and their sound was heralded in fanzine *Noise* as "cleaner and more polished . . . but just as fast."[43] Producer Skip Groff claims *In My Eyes* is "one of the greatest punk records of all time, from start to finish";[44] *Spin* rates Minor Threat's Complete Discography one of the fifty most essential punk albums, "Out of Step" as one of the twenty best punk songs, and *Out of Step* rounds out Pitchfork's top hundred albums of the 1980s (asking "How were Minor Threat this fast and this tight, this judgmental and this inviting, this minimal and this expansive?").[45] Even Teen Idles, whose musical ineptitude was not only widely known but also was a badge of pride, was honored for their chops: their single "Get Up and Go" was called "this year's best single" by Michigan's popular fanzine *Touch and Go*, and San Francisco punk radio show *Maximum Rocknroll* made the song its number one for several weeks in a row. The praise went beyond their recorded music into the arena of their live performances. Village Voice writer Tom Carson was impressed by how professional and tight Minor Threat played, which Baker says was deliberate: "Yeah, we strove for that. We rehearsed constantly. Those little bursts of 35 second songs became a lot more effective if it's more of a precision thing."[46] And, in a 1982 review, *Washington Post*'s Howard Wuelfing called Minor Threat shows an "irresistible force meeting implacable beauty at impossible velocity" as they "displayed the sort of style and strength associated with a class act."[47]

What's so simultaneously fascinating and paradoxical is the classed language and system of valuation Minor Threat and Teen Idles' music engendered. Attempting to escape the hierarchal system of conventional culture and the accompanying industry of music, Minor Threat ends up ensnared in and elevated by that same hierarchy, partially *because* of their mold-breaking sound and style. The seemingly infallible American values of economic and social ladder climbing and a never-ceasing zeal for fame and fortune were the core of what Minor Threat and Teen Idles were raging against. The irony is their musical reactionary response brought about the glorification and adulation the band was trying to subvert. Even the vocabulary used to describe their playing—"precision," "accuracy," "best"—conjures images of a level of fastidiousness and achievement that seem to correspond more closely to upper-class values. Indeed, the paradox is almost laughable when Wuelfing describes the band as "a class act" in his review, ostensibly linking their showmanship and technical skills with an upper-class act rather than the working-class act the band so constantly attempted to represent.

A certain amount of classed contradictions is also present in the lyrical subject matter of the bands. Almost unilaterally, the songs of Teen Idles and Minor Threat describe the personal rather than the overtly political. And if their approach to the personal is in itself a political statement,[48] a certain privilege and freedom is inherent in the ability to ignore politics and focus nearly exclusively on the "me." In *Minor Disturbance*, the eight songs may touch on sociopolitical concerns—drug culture in "Deadhead," rampant consumption in "Fiorucci's Nightmare," youth culture in "Teen Idles," and "Sneakers"—but all these references are specifically constructed around how and why they affect the band and its members, rather than the outward-looking political implications. The band bemoans the hippie music scene ("Riding that train high on cocaine/the music is really lousy, the fans are a pain") not for the way the social justice idealism of the 1960s was sublimated by drugs, but instead for the aesthetics of the music itself and the fans who are "a lousy joke." Similarly, "Teen Idles" and "Sneakers" scorn contemporary youth culture as "teenage ignorance" and youths (including themselves) who are "fuckin' bored to tears . . . with nothing to do." Yet this contempt is not for the ennui of youth as an institutional crisis or for the class-based leisure system that perpetuates class inequality; instead, it is a complaint about their own lives and the lives of their friends. In these instances, the personal dictates the political rather than the reverse.

The same is true of Minor Threat's three '81–'83 albums, which focuses on the dystopian reality of relationships. With their lamentations about friends who are no longer the same people they used to be ("Filler," "Screaming at a Wall," "Look Back and Laugh," "No Reason"), their rages about betrayal ("I Don't Wanna Hear It," "Betray," "Stepping Stone"), and their painful eruptions of feeling misjudged by the outside world ("Seeing Red," "Minor Threat," "Guilty of Being White," "It Follows"), Minor Threat seems to ignore explicit politics in favor of personal politics. As MacKaye explains in punk zine *Maximum Rocknroll*, "every song I've written is about me and you. Every song . . . it was me. First person."[49] And although one might argue, rightfully, that these albums were the impetus for a straight, highly politicized social movement, my contention is that the purpose, the motivation, for writing them was not an attempt to make a political statement but instead was an outlet for personal, emotional catharsis. As with Minor Threat's other songs, which are positioned as an anticonsumption, anticapitalist manifesto of sorts, the personal *always* precedes the political.

This privilege—of valuing the me over the we—was a function of the band's sociocultural location and a specific time and place. As Tom Berrard, a member of the DC hardcore scene, said, "Most DC Hardcore kids came from well-off families. The whole joke in the media was 'Georgetown Punks' since that was one of the richest parts of town. It was seen as hypocrisy, but you can be unhappy if you have money—it's not your money anyway."[50] This privilege granted the band space to explore the politics of the personal, rather than the politics of the many. Not encumbered with the more blue-collar burdens other DC families shouldered, including challenges and intersections of race and class, Teen Idles and Minor Threat were free to express their own problems. At the same time, for those growing up in DC, politics was second nature. It was a part of the culture and the economy. The drinking water was spiked with it. During Nelson's childhood, his father worked for the Foreign Service and was stationed at diplomatic posts in Iran, Hungary, and Afghanistan. MacKaye's parents wrote for the *Washington Post*, and the machinery of politics seemed like "the same story, it's the same fuck-ing plot lines," which led to what MacKaye calls a "desensitiz[ation] to politics to the point where I don't have any interest in politics."[51] This disgust with the interminable and unchanging nature of politics, coupled with the privileged ability to disconnect from the material realities such policies and politics often necessitated, guided MacKaye to writing and creating music that spoke to the self. As he explains, "If you want to keep an eye on what's going on, that's cool, but you are not as capable of changing politics as you are capable of changing yourself."[52] This power to circumvent politics in favor of the private was a function of a specific form of class- and place-based privilege.

This near single-mindedness on the personal over the political was unique to Teen Idles and Minor Threat. On the West Coast, Black Flag was raging against the Los Angeles Police Department ("Revenge") and race ("White Minority"); Adolescents lamented the death of our political system ("Democracy") and classed society ("No Way," "Kids of the Black Hole"); in New York, Agnostic Front seethed about war ("Final War") and class discrimination ("Discriminate Me"); and Reagan Youth, besides the name of the band itself, warned about white supremacy ("New Aryans") and the death of US democracy ("USA"). This is not to say, of course, that these hardcore bands' albums were nothing but political songs. On the contrary, the majority of their albums do focus on the personal—relation-ships, the hardcore scene, ennui, and the anxieties of youth. However, at least two songs on each album look externally, nationally, to the socio-political issues of the time. Even Minor Threat's DC hardcore brethren had some political songs: S.O.A's "Public Defender" shouts about the evils of cops; Bad Brains warns about the evils of capitalism ("Fearless Vampire Killers") and race ("The Big Takeover" and "Don't Need It"); and Government Issue (GI) laments the police ("No Rights," "No Way Out"), religious hypocrisy ("Religious Ripoff"). It is interesting to note that Faith, featuring Ian MacKaye's brother Alec, is the other DC hardcore band in this book whose album solely concentrates on the personal, rather than the political.

It becomes evident, then, that in many aspects of the performance of class within Teen Idles' and Minor Threat's music—the selection and use of instruments, the hardcore sound and musical composition, their lyrical content—enact a kind of downward class-passing. Class-passing is most often associated with upward mobility, the naturalized assumption being that wealth and cultural capital are the desired end. As feminist cultural and film theorist Gwendolyn Audrey Foster explains, there is a "fixation with class mobility because it insists on the social negotiation of desire . . . into the capitalist fantasies of the American Dream, including fantasies of upward mobility."[53] Yet it is precisely this cultural supposition—that money, power, and fame are compulsory as seen through the promotion of the American Dream—that Teen Idles and Minor Threat sought to rebuff. Downward passing becomes then, not emulation, but an alteration, of power.

By denying the tacit desirability of being rich, MacKaye and company repudiate what sociologists Karen Bettez Halnon and Saundra Cohen describe as "gentrification" of the body, instead using downward passing to "renegotiate authority, and indeed the right to author" their own bodies.[54] Although gentrification, as Halnon and Cohen describe it, implies the "invasion" and the appropriation of working-class aesthetics and material goods by the middle class, with the consequences being the eradication of the working class's power, these bands both rejected material goods as a distinction of class and simultaneously sought to achieve a balance of power they saw missing in the city's power-laden, white, upper-class system. Rather than using consumption as a tool for "playing" lower class, that is, borrowing and sporting symbols of the working class and thereby neutering its power, as Halnon and Cohen define aesthetic gentrification,[55] Minor Threat and Teen Idles embraced the performance of downward class-passing through sound as a celebration of working-class values, or at least a repudiation of the dictates of upper-class ones. Their downward passing was used to "express an ambivalence toward the self-identity of a class structured in dominance [and] highlight the colonizing moment of a ruling class"[56] by exposing, and discarding, the sociocultural necessity of achieving the American Dream in one particular way.

LYRICS AS ANTICONSUMPTION

My previous argument has a glaring and significant exception about the privileged nature of the personal lyrics of Teen Idles and Minor Threat: conspicuous consumption. This lyrical vitriol was particularly pointed at the consumer-obsessed culture the band members saw among their peers both in Washington, DC, and in the British punk scene preceding the hardcore scene. "Fiorucci Nightmare," the sixth song on Teen Idles' *Minor Disturbance* EP, a mocking ode to the high-stylings of their George-town peers, addresses the pretentious privilege of Washington: "Fiorucci nightmare/asshole's dream/spend all your money on the fashion machine/spots and stripes and spandex pants/pay a hundred dollars to learn how to dance/ . . . Down in Georgetown in a fashion race/For the guys to see how high you rate." MacKaye himself had two afterschool jobs in Georgetown, working at the movie theater and at the Haagen-Dazs ice cream shop, where he was familiar with the quickly gentrifying neighborhood. Teen Idles were not alone in their lyrical disdain for fashion-based consumption. GI similarly mocks the status and class-infused hypocrisy ingrained in their peers' behaviors, centered in Georgetown. In "Fashionite," they scorn "Shops in all the high class stores/All you are is high class whores/Georgetown's where you spend your time/Think you're cool but you're just slime." Until around the late 1930s a mainstay of African American culture, Georgetown had priced out its original inhabitants and remade its streets into a primarily white, upper-class bastion of consumerism and capitalism. "Fiorucci Nightmare" and "Fashionite," if not a direct attack on the gentrification of formerly black neighborhoods, still is a personal censure of the outcomes that urban redevelopment produced. Material goods, in this song represented by clothing, are castigated as privileged trappings void of any meaning but that of economic spectacle.

In a similar way, Minor Threat addresses, and ultimately reviles, the theoretical consumption-based mainstay of outward appearance as a representation of identity in "Seeing Red." The lyrics bemoan their peers' fixation on conformity, particularly one based on looking and wearing the same items as everyone else: "You see me and you laugh out loud/You taunt me from safe inside your crowd/My looks, they must threaten you/To make you act the way you do. . . . You see me and you think I'm a jerk/First impressions without a word." The band clearly acknowledges the culturally mandated routine of identification and subsequent clas-sification by appearance. Continuing in the vein of Teen Idles' "Fiorucci Nightmare," Minor Threat scorns not just those who buy into—literally and figuratively—the consumption-based model of class identity but also those who use that system to belittle, berate, and isolate those who do not conform to those standards. The band understands that their unwillingness to participate in such a class- and consumption-based identification system is a threat (albeit, given their name, only a minor one) to the accepted cultural paradigm.

Part and parcel of this concept of the performance of consumption as a performance of a classed identity was the concomitant ideal of upward mobility. Teen Idles and Minor Threat habitually and intentionally participated in the contrary act of downward passing, while mainstream culture and their DC peers, who often were the children of rich and powerful senators, lobbyists, and assorted political glitterati, partook in the new American Dream of cultural ascendency. "Stepping Stone," from Minor Threat's 1981 *In My Eyes*, addresses the interwoven desires for consumption and celebrity: "You're trying to make your mark in society/Using all the tricks that you used on me/You're reading all those high fashion magazines/The clothes you're wearin' girl are causing public scenes/I said/I'm not your stepping stone/I'm not your stepping stone." Despite the fact that Minor Threat is covering this song, which was originally written by Tommy Boyce and Bobby Hart, recorded and released by Paul Revere and the Midnight Raiders in 1966, the song still acts as a statement against consumption-based mobility by Minor Threat in two ways. First, it continues the band's disparagement of people (or, in this case, a specific girl) who believe that blindly following the demands of the culture industry (fashion magazines, advertising, the commodification of the body as a sexual object) will elicit fame and acclamation. Second, the song acts as an anticommodification statement about the band itself. MacKaye is demanding that he, and his band, is not a stepping-stone—ostensibly to that sought-after acclaim and social mobility. This is not simply a condemnation of being used, as love-gone-wrong songs often evoke (though, clearly, the song has undertones of that as well) but is also a denunciation of the way music itself has been commodified and, subsequently, deified.

The bands' antipathy to the music industry's obsession with money and possessions was not, however, confined to the mainstream. Yes, their anticonsumption stance was formulated in large part as a reaction against the luxury and affluence that enclosed DC punks in Georgetown, but it also was a response to the commodification of British punk rock in the 1970s. Although British punk rock is often idolized as an expression of the anger and aggravations of working-class British youth during years mired in inflation and unemployment, the scene, particularly exemplified by the Sex Pistols, quickly transformed. Sex Pistols' lyrics were indeed reflective of the working-class anger occurring in London at the time, and punk music—by virtue of its focus on amateur musical ability—lent itself (at least, hypothetically) to any class, but the band's puppet master, Malcolm McLaren, was more interested in the aesthetic and revolutionary possibilities of shocking the upper class, rather than opening an avenue for working-class values to be espoused. And the band itself—Rotten, guitarists Sid Vicious and Steve Jones, and drummer Paul Cook—seemed to be more interested in acquiring the fame and money it sang so despairingly about than staying insular in its working-class message. They were caught in the conundrum of a music that promulgated an anticommercial ethos but a band that pursued commercial triumph. As Rotten said on a British rock program, "I am against the whole of the middle-class bit: tellies, cars, possessions. But that don't mean I won't get corrupted by middle-class values."[57] Such contradictions spurred the fervent anticonsumer stance of Teen Idles, particularly in their song "Fleeting Fury." Clearly directed at the Sex Pistols, the song hollers

> Cries of anarchy, cries of freedom
> Cries of fury in the United Kingdom
> Started out loud, started out young
> Started out poor and just for fun
> Tales of youth fighting back
> Just another load of crap
> The clothes you wear have lost their sting
> So's the fury in the songs you sing
> Walking with a goose-step, rose up high
> Making sure you're seen in the public eye
> You're acting mean, you're acting tough
> You should have been happy with just enough.

Even the original punk heroes seemed no match for the machine of capitalism and consumerism. This danger, of "selling out," of not being authentic, which was palpably linked to the performance of a downwardly classed identity, whether it was as a teenager in DC or as a punk band in the echelons of music history, was a recurring theme in Teen Idles' and Minor Threat's lyrics and a tenet of how they lived their lives and created their music.

Of course, this was the 1980s in Washington, DC, so I would be remiss to not mention the huge red elephant in the room: Ronald Reagan. Touting "supply-side economics," or what we refer today as trickle-down economics, Reagan's first term in office oversaw the widening and deepening gap between the rich and the poor, cutting taxes in an effort to jump-start the economy, but ultimately slashing the middle class. Despite the golden halo retroactively applied to the president, particularly surrounding his economic policies, his policies achieved unimpressive GDP growth, poor productivity performance, and an astounding rise in the deficit.[58] Only two songs by a DC hardcore band addressed the president: GI's "Hey Ronnie," whose lyrics are constrained to two lines that do not start to skim the surface of poverty, economic inequality, or capitalism: "Hey, Ronnie!/You ain't no fun!/Hey, Ronnie!/You ain't no fun." The second song, "Moral Majority" was written by Youth Brigade's Nathan Strejcek (formerly of Teen Idles), and eviscerated the right wing in its many forms, including racism ("You wanna move the country to the right/You wanna make the country bright white"), religious zealotry ("A godless society full of moral decay/But Jerry Falwell says he knows the way"), and, of course, Reagan himself ("Ronald Reagan is quite a man/A part of the new morality trying to ruin this land").

Although Reagan's economic policies did not make its way into DC hardcore in any profound way, it did infuse hardcore scenes around the country. Houston's D.R.I. (Dirty Rotten Imbeciles) sang on their 1983 album *Dirty Rotten EP/LP*, "Smell the power/smell the health/Smell the poverty of America's wealth/Money smells of evil, greed/Capitalist wants and pumped up needs" (on "Money Stinks") and were even more transparent on "Reaganomics": "Reaganomics killing me/Reaganomics you," which was the totality of the song's lyrics. In Austin, MDC (Millions of Dead Cops) ranted on their 1982 album *Millions of Dead Cops*, "Ronald laughs as millions starve/And profits forever increase" (on "Corporate Deathburger") and "Crumbs for the poor/Rich man's profits soar/Government by the rich/Poor man's life a bitch" (on "Business of Parade"), and

Wasted Youth in L.A. sang in "Reagan's In," "Kill that man his values are wrong/It ain't movies it's not T.V./It's pretty rough man you will see." New York's Reagan Youth was the clearest political statement to and about the president in their name and in their eponymous song: "We are the songs of Reagan heil/We are the godforsaken heil/The right is our religion/ We all watch television." Even DOA in Vancouver got in on the Reagan-bashing with the song "Fucked Up Ronnie," singing, "You're fucked up Ronnie you're not gonna last."

This gap—between hardcore and Reagan writ large and the DC hardcore scene—exemplifies the contradictions that imbue DC as a national and local space and place. On the one hand, Washington is the nation's capital and Ronald Reagan was the face of that capital city—including the economic policies and realities that emerged from those policies. On the other hand, Washington, DC, is home to thousands upon thousands of individuals—adults and teenagers alike—that have lives separate from or not primarily based on the city as the face of the US government. That is not to say, of course, that these two conceptions of the city are disparate; they are constantly and continuously intertwined and interdependent. Yet the songs of Minor Threat and Teen Idles (and of GI, with the exception of "Hey Ronnie!") are centered primarily on the city as the home of its people, the personal and local DC, the DC where they worked, went to school, skateboarded, and lived. It wasn't that Ronald Reagan did not exist for them; it was instead that other people were more relevant and meaningful in their lives.

4

Masculinity as Music

DC Hardcore and the Implications of Gender

In many ways, gender roles were in flux during the 1970s and into the early 1980s. Perhaps more precisely, gender roles seemed paradoxical, at once subverting and reinforcing conventional constructions of both manhood and womanhood. For both genders, the paradox can be firmly located within the (still) ever-present tension between the deconstruction of male hegemony and the consequential fear of that deconstruction, a power-laden, gendered pendulum swinging toward progress and then back toward conventionality. This first pendulum swing headed toward the subversion of conventional manhood, propelled by the sociopolitical gains of the civil-rights, gay-rights, and women's movements of the 1960s, which made some cultural progress in recentering nonwhite, homosexual men and women and taking to task the oppressive and marginalizing forces of white heteronormative masculinity. But this vacillation was halted to some degree by yet another chink in the armor of masculine dominance: political and economic crises in the form of a rise in unemployment in the 1970s as a result of recessions, oil emergencies, deindustrialization, and the accompanying weakening in manufacturing, as well as a government waving the flag of inflation rather than unemployment. What's more, women were entering the workforce in larger numbers and in fields that had formerly been dominated by men. Such shifts in the workplace seemed to presage shifts in the home too; if men were not employed (or not the only one employed), who was to say the privileges and hierarchies at home would remain the same?

In what amounted to a crisis of traditional manhood, with sociopolitical dominion of men challenged and the prestige of the breadwinning role under siege, one might expect that masculinity as a category transformed in the 1970s into a more malleable and less rigid one. One would, for the most part, be wrong. Indeed, the 1970s made little dent in the history of patriarchy. Instead, masculinity in the 1970s merely adapted and reestablished its dominance. Men—and the slippery but clearly binarily defined characteristics of masculinity—were still "ubiquitous in positions of power everywhere."[1] And those positions of power—be they military, political, scientific, or musical—were, by default, masculine positions, with successes attributed not to gender but to an assumed invisibility of dominance because of that gender. At the same time, as men studies vanguard writer Michael Kimmel describes it, "the quest for manhood—the effort to achieve, to demonstrate, to prove their masculinity—is one of the animating experiences in the lives of American men."[2]

Such omnipotent masculine ideals are then embedded, subconsciously or not, within nearly every aspect of our social and cultural lives. Which includes, of course, music. How we understand what it is to be a man or a woman informs our physical and emotional reactions to certain sounds and their associated music. At the same time, gendered sounds and music work to reinforce and reproduce the culturally constructed gender roles. Hardcore was not immune to the gendered contradictions playing out on the cultural, political, and economic stage. In this chapter, we will explore how DC hardcore sonically reinforces the culturally constructed gender of sound, which subsequently replicates socially formed understandings of masculinity, using State of Alert (S.O.A.), Government Issue (GI), and Faith as the primary paradigm. Although Bad Brains and Minor Threat were, and in many ways, still are, the two most definitive DC hardcore bands, these three highly influential and emblematic hardcore bands, even with their slight derivations in sound, lyrics, and style, all perform a very specific construction of masculinity.

State of Alert, Government Issue, and Faith: Hardcore's Sonic Masculinity

The music of DC hardcore, as well as the physical makeup of the band members themselves, continued the long history of rock's male-centric tradition. As will be discussed in subsequent chapters, the DC scene more generally, and DC hardcore bands more specifically, were dominated by males. Such gendered homogeneity, however, is not particularly surprising in the gendered narrative of rock 'n' roll, which is fundamentally marked by its often surreptitious (and other times glaringly obvious) designations of gender roles. There's the music industry—the producers, studio engineers, executives, business managers, musicians, and performers, not to mention the myriad others involved in the composition, production, and dissemination of music—all of which has long been understood as a field predominantly occupied by men. Then there are the performers themselves: in early R&B (Chuck Berry, Little Richard, Elvis Presley, Chess Records), Motown (Berry Gordy, Stevie Wonder, the Temptations, the Four Tops), folk (Arlo Guthrie, Pete Seeger, Bob Dylan), British blues-rock (the Animals, the Beatles, the Rolling Stones), heavy metal (Led Zeppelin, Deep Purple, Black Sabbath), and glam rock (Kiss, T. Rex, Bowie), the creation and performance of music has been near uniformly associated with and ruled by males. And though clearly exceptions to these male-dominated genres exist—including, for a few examples, the girl groups of Motown, Joan Baez and Mary Travers of folk, and Janis Joplin of blues rock—women were not only rare instances as performers but also were frequently managed and overshadowed by their male managers and counterparts or relegated to mere mouthpieces for male-written tunes. This history of music naturalizes the way gendered music is recognized. As feminist music critic Ellen Willis remarks, "Rock is, among other things, a potent means of expressing the active emotions—anger, aggression, lust, the joy of physical assertion—that feed all freedom movements, and it is no accident that women musicians have been denied access to this powerful language."[3] Over and over again, males were the designated possessors of musical prowess, as both technical musicians and as passionate performers.

Although the gendered character of musical history is widely acknowl-edged and immensely important in understanding the construction of both gender and music, it is equally important to recognize how sound itself, the building blocks of music, has been culturally constructed as a gendered paradigm. Music has frequently been regarded as a "neutral enterprise . . . because of the desire not to acknowledge its mediation through actual people with gendered bodies,"[4] but we cannot separate our conception of music from our experience of that music. When we (try to) do so, we recognize that the body acts as a contested terrain, a space in which cultural expectations and emotions are confronted and processed. *What* these expectations and emotions are and *why* they cre-ated, recognized, and felt is in no way a natural or essentialized explana-tion. That is, there is no biological or physiological reason why a certain pitch, timbre, volume, or frequency would evoke sentiments of alarm, excitement, or tenderness; nor is there an *a priori* set of innate identity markers in sound indicating a feminine or masculine (or for that mat-ter, racial, sexual or geographic) constitution. The lack of intrinsic social meaning in music is, in part, its most formidable and influential aspect. Much like the institutionalized assumptions that form sociopolitical he-gemony, gendered structures are taken for granted, working "below the level of deliberate signification and . . . thus usually reproduced and trans-mitted without conscious interventions."[5] By exploring the sonic color of S.O.A.'s, GI's, and Faith's music, by investigating their songs' musical texture, the accumulation of timbres, ambience, amplitudes, and rhythms, we can discover how their specific form of masculinity is constructed and communicated. In addition to the technical aspects of sound—physical qualities like pitch, rhythm, or timbre—we will consider the rhetorical aspects of sound, that is, "how the conventional associations that sounds have . . . allow them to stand as symbols suggesting dialogues and reso-nances beyond the boundaries of the track."[6]

AGGRESSION AS/AND MASCULINITY: THE ELECTRIC GUITAR AND BASS

Hardcore is aggressive. It is loud and hard and driving and, in the words of one *Washington Post* writer "brutally fast" with a "ferocious blur"[7] of sound. Anyone listening to S.O.A., GI, or Faith—or, for that matter,

Agnostic Front, Cro-Mags, Black Flag, or Circle Jerks—in the early 1980s would agree: hardcore is belligerent, provocative, and relentless. But why? Or perhaps more to the point—how? How does the sound of hardcore, the music of GI and S.O.A. and Faith create the sensation of aggression? How does music create emotion and how does that emotion get linked to gender? One pathway is directly through the choice and use of instruments and the associated connotations of both the instruments themselves and the individuals playing them. Sound and body work concurrently to perform a certain form of masculinity.

Instruments by themselves, and the sounds they produce, have no essential meaning; instead, "the instrument is used to invest the body of the performer with meaning, to confer on it a unique identity whose authentic, natural appearance works to conceal its reliance upon artifice and technology."[8] The combination of an instrument's physical form and its sound help articulate a culturally produced understanding of gender. For instance, flutes, clarinets, and pianos are traditionally seen as feminine instruments, mainly because their small physical size and high-pitched tone make them an acceptable purview of women rather than because some aspect of those instruments is inherent or essentialistic femininity. On the other hand, instruments like the tuba, the bass, and the horn are taken to be in the masculine musical terrain because of their deep and resonant sound.

Let's take one of the crucial (and one of just three) instruments in hardcore, the electric guitar, which often parallels the construction of masculinity: loud, powerful, aggressive, and dominating. The meanings created by the electric guitar are inextricable from the males who play and perform on this technophallus, often seen as an extension of the male body[9]—the hyper-heterosexuality of Jimi Hendrix, Keith Richards, and Jimmy Page. The correspondence between masculinity and the electric guitar is confirmed and perpetuated by music critics and analysts who, in *Rolling Stone* magazine's Hundred Greatest Guitarists, list merely two women (Bonnie Raitt and Joni Mitchell), both of whom are known for their acoustic guitar playing.[10] The electric guitar has, to a certain extent, always been understood as a binary to the acoustic guitar. The acoustic guitar is mellow, warm, earnest, and refined, relegated to the passive, subdued realm assigned to women; the electric guitar is the opposite, symbolizing distortion, vulgarity, and domination, allowed to be played by men who "wield [this] technology to display their transcendence of nature, and their power to order the world according to their will."[11] It is in part the method of amplification—that is, the deliberate manipulation of sound—that acts as this expression, "so when Neil Young straps on an electric guitar, it is because he has something to say that cannot be said with an acoustic. . . . Young recognizes that his electric playing is the vehicle for his feelings of anger, violence, and frustration."[12] These expressive emotions can be understood by the audience mainly because the two guitar types' timbral differences, which immediately indicates to the listener the genre and effect, and because the aforementioned gendered musical history of the acoustic versus electric guitar—before lyrics, melody, or harmony—act as an emotional and thus gendered weathervane.

This is especially true of hardcore, and of S.O.A., Faith, and GI more explicitly. The bands' recurrent use of the eighth-note pulse in both their guitars and basses generate the overwhelming feeling of force and momentum, and with and because of that, hostility and anger. S.O.A.'s Michael Hampton is crucial in achieving this sonic electric guitar assault with his "aggressive flair on guitar"[13] and ferocious tempo. The blitzkrieg of "Draw Blank," the second song from S.O.A.'s *No Policy*, is an example. Opening with only a two-second guitar riff, the mind-boggling speed and distorted reverberation of the guitar portends the dark, pounding attack of Hampton's solo eighteen seconds into the thirty-six-second song. The solo itself is a mere five seconds, but it explodes with a high-pitched, atonal offensive, like shuddering, unsteady nails on a chalkboard, demanding attention. The tempo alone suggests what *Washington Post* critic Richard Harrington described as "staccato bursts of aggressive black noise that come and go like machine gun bursts,"[14] but also the intensely high pitch of the screeching guitar solo connotes warning, a cautionary sound that conjures associations of police sirens, ambulances, and fire alarms, a premonition of the danger, chaos, and frequent savagery to come. Part of these connotations are specifically linked to our already constructed understandings of high-pitched tones. Sounds in the form of alarms regularly designate panic, agitation, and distress. And although this sound is sometimes connected to our cultural construction of femininity grounded in the cliché of the hysterical, overwrought woman screeching, Hampton's manipulation of the guitar points not to a defenseless woman in fear but instead a powerful man wielding an instrument designed to sonically maim.

Hampton's musical warning is complemented and intensified by Wendel Blow's accompanying bass line (E/B/G/D/A/E), which offers a low hammering counterpoint riff of authority and control. It is the combination of the song's two stringed instruments—Hampton's maniacal speed, fuzzed-out distortion, and high-pitched, discordant electric guitar solo and Blow's steady, regimented gruff riffs on the electric bass—that simultaneously suggests agitation, a cause for alarm (which can be understood as a masculinized threat of the typically feminized hysteria) and a promise of militant authority. In both cases, the guitar and bass work to typify dread and underscore the risk of violence.

Similarly, Hampton's use and punctuation of guitar slides in "Gang Fight" and "Warzone," whose overt lyrical expression of anger will be explored in subsequent paragraphs, perform as a symbol of disorder and a promise of uncontrollability. "Warzone" begins with an onslaught of electric guitar, a breakneck riff of E/B/C#m/A asserting menace with its frenetic tempo and combative tone, and "Gang Fight" opens with ominous plucking of chords before churning into a similar rough and reckless guitar and bass line, affirming a foreboding and sinister sound. This arrangement of uncivilized speed and brutish, angry timbre is archetypal, indeed emblematic, of hardcore and of S.O.A. Frustration, aggression, and anger were a product of both youth and the sociopolitical milieu of DC. Yet this overt expression of belligerence is interrupted, and even augmented, by the jarring, startling guitar slides in the middle of these seemingly hostile riffs. Bursting through "Warzone" at 0:16 and 0:32 (of a fifty-two-second song) and at 0:05 and 0:40 in "Gang Fight" (clocking in at a lengthy fifty-nine seconds), these slides function as another type of sonic warning—the inability to anticipate or control. Hampton's guitar slides themselves are discordant, feverish, almost shrill; by appearing in quick, unexpected torrents between the steady militancy of bass and guitar lines, they lend a wild unpredictability to the already formed sonic bellicosity. The slides perform as a different kind of threat: you may think you know us, our music, and our anger, but you don't. This rage can explode at any moment; it can be messy and overpowering; it is disobedient and unmanageable, and it is *in addition* to the pugnacity already promised by the guitar and bass riffs. As social theorist Jacques Attali insists, "Noise is violence: it disturbs. To make noise is to interrupt a transmission, to disconnect, to kill,"[15] and in the case of "Warzone" and "Gang Fight" it is noise upon noise—a doubly assertive dose of disruptive sound. Supplementing the aggression of the guitar's and bass's speed and tone that surprise the listener, S.O.A. intensifies their sonic expression of rage with the unpredictable threat of guitar slide, adding to it the menace of randomness and abandon.

It is unsurprising that Hampton reprised his status as guitarist in Faith directly after the dissolution of S.O.A. and the sonically extreme expressions of antagonism continue in his second band. Still revered as a hard-nosed guitarist, Hampton exploits and worships the use of guitar distortion—in addition to his distinctive excessive speed and uncompromisingly brutal style—as a symbol of unruly and anarchic mutiny. "It's Time," Faith's first song on their Faith/Void Split LP, uses fuzzed-out guitars throughout the track, giving the guitar riff (the prototypical hardcore progression E/B/G/D/A/E) and Chris Bald's parallel bass line a heavy, sinister effect. The muddy, blurred sound garbles the rich and well-defined sound of the electric guitar, an effect that is intensified in the last six seconds of the song, when Hampton peels into a three-second distortion-free, high-pitched solo, which peters out into a cloud of guitar feedback and sonic haze.

This menacing ambiance is replicated in "You're X'ed," the ninth track on the album, this time with Bald's insistent bass line underscoring the murky distortion of Hampton's guitar. Opening with a full three-second detonation of piercing guitar feedback, the bass sneaks in a shuddering, dejected progression, offering a steadfast counterpoint to the dirty sound of the electric guitar. Faith's use of sonic manipulation continues through-out the album, particularly as a disquieting intro and outro to their songs, punctuating the already vicious guitar shredding and bass lines with an added dose of cacophonous auditory aggression. The last nine seconds of track eight, "Confusion," is simply the shrill shriek of guitar distortion and feedback, a complete tonal reversal from the rest of the song, which slogs through a dark, heavy, low texture; and the opening strains of the LP's final track, "In the Black," launches into a twelve-second slow-motion interlude of distortion, with Alec MacKaye's vocals indecipherably slurred through the sliced-up discordant sound of guitar until the ominous bass line kicks in at 0:13, a portentous prelude to the rest of the song.

We should understand Faith's emphasis on and sheer pleasure in the manipulation of guitar sound as musical and social insurrection, an act of aggression and defiance. Musically, the act of distortion itself is a measure of extremism—distortion occurs when the guitar's volume goes beyond its capacity or if the amplifier itself is slightly damaged. Traditionally, tube guitar amplifiers were intended to provide the utmost in clean sound; if there was a woolly or fuzzed-out sound, it was considered a mistake and engineers endeavored to eliminate any such imperfections from the final tracks. But by the early 1950s and into the 1960s, musicians began intentionally pushing their instruments past their normal or socially acceptable sonic boundaries, and, in doing so, they began to achieve a meaner, louder, and more dissonant sound. This was not just an aesthetic choice but also an expression of cultural distortion. Just as the Chicago electric bluesmen intentionally used loudness and distortion as a statement of racial independence and musical originality, Dave Davies of the Kinks intentionally slashed his amps to realize the gritty, muddled sound that signified the British youth revolt of the 1960s, and Jimi Hendrix famously used guitar feedback as the foundation of his Woodstock performance of the "Star-Spangled Banner" as a commentary on the warped, grotesque, almost unrecognizable, sociopolitical state of affairs in the United States, so too does Faith's use of guitar feedback and distortion work as an expression of wrath and repudiation. Their purposeful use of distortion and feedback is both a literal and musical rebellion. In the more literal sense, distortion—of any kind, whether it be visual, verbal, or physical—functions as a commentary on what one, or society, perceives as normal. In order for something to be *distorted*, it must, of course, deviate from what is considered the standard. And Hampton and Bald's guitar and bass playing—their hard-driving style, their lightning-fast tempo, their deafening volume, and their actual use of distortion—is an intentional aberration. Their distorted sound, their aesthetic of confusion, haziness, and pure discordant noise, is their statement about DC. It's not their music that's distorted; it's the world around them.

Faith uses feedback in the same way. Most conventionally, we understand feedback as a response to a particular situation, process, or activity, often with a component of assessment or appraisal inherent in those reactions; we receive feedback from our teachers, our parents, our bosses, our therapists. With that straightforward definition, Faith's musical use of guitar feedback can be recognized as, well, literal feedback. They are responding, with an earsplitting, antagonistic, sustained stream of guitar feedback, to their particular circumstances. The underlying emotions then, both in Faith's use of guitar distortion to represent the distortion of reality and in their atonal musical feedback, are clearly ones of antagonism, manifestations of aggression. Hampton does not use his guitar to capture a psychedelic distorted haze of love, calmness, and peace; Bald does not pluck his bass in a strong, supportive way. Instead, Faith's guitar and bassist act as instruments of hostility, attacks on the musical and social world from which they feel marginalized.

The use of the electric guitar in DC hardcore and the threat, extremism, and out-of-control-ness of that use, is a reinforcement of the traditional role of male sexuality. Much like the nearly three decades of music that preceded it, DC hardcore continued not only the socially constructed equation of rock 'n' roll equals male (hetero)sexuality but also that rock 'n' roll equals dominant, aggressive male (hetero)sexuality. As rock came into mainstream culture in the 1950s, it was feared not just for its racial associations but also for its tacit (racialized) sexualization. The disruptive sound of amplification—the electric guitar—connoted black masculinity, which in turn was equated with a threat, particularly sexually. Musicians like Chuck Berry and Little Richard functioned as both a new model of masculinity, embracing a freedom and lack of inhibition that assumed a certain amount of self-possession and the privilege of nonconformity and danger, exhibiting an overt sexuality and expression of desire.

A considerable aspect of hardcore's and rock's suggestive sexuality is a kind of anthropomorphic function of the instruments mingled with their aural affectivity. The electric guitar and bass are central to this sonic sexualization: the fleeting, squealing guitar solo of S.O.A.'s "Draw Blank" and Hampton's shuddering opening guitar riffs of "Blackout" and "Girl Problems," the jagged, short bursts of guitar spray in GI's "Rock 'n' Roll Bullshit" and the assertive screeching of discordant guitar slides in their "No Rights," and the booming, lurching, insistent combination of guitar and bass in Faith's "It's Time," "You're X'ed," and "In Control" perform, apparently contradictorily, as an act of sexual control and of sexual wantonness. In one way, the guitars function as a sonic display of male domination over the female. This results in part from the feminine personification of the electric guitar. If the guitar can, at least partially, be understood as the female body, then the male command over it (her), his ability to play (her), fold and bend (her) notes to his will, make her wail and quiver, all in front of an audience or recorded in perpetuity, cast the male as sexual aggressor and the female as his submissive instrument.[16] The physical reality of the male lead and bass guitar players in S.O.A., Faith, and GI, and their attendant grating, grinding, and manipulation on that instrument, links back to, and thus always performs, an engrained male sexuality based on the female/male submissive/dominant paradigm preconstructed by cultural norms.

Seemingly paradoxically, though still within the clearly constructed male purview, the sounds of these hardcore guitarists also connote an uncontrollable wild sexuality. The scorching speed of S.O.A. and Faith's Hampton and GI's John Barry and Tom Lyle, the theretofore unknown brevity of their explosive guitar solos, the abrasive, mutinous loudness, and almost defiant simplicity of composition, all raise the bar on rock's rebellious, uncontrollable streak. If parents were concerned about the inflamed abandon that Chuck Berry, the Beatles, or even Elvis Presley would arouse, then the hard-driving, feverish guitar-based hedonism of Faith, S.O.A., and GI would seem to presage the return of the chastity belt. The *way* these male, hardcore guitarists played—renouncing musical moderation or attention to the "rules" of sonic aesthetics—embodies their aversion to, and rejection of, those same corresponding cultural rules. Their guitar playing was aggressive, powerful, and out of control, adjectives that can, and often are, similarly applied to males and their sexuality. As Garfield asserts, "Guitars with politics bore me. I relate to music on the level of sex and death—sweat, blood, cum, sleepless nights, insecurity."[17] The frenzied recklessness of guitar sound parallels, or at least represents, the frenzied recklessness that men's (hetero)sexuality is allowed to enact.

AGGRESSION AS/AND MASCULINITY: THE DRUMS

The aggressive masculinity of DC hardcore's guitars and bass lines are only strengthened and hardened by the only other instrument in hardcore: the drums. In cultures worldwide and throughout time, drums have performed as a musical symbol of traditional masculinity. Historically, men played drums in preparation for battle and contemporaneously men battle in drum contests to prove their manliness, advancing the culturally constructed male characteristics of competitiveness and belligerence. Sonically, the deep, pounding backbeat of the drums evokes an aesthetics of command. Its rhythmic tension and anticipation suggest an undertone of sexuality, and how the drums are played is habitually referred to as an attack, with the bite or snap of the cymbal, tom-tom, or snare—further symbols of traditional masculinity. At the same time, these properties are strengthened and reimagined through the bodies of such rock drummers as Keith Moon, Ginger Baker, and John Bonham, whose sweaty, often shirtless, explosive, vigorous performances on the drums reaffirm this masculinity.

Certainly, the underlying sensation of Simon Jacobsen's drumming in the entirety of S.O.A.'s *No Policy* is a menacing defiance, coupled with the implied threat of violence. This is partially achieved by the use of the drumroll, used in four of the EP's ten tracks: "Girl Problems," "Gang Fight," "Gonna Hafta Fight," and "Gate Crashers." In two of these—"Girl Problems" and "Gonna Hafta Fight"—Hampton's blistering electric guitar riffs actually open the first few seconds of the songs before Jacobsen's assertive, militant-like roll explodes, acting as palpable partner, a musical two of one-two punches, with the antagonism of the guitar. In these two tracks, the speed and aggression of the electric guitar, with its high-pitched metallic sound, is compounded and magnified by the deep, ominous, and equally fast, drumroll. The striking timbral contrast of the guitar and drums, particularly since they are first played independently of each other, heightens the sonic spectacle of assault.

In a similar way, but with a slightly different effect, "Gang Fight" and "Gate Crashers" use Jacobsen's drumroll in conjunction with Hampton's guitar to open the songs, suggesting an equally aggressive two-pronged attack. Unlike the previous two songs, however, "Gang Fight" and "Gate Crashers" have a prolonged intro. "Girl Problems" begins with just three seconds of guitar before Jacobsen's drumroll kicks in, and "Gonna Hafta Fight" has just one scorching second of guitar before the drums; in contrast, the combined guitar-and-drumroll attack of "Gang Fight" is a full five seconds, and the intro on "Gate Crashers" is an extended eleven seconds.[18] These protracted introductions have a hard-hitting, antagonistic effect comparable to the two previously mentioned songs but lack the timbral contrast, which makes the result more immediate and, because of their length, more extensive. In part, the violent undertones of Jacobsen's drumrolls stem from the physicality of the actual technique, which demands a near-continuous right-left-right-left thumping, with added force to the fulcrum on impact, allowing the drumstick to bounce multiple times on the drumhead. The material force of the drumroll sonically translates into metaphorical force. Jacobsen's ability for sustained pounding signifies his masculine ability for corporeal pounding—just imagine the muscles it takes to maintain that kind of drumming, and then imagine those drums as your face. The material-physical equivalence of the drumroll performs as a threat, and one that exaggerates the one already posed by the electric guitar.

Marc Alberstadt's use of the cymbals throughout GI's 1981 *Legless Bull* EP represents the aural codeclaration of force of hardcore's drumming. Alberstadt's punishing abuse of his hi-hat is unrelenting throughout the album, with seven of the ten tracks ("Religious Ripoff," "Fashionite," "Rock 'n' Roll Bullshit," "Asshole," "Bored to Death," "No Rights," "Cowboy Fashion") featuring the double-barreled assault of drums and prominent hi-hat, maintaining a viciously aggressive eighth-note beat.[19] Even on GI's other three tracks—"Anarchy Is Dead," "Sheer Terror," and "I'm James Dean"—the crashing cymbals are present, but simply are neither as heavily prolonged nor as domineering as the previous seven. Like the collaboration between electric guitar and drumroll in S.O.A.'s tracks, the relationship between drums and cymbals in *Legless Bull* poses a sonic, textural juxtaposition and, in doing so, asserts an assault based on a full range of pitch and multiple timbres. The sound of the hi-hat is rapid, brusque, and brassy, with a clanging noise that sounds like, and is known as, a "chick"; in conjunction with the low, dark sound of the drums, this arrangement behaves like an attack on both sides of the pitch and timbre spectrum. If the drumbeat is the portent of future aggression, its rhythm echoing the metaphorical drumbeat toward war, the hi-hat cymbals are the promised outcome of that sign—a crashing, deafening dénouement, scattering sound in a higher-pitched frenzy.

This dual effect depends also on Alberstadt's stunning technical speed. His fever-pitched tempo connotes a sense of wild fractiousness; the speed at which he pounds the drums and hi-hat reeks of an out-of-control impulsiveness, a power that can be neither reined in nor contained. What's more, this unrestrained speed seems never-ending; it's sustained not only throughout every song (which average a tad longer than S.O.A.'s, at around one minute) but also throughout every song on the album. Although Alberstadt's percussive danger may seem a mere rapid blasting burst, a passing storm (given the short duration of the songs), in its totality, over the album's ten songs, each of these quick-fire incursions adds up and together perform as an unremitting assault.

But the drums are not just representative of anger and violence. They also signify sex and a powerful male (hetero)sexuality. Indeed, rhythm itself, manifest in the drums as the persistent, strong, and regular pounding beat thumped out, is often cited as the primary representation of this male-centric (hetero)sexuality in its sonic physicality and emotive ability.[20] In "Blackout," the insistent rhythmic throbbing of Jacobsen's drums engulfs nearly every other recorded instrument, and his fierce, muscular thudding evoke a pulsing carnality. Accompanying this pounding physicality is the shimmering attack and penetration of Jacobsen's hi-hat, which is sometimes juxtaposed with the drums (0:03–11 and 0:23–29), at other times is used to punctuate the end of a drum pattern (0:12–17), or is absent all together, letting the drums themselves dominate (0:18–22 and 0:30–42). If Jacobsen's drums exemplify the male proclamation of sexual prowess with his unchecked physical aggression and grinding backbeat paralleling the phallic penetration, then the cymbals, with their jittery, glassy, high-pitched cut, connote femininity, or the submissiveness of female sexuality. "Blackout," then, performs a form of male-dominated sexuality; the male-infused drums overtake, direct, or simply exclude the feminine sounds of the hi-hat.

Ivor Hanson's drumming in Faith performs male sexuality in a slightly different way, using tempo and meter. "Face to Face" is rife with Hanson's unrestrained, frenzied speed and pugnacious pummeling on the drums. Completely free from any use of hi-hat, the walloping blows of his drums are absolute—persistent, unadorned, and wickedly fast. And although the recording of the song tends to somewhat undercut the prominence of Hanson's sound, as Hampton's electric guitar is sonically overbearing, the drums' physicality is no less diminished. In fact, the snaking coil of noise blurting from Hampton's guitar offers a musical counterpoint to Hanson's feverish, lightning-quick drums. It is this speed and rhythm that suggest a latent masculine (and racial) stereotype of unchecked male sexuality tied to the cultural constructed image of sexual savagery and tribal primitivism. In the cultural production of musical history, the drums have been nearly exclusively relegated to the purview of African, Native American, and Othered tribes. And although their use in these communities was primarily ceremonial or communication,[21] the Westernized designation of those places and tribes as uncivilized and savage, in binary contrast to and construction of the West as civilized and refined, produced with its implications irrepressible and uncontainable sexuality. In this way, Hanson's feral, relentless thudding arouses cultural memories of both tribal abandon and the associated sexual depravity.

AGGRESSION AS/AND MASCULINITY: THE VOICE

Yet the most perceptible, and perhaps the best known, sonic expression of anger in DC hardcore clearly comes from the vocal timbre and style of the bands' singers. As I have discussed in this chapter, not only is musical gender association a derivative of the particular sociohistorical moment in which the music is created and consumed but it is also linked to the history of the sound of music, and how that has historically and culturally been linked to men and manhood. In the case of the lead singer, just as it was with the electric guitar and drums, that history is firmly entrenched in the male body. Our rock singer idols of decades past set the mold for the ways in which lead singers perform a particular form of manhood with both their voices and their bodies: Mick Jagger, Jimi Hendrix, Robert Plant, James Brown, Jim Morrison, Elvis Presley all growled, begged, snarled, and pleaded with their low, deep, dense-sounding tone, signifying authority, confidence, virility, and sexual power. But they also shook their hips, wore skin-tight pants to accentuate their genitals, and swaggered around the stage, caressing the microphone and stand in an intimate embrace. DC hardcore vocalists followed in this tradition of using their body and their voice to signal strength and command, power and sexuality, albeit in a sonically and physically different style than the R&B and rock singers before them.

By eschewing the conventional melodic singing style and refocusing their vocal efforts on the expression of emotion rather than pitch, Garfield, Stabb, and Alec MacKaye manipulate their voices as another form of instrumentation and as a focal point for their manifestation of rage. In small part, this vocal effect can be attributed to the singers' use of the natural minor scale in their singing, which tends to have a bleaker, heavier sound, with a more dissonant and melancholy quality. More noticeable to both the casual listener and the music critic, however, is the hardcore singers' "impassioned but rough-hewn, almost amelodic vocals,"[22] which produces a shouted, rather than harmonic, form of singing.

S.O.A.'s Garfield does this by blending his already husky tone with a pugnacious pace to deliver his lyrics. His voice is naturally gruff and semihoarse, and in each song on *No Policy* he sounds as if he has popped a vocal cord or has at least already been shouting for hours on end. This grainy vocal quality, in part a function of his lack of formal vocal training, in part a consequence of his inherent tone, and in part because he is in fact yelling over a sustained period of time, contains a coarseness, a crudeness that acts as a symbol for the brutality he is attempting to convey. Just as the smooth and intimate vocal tone of the crooners of the 1940s and '50s suggested seduction and tenderness and the girl groups of the '60s sang in a calculatingly girlish tone to indicate naivety and acquiescence, Garfield's grating, rasping vocal quality denoted fury, ache, and strain. Furthermore, his vocal speed and cadence perform as yet another indication of militant rebellion. Expelling words in a near blur of sound, Garfield crams verses into a mind-numbingly short time; in the opening track "Lost in Space," he shouts the first two verses—

> Up in smoke, I laugh in your face
> Fucked on drugs, lost in space
> See your friends, they laugh at you
> But don't get mad, 'cause they're drugged too.
>
> Spend your time on the floor
> Go throw up, come back for more—

in a mere ten seconds. "Blackout" squeezes in two full verses and two choruses in less than forty-five seconds, while Garfield expels the first verse of "Riot" in just four seconds. His speed, particularly in conjunction with his harsh vocal quality, communicates a frenzied, outraged need. The tempo specifically evinces this need; the pace one talks at is an indicator of exigency—a slow drawl suggests easygoingness, a fast-talking rhythm, urgency. Compounded by Garfield's vocal tone, the urgency becomes hostile and demanding.

The vocal exigency is intensified by Garfield's martial-like modulation, which creates the vocal image of a blaring drill sergeant or a "bellicose auctioneer."[23] In "Public Defender," Garfield trades his typically excessively speedy vocal delivery for a more measured, deliberate expectoration of lyrics. With a clarity not often associated with hardcore punk singing, he spits out each line with purposeful yet commandingly intimidating enunciation, his voice rising on the last word of each line, and more authoritatively and protractedly on the last word of each verse:

> See 'em coming
> You'd better move quick
> He's gonna hit you with a stick.

Each of these words is punctuated by Garfield's aggressive intonation and articulation, and "stick" is drawn out in an extended growl, emphasizing the violence of the line with the violence of his voice and cadence. In a similar fashion, Garfield relies on a rising intonation in "Warzone," albeit with less of a formal elocution. Using his characteristically brisk delivery, with its accompanying muddling of words, Garfield uses the last word of each line to punctuate and skewer; these words—"beware," "care," "apart," "start"—are barked like commands, demanding not only attention but also no small measure of fear. Though the majority of S.O.A.'s lyrics are, to be sure, jumbled by the speed and yowl of Garfield, his regulated and controlled phrasing, in combination with his obviously vicious tone and articulation of a few key words, embodies the ire and wrath he is trying to convey.

In a related, though slightly modified way, GI's John Stabb uses his vocal tone, as well as his penchant for screaming, to communicate rage. Unlike Garfield, Stabb has a more refined, higher-pitched voice. There's no gritty coarseness to convey turbulence, no deep pitch to suggest a threat; yet his reedy, piercing tone still conveys alarm and danger. Like sirens erupting in an air raid, Stabb's voice stabs (pun intended) the listener, impaling his wrath with his pitch. As previously mentioned, this high pitch has been frequently associated with women, and so it may seem contradictory to argue that such a tone suggests an explicitly masculine form of aggression. Yet two factors transform the feminized pitch into an overtly masculinized type of anger. First is the most obvious explanation: if Stabb's voice is indeed higher-pitched than Garfield's and lacks the socially constructed archetype of a low, deep tone representing masculinity, his pitch is still considerably lower than that of a female and we as listeners instantly understand the sound to be of and from a man. Stabb is not employing a falsetto; therefore, although his vocal timbre may suggest a higher, sharper sound, it is still clearly identifiable as masculine, with all its accompanying cultural privileges and connotations. Second, and perhaps even more crucial, Stabb's pitch cannot be extricated from his vocal delivery, which can only be described as squawking shout, a sonic amalgamation of jeering and baying. Indeed, as *Washington Post* music critic Richard Harrington said in a 1983 review, GI's lyrics are "virtually unintelligible . . . but their meaning is quite clear."[24] Vocal emotion trumps lyrical comprehension.

Besides the spoken-word opening of "Rock 'n' Roll Bullshit," the listener is effectively unable to understand any other lyrics of this song on first or second listen; what comes through, however, is Stabb's resentment. The same can be said of "Anarchy Is Dead," which is indecipherable except for the chorus, which is the song's title, or "Bored to Death," on which one or two errant words can be untangled, but which otherwise becomes a miasma of Stabb's sneering shouts. What is principal in these songs, and how his anger is transmitted, is not simply through the lyrics, but viscerally through his tonal quality and delivery. The attitude of Stabb's singing, flippant, scornful, and inscrutable, along with the vocal quality—the high-pitched intensity—performs as aggression, violence to the customary etiquette of conventional music and conventional manners. Obliterating the concept of harmony or melody (with its corollary implications of peacefulness, accord, and mainstream acceptance), Stabb's vocal styling is loud, dissonant, and ultimately a "screw you" to the established norms of music and society.

Faith's Alec MacKaye, interestingly, fuses many of the vocal stylings of both Stabb and Garfield, besides inserting his own heavy metalesque technique of merging spoken word with singing, to establish his vocal belligerence. Like Garfield, Alec's tone is low and harsh (though without the distinctive hoarseness of the S.O.A. singer), announcing his maleness and its attending forcefulness. Like Stabb, Alec uses a curt, snappish delivery, manipulating his inflection to suggest contempt and a lack of care for the traditional forms of singing. Yet, unlike both Garfield and Stabb, Alec's delivery is nearly entirely comprehensible, with the lyrics enunciated lucidly, but no less vehemently. In fact, Alec relies quite often on the elongated shout of a word to emphasize not only the violence inherent in his diction but also in his tone. On "In Control," he stretches out his vocal screaming articulation of specific words—"control" and "know" are extendedly screeched twice in two verses. "You're X'ed" starts each line with Alec's biting yelp but ends in a protracted yowl, as the chorus begins, in a terse shout, "you're X'ed, you're X'ed, you're out of my" and ends with the raucous howl of "liiiiifffe." And the final word is lengthened in a guttural bawl of the repeated chorus line in "Nightmare"—"suffering in agony"—as if to vocally represent the agony of which he speaks. These vocal expansions, with the quavering discomfort of Alec's strained voice, express the intensity and extent of the singer's pain and anger.

Faith's use of echo and spoken word underscore the insistent onslaught of Alec's tone and attitude. "Don't Tell Me" features Alec speaking, with rigidity and his typical derision, all the song's lyrics. This stylistic choice works to emphasize the rantlike nature of the song; despite the decidedly unharmonious singing on the other tracks, the song doesn't even participate in the patina of conventional singing. Alec accuses the listener with his spoken word; furthermore, his lead vocals are augmented by the backup vocals of the rest of the band, who shout in unison at the end of every line "don't tell me!" In a way, these vocals represent a musical one-sided argument—an antagonistic outburst of anger, replete with bluster and bellowing.

Relatedly, "In the Black" uses a combination of spoken word, singing, reverberation, and distortion to accentuate the dark aggression of Alec's voice, echoing the vocal techniques of the heavy-metal genre. The opening strains of the song are heavily distorted, with Alec's voice completely unrecognizable and his words indecipherable, as if the tape has been slowed down and then sped up. Immediately, this has a disorienting effect, challenging the listener to readjust both their auditory expectations and the conventional musical norms, which had seen a great deal of guitar distortion but a near dearth of vocal distortion. After the beginning eleven seconds of distortion, Alec enters with his spoken-word verse, awash in booming reverberation in each word, lending a sinister, ominous tenor to his voice; each of these spoken verses is then followed by a prototypically hardcore-sung chorus—spat out with a cutting, slightly discordant singing style. The overall effect is like that of the electric guitar and drumroll sequence in S.O.A.'s instrumentation—the promise of a threat (in the form of Alec's spoken word, echoed in reverb) and the fulfillment of that threat (in the biting aggression of the sung chorus).

Undeniably, all these DC hardcore singers, Garfield, Stabb, and Alec MacKaye, used their voices—their pitch, their delivery, their tempo, and their sound effects—to communicate rage. What's more, they sang, blurted, yelped, and barked deafeningly. Indeed, it was this volume, this irrepressible noise, that worked in concert with their voices to express their fury because "*loud* meant passion, *loud* meant the pent up anger of the age, and loud rock n' roll thus became an acting out of that anger."[25]

AGGRESSION AS/AND MASCULINITY: THE LYRICS

Examining the expression of aggression in DC hardcore music would be impossible without including the most literal and most verbal communication of the songs' feelings: lyrics. Despite the aforementioned obfuscation of many, if not most, of the words from S.O.A.'s, GI's, and Faith's songs as a result of their vocal delivery style, tempo, and volume, there are a number of compelling reasons to explore the lyrics. First, notwithstanding the intelligibility of the words, they are a central aspect of the music. Much like instrumentation and vocals, verbalized language performs an emotional and political function in their sonic interpretation. For instance, plosives (/b/ /p/ /t/ /d/ /k/ /g/) have a harsh, abrupt, and sharp sound, sibilants (/s/ /sh/) create a more sinister, hissing, or sometimes soft sound, and fricatives (/f/ /v/ /th/) can produce a light, buoyant sound.[26] These sounds, and their attending expressive nuances, become meaningful in context with the constructed denotations and connotations of the actual words, as well as the other forms of musical implications.

Second, the lyrics are a direct product of the band members themselves (in most cases, the lead singer, but often songs are cowritten by other band members as well), and as such, stand as the most explicit, transparent documentation of what feelings, ideas, and beliefs the musicians were attempting to share. Unlike an analysis of musical structure or instrumentation, which depends heavily on the privileged position of the academic (me) superimposing her own sociopolitical interpretation, lyrics serve as *prima facie* proof of the writers' sentiments. Of course, this line of interpretation has its own limitations: postmodern analysis expects the ascendency of the audience as arbiter of meaning, relegating the author to a less direct and less central creative role in meaning, and, relatedly, audience members may interpret the writer's meaning in highly subjective ways, each skewing the "intentions" of the writer to fit her own social schema. In addition, no assurance can be given that what is written—whether it be a poem, book, or song—represents the unmitigated, all-inclusive feelings of the author. However, as subsequent sections will explore, the members of S.O.A., GI, and Faith themselves saw their music as a form of personal expression, and their songs became a form of agency in a town in which power was at a premium. In that way, we can and should understand their lyrics as a type of, though certainly not the only, personal and musical communication.

Third, the difficulty of making out these bands' lyrics, even after multiple listenings, for the most part did not preclude their ardent and loyal fans from learning them. Lyric sheets, zines, live shows, incessant playing of the albums, and friends' assistance are only some of the ways that fans discovered and frequently memorized every word of their favorite hardcore bands' songs. The audience's reception of these lyrics, and their subsequent recitation of them—at shows, in bedrooms, at record shops— offers yet another component of why words matter.

Even with the possibility of mis- or reinterpretation of meaning, almost every single one of the songs from S.O.A., GI, and Faith are, as *Washington Post* music critic Richard Harrington notes in 1981, "baldly aggressive, self-centered, a bit paranoid and certainly hard to put up with if you're not in agreement with the philosophy."[27] Although it might be more efficient (not to mention quicker) to simply list the songs that *don't* deal with feelings of aggression, hostility, and rage, I'll instead categorize the songs by the object of their wrath: their peers, those in authority, and themselves. Before diving into the categories, I think it is significant to note what is absent from the lyrics. Unlike the implications of male potency and sexual prowess constructed by mainstream culture and performed by the guitars and drums of Faith, S.O.A., and GI, such subject matter is virtually nonexistent in the lyrics of these bands. Indeed, every single song on S.O.A.'s *No Policy* (1981), Faith's *Faith/Void* (1982), and GI's 1981 *Legless Bull*, its 1982 *Make an Effort*, or its 1983 *Boycott Stabb* is utterly and, perhaps astonishingly, lyrically devoid of any overt sexuality. In fact, through the span of three years, five albums, three bands, and forty-nine songs, women are mentioned just *three* times, once by each band. GI refers to the opposite sex implicitly in 1983's "Puppet on a String"—"I don't know how I'll live without you/Now I find myself so sad/Hard to deal with all the pain/I say I'll never do it again/but I keep on searching for my dream girl"—and does so even more obliquely in "What's Wrong with Me?": "Why do I care when you don't/Why can't I see you don't want me?" Yet both these instances are clearly about love gone wrong, relationships that have failed, rather than the sex, desire, or unadulterated lust. S.O.A.'s brush with the female sex is even less sexual; Garfield blatantly rejects women and the ensuing relationship woes they bring in "Girl Problems":

> You lower your fuckin' pride 'cause you think she's what you need/You don't mind the pain or the way you always feel/It's just a fuckin' game, she's got you on a line. . . . I don't need no girl problems/I got troubles as it is/I don't need to waste my time/I don't need more shit.

Of course, this lyrical elimination of sex, or any insinuations of carnal yearning and desire, can and should be seen in part as a manifestation of these bands' adoption of the straightedge lifestyle, which will be discussed in more detail in chapter 6.[28] Their eschewal of rampant, and therefore in their eyes meaningless, sex is on prominent display in their lyrics. Such a positioning, like the straightedge tenets of no drinking, smoking, or drugs, finds its motivation in a deep-seated respect for the body. In this way, S.O.A., Faith, and GI subvert the cultural mandate of aggressive and ubiquitous male sexuality. Of course, their subversion exists side by side with the sonic sexuality of their music. And, because bands' lyrics are very often distorted and indecipherable, any lyrical destabilization of male sexuality is somewhat undercut by the overpowering force of the traditional, instrumental performance of potent, commanding male sexuality.

Passing from the lack of sex-based lyrics, we will return to the preponderance of songs that deal with anger and aggression, the most numerous of which express resentment, contempt, and outright anger toward their peers. Their lyrical loathing is, within their peer group, reserved primarily for three groups of people—those who are not straightedge or those who are disapproving of that lifestyle (see chapter 6), their disappointing friends, and those who fall outside the punk purview but are still their peers. GI rages against friends' manipulations in "Twisted View" (1982) and the destructive toxicity of rumor-mongering in "Partyline" (1983); remarkably the same subject matter appears in Faith's "In Control" and "Trapped," the latter of which warns, "You sit around and talk/Behind each other's backs. . . . You think you'll be safe/Hiding behind your friends/Remember nothing's real/About the way they feel." Finally, intense contempt is widened to the bands' peer group at large, from those who criticize and defame hardcore punk rockers (GI's "Sheer Terror," S.O.A.'s "Gang Fight") to those enraptured by popular culture ("Fashionite," "Rock 'n' Roll Bullshit" from GI's *Legless Bull*) and the fame monster of the music industry (S.O.A.'s "Gate Crashers" and GI's "Anarchy Is Dead"), or even to the generalizable, anonymous masses (S.O.A.'s "I Hate the Kids," Faith's "Face to Face," and GI's "Here's the Rope"). It is not surprising that these lyrical themes—betrayal, ostracism, and the disappointment and unraveling of friendships—are nearly universal to teenagers and to the subject matter of popular music of virtually any decade. There's nothing particularly unique about these themes. Once again, however, it is form, rather than content, that sets apart DC hardcore. Rather than addressing these tribulations with nostalgia, heartache, yearning, or even despair, GI, S.O.A., and Faith use militancy, fury, and disparagement.

The lyrical violence is also directed more outwardly, toward society and the hegemonic institutions of authority that these DC bands see as oppressive. Religion is the object of ridicule in GI's "Religious Rip-off" ("T.V. evangelists put on a show/Trying to tell me what they know/Just send us money and you'll be saved/Pretty soon you'll be our slave") as are the cops in "No Rights" ("Cops say shut-up or you'll get hit/I'm sick and tired of taking their shit"), while S.O.A. focuses on the many faces of authority, such as club owners ("Warzone"), the local government ("Riot"), and the police ("Public Defender"). Each of these songs plays a dual function in the expression of anger and brutality: they all communicate the savagery of the institution ("Destroy the city, smash it [to] bits/They won't stop, they don't give a shit," "See 'em coming/You better move quick/he's gonna hit you with a stick"), but they also reflect and redirect the violence toward the institution itself ("Sticks and stones—Riot/Break your bones—Riot/Stores in Flame—Riot," "Here they come, club owners beware . . . they're gonna rip this place apart/Trash to the finish, trash from the start," "Somebody better kill 'em [cops] quick/Somebody hit 'em with their own stick"). Ironically, in this way the destructiveness that these bands embrace and use as a warning toward a society that does not accept them is concurrently a product of that same society.

The final prong in this triad of aggression is the self. After directing a large dose of anger at friends and contemporaries who have disappointed and enraged them, along with the society who helped construct those expectations and the violent reactions they induce, S.O.A., Faith, and GI turn the anger inward, an emotional accumulation of the other two realms' perceived dissatisfactions. Faith's "What's Wrong with Me?" ("How come it's me that's always hurt/How come it's me that feels like shit?"), "Nightmare" ("Can't get no sleep/I can't close my eyes . . . Twist and turn/cringe and burn/Feel the pain inside of me/Suffering in agony"), "Confusion," and "In the Black" all articulate the pain and acrimony that come from the attempt to reconcile one's perception of self with the expectations of others and the failure to do so.

This violent despair is echoed in two of S.O.A.'s ten songs, "Draw Blank," in which Garfield obstinately refuses to show any straightforward emotion ("You'll never know/I'll never show/I'm not a book/You can't read me") and "Blackout," where this self-society congruence takes a self-destructive bent ("War going on inside my head/I can't get to sleep, I'd rather be dead. . . . I don't know what to say, I don't know what to do/Everyday seems the same, I might as well die"). GI's Stabb goes from manic boredom on his 1981 Legless Bull ("My life's a drag/I'm just a waste/Put me in a bag . . . When boredom sets in/I just wanna die/I can't move/No matter how I try") to a more explicit and personal form of resentment in his 1983 Boycott Stabb, including "Puppet on a String," "Hour of One," and

"Insomniac." Much like the marginalization from friends and peers, the underlying emotion of the self-directed lyrics is pain, uncertainty, and isolation; however, also much like the bands' response to that marginalization, their primary lyrical emotion toward their own chaos of self-perception is a male-approved outward reaction of anger and violence, rather than the culturally constructed feminine emotion of hurt.

Accordingly, we can understand these musical declarations of rage—through instrumentation, vocal delivery, and lyrics—as a performance of gender, and, in this instance, the culturally constructed and accepted masculine attribute of anger. Anger was found not just in DC hardcore but was paralleled in hardcore scenes around the country. Black Flag (Los Angeles) railed against friends' betrayals ("Revenge," "You Bet We Have Something Personal against You!"), themselves ("What I See," "Damaged II," "Nervous Breakdown"), and society ("I've Had It," "Spray Paint," "Police Story"); Necros (Detroit) inveighed against their peers ("Peer Pressure," "I Hate My School," "Past Comes Back to Haunt Me"), and institutional violence ("Police Brutality," "Youth Camp," "War Game"); Agnostic Front (New York) attacks society's standards ("No One Rules," "Discriminate Me"), nonhardcore peers ("United Blood," "Fight") and friends ("Friend or Foe," "Traitor"); and Circle Jerks (San Francisco) complained about capitalism and consumption ("Beverly Hills," "Red Tape"), society and hypocrisy ("World up My Ass," "Question Authority," "Product of My Environment," "Moral Majority"), and the pressures of adolescence ("Leave Me Alone," "Trapped," "High Price on Our Heads"). However, the aggression of DC hardcore was not the same as in San Francisco, L.A., New York, or Detroit—or anywhere else, for that matter. DC hardcore's violent emotions were molded and reinforced by the specific realities of these young males living in Washington, DC, in the late 1970s and early 1980s, as well as the cultural mandate of masculine expression.

DC, as a national symbol of government and power, had an even more explicit effect on the people who lived there than perhaps the country as a whole. So although the Watergate scandal and the never-ending Vietnam War were fuel to the disillusionment flame of Americans who had exhausted the 1960s idealism of people power, peace, and a government who worked for good, such suspicion and cynicism were more acute for those who called DC home. Any sort of distancing that the nation as a whole could assume—whether geographic or emotional—was much more difficult if not impossible to maintain when living in the city that represented that very angst. Sure, the Circle Jerks could sing about the red tape of Washington, DC, and Agnostic Front could warn of the draft and Uncle Sam coming to get you, but people in DC were physically, if not psychologically and intellectually, a part of it.

The presence of the administration housed within the city was a major contributor to the city's atmosphere. The ascent of Reagan and his particular brand of conservatism intensified the ossification of anger toward and distrust of the government, whose "bootstraps" mentality, anti–affirmative action policies, and fiscal conservatism tempered and nearly eradicated the revolutionary air of social equality wrought by the late 1960s and early 1970s. Though only teenagers, band members and scene participants alike were highly aware of and reactionary toward the sociopolitical quagmire surrounding them. As Garfield himself notes, "I was an angry kid, an angry adolescent. . . . Washington DC was an intense place to be a young person in the '70s and '80s. . . . In my opinion, to be a conscientious American, you should be pretty damn angry."[29] Participants in the hardcore scene I interviewed reinforced this view of this political morass. As Tim said in a participant interview, "We saw Reagan creating a poor class in America so there was a lot to protest." Malcom, another interviewee, added, "Marion Barry and Reagan being in town stirred up a lot of anger." Yet another participant I interviewed, Mike, agreed, saying, "The politics of the time— Ronald Reagan, for example—naturally fed our anger and our sense of rebellion."[30]

But more than simply overt political hostility, the rage contained in and expressed by DC hardcore was also a musical manifestation of the physically violent realities these teens faced on the streets, which itself can be, in part, attributed to the social consequences of the city's escalating conservatism. Along with the influx of money and the city's gentrification efforts in Georgetown discussed in chapter 1 and DC's lowered drinking age came the arrival of an entire collection of new youth: suburban teens, children of the new administration, Georgetown University students, and marines from the local bases, or as DC hardcore historians Mark Andersen and Mark Jenkins call them, "a veritable rogues gallery of punk archenemies."[31] Violence against punks, who were detested for their rebellious, defiant appearance, and cocksure attitude, as well as for being different, being freaks, became a daily occurrence. DC punks often took different routes and streets in order to circumvent any such hostilities; they also understood the realities of the potential and likelihood of violence, wearing chains not just as a rebellious fashion statement but instead as a form of self-protection.

The reentrenched traditionalism of the federal government trickled down to the community, merging with the already violent history of both the city, including the riots of 1968, and the government, acting as an impetus for aggression both toward and by band members and scene participants. In this way, antagonism and aggression were appropriated and reexpressed as their own rage. As performance scholar Joseph Roach explains, violence should be understood not as merely pointless, but instead as a meaning-laden act that "exist[s] as a form of cultural expression that goes beyond the utilitarian practices necessary to physical survival."[32] For the music and lyrics of S.O.A., GI, and Faith, violence was meaningful in both its symbolism and its practicality, articulating a message Garfield called "Kill the World."

Of course, connected to these punks' particular performance of violent masculinity is the more overarching sociocultural expectations of emotional expression that was discussed in the introduction to this chapter. That is, DC punks' masculinized sonic and physical expression of anger is always-already joined to the cultural construction of manhood. Customarily, "anger in men is often viewed as 'masculine'—it is seen as 'manly' when men engage in fistfights or act their anger out physically,"[33] a sentiment that is reiterated and validated not just by the traditional social and familial model but also by the inundation of this representation in the popular culture of the 1970s and early '80s. Leading men like James Bond, Clint Eastwood's array of cowboys, and Steve McQueen's on- and off-screen tough-guy persona, as well as television's representation of aggressive males in the form of Magnum P.I., Starsky and Hutch, and Michael Knight, reproduced the stereotype of the aggressive male. The violence of their personae was not only an unquestioned day-to-day reality (which is often simultaneously linked to their sexual prowess), but also an effective method of getting the job done and was consequently glorified. It is necessary to recognize the collective climate of gender in such societal constructions that permeated and indubitably affected the representation of violent masculinity assumed and enacted by the male DC hardcore bands.

POWER, CONTROL, AND AGENCY AS MASCULINITY

The expression of violent emotion both musically and physically is a distinctive form of power. And power itself stems from the ability and privilege to act and express such sentiments in a shared, public forum. Of course, not all such configurations of power are or must be aggressive or destructive. It might be argued (rightfully so) that the connotation of power, control, and agency has inherent in it the characterization of some form of domination, and with that an asymmetrical articulation of force, but these concepts and their corollary expression in music do not have to be overtly hostile. As philosopher Antonio Gramsci explains, hegemony is both perpetuated and invisible precisely for its lack of explicit coercion; the consent of the governed is given obliquely and dominion is maintained nearly imperceptibly.[34] The naturalization of power to and for a certain group or institution or ideology, because of the cultural assumptions of neutrality, historical detachment, or evolutionary essentialism, allows for the continuation and unquestioning conviction in imbalanced structures of power. The same is true of music. Just as this chapter has attempted to unravel the concealed structures of gender in the performance of aggression in DC hardcore, so too do we disentangle other covert forms of gender coding in DC hardcore, including one of the primary forms of patriarchal hegemony—the privilege of power and the freedom of expression.

POWER, CONTROL, AND AGENCY AS MASCULINITY: THE INSTRUMENTS

As discussed earlier in this chapter, instruments are frequently endowed with anthropomorphic qualities, elevating a mere cultural object and bestowing it with agency or what social anthropologist Alfred Gell describes as the ability to function as social actors in human culture, including the concomitant gender ideologies.[35] Even our basic descriptions of instruments suggest personhood, labeling the "body" of the instrument and its associated humanlike parts: the "neck," the "head," and the "belly" indicate human identity and, necessarily, a gendered identity. It is interesting that the instrument itself can be, and often is, associated with a different gender than both the musician who plays it and the sounds that emerge from it. We turn back once again to the quintessential hardcore instrument—the electric guitar. In its anthropomorphic form, the electric guitar can be understood as feminine,[36] with a curved hourglass-shaped body and a well-rounded bottom. Indeed, musicians often refer to their guitar as "she" or "her." Albert King named his "Lucy," Jimi Hendrix's was "Betty Jean" and B. B. King had "Lucille." In this view, the guitar-as-woman would seemingly afford at least some scintilla of power to females, as an instrument both literally and figuratively of noise, containing within its form the capacity to inspire, disrupt, arouse, warn, and thrill. Yet it is the male musician—in both the history of nearly all popular music up to DC hardcore and in the actual composition of every DC hardcore punk band, including Faith, S.O.A., and GI—who has dominion over this instrument and its potential power. Like ships, which are given women's names and referred to as female but are navigated and controlled by males (who historically believed women aboard such ships were bad luck), the electric guitar is conquered and appropriated by men's indomitable potency, one that, it should be said, is clearly grounded in heteronormativity. In this way, the potential for female power is subsumed by and ultimately recast as male.

The dichotomy between instrument and musician is further complicated by the culturally conferred perception of its value. In the genre of rock 'n' roll, the electric guitar is king, recognized not just as the most technically demanding of instruments but also as the personification of the entire band itself, where "the star status of the guitar is conflated with its gendered character."[37] This male-dominated, guitar-centric understanding of rock was magnified in the 1960s and '70s with the formulation of the guitar-god concept, elevating the playing of guitar to a near-religious fervor (many a Cream fan proclaimed "Clapton is God"), a hierarchy that was, and still is, perpetuated by music magazines' obsessive ranking of the top guitarists of all time. What qualified as guitar-god-worthy was the highly masculinized, and implicitly control-based, quality of technical prowess: "To be in command of the very latest technology signifies being involved in directing the future, so it is a highly valued mythologized activity."[38] Thus, idealized models of masculinity, particularly within the subcategory of music, were based on technical dexterity, and in contrast femininity was associated with "non-competence and, therefore, dependence on men's skills and knowledge."[39]

Yet S.O.A., Faith, and GI clouded this masculine ideal of the fetishization of technical mastery, and, with it, the implications of gender. Despite the more obvious relationship of male musician commanding both a semifeminized instrument and its capacity for power (which should not be ignored or automatically discounted), these three bands asserted an antigendered stance in their veneration of lack of technical musical skills. Musical simplicity and the celebration of emotion over professional skill as a mainstay of punk rock has been examined in all the previous chapters, particularly in reference to its performance—or upheaval—of race and class. Guitar-based minimalism, also found throughout the albums of S.O.A., Faith, and GI, was no different and can likewise be understood through the lens of gender. Almost identical to the chord progression of nearly every Teen Idles and Minor Threat song, the B/G/D/E/A sequence is virtually invariable in S.O.A.'s *No Policy*, Faith's *Faith/Void Split*, and GI's *Legless Bull* and *Make an Effort*. Their reliance on and respect for only the most basic of chords seems to indicate a nod toward gender parity. If "noncompetence" was classified as decidedly feminine and technical mastery was categorized as not only masculine but as an aspiration that would ultimately generate accolades and musical glory, then Faith, S.O.A., and GI perform a sort of gender reversal, interrogating the naturalized assumptions of gendered guitar playing.

Bad Brains, as the master technicians of hardcore, and Minor Threat as their progeny, did undercut such characterizations insofar as their virtuosity seemed to simply reinforce the culturally constructed power and mastery afforded to traditional masculinity. In the case of Minor Threat, however, power was ceded to a certain extent by the minimalism of their compositions. Even though their technical playing performed an authoritative masculinity, their musical structures undermined that power. It's a sort of gender wash, with assertive masculinity neutered by simplistic femininity. However, there was no such compositional minimalism with Bad Brains. Their songs used a significantly more expansive range of chords and their technical skills were widely recognized as the best in the national hardcore scene; there is no diminishment of power and control in their music. Their assertion of masculinity was prioritized, which makes sense in light of the devaluation of their black bodies. As black men, the members of Bad Brains lacked not just the privilege of whiteness but also a sense of control and power; instead, the hypermasculinity of their music worked to compensate for their lack of sociocultural power.

Yet all of DC hardcore, regardless of any semirenunciation of strictly gendered minimalism and technical skills, still performed the masculinity of guitar godliness in their use of tempo and volume. Their songs' frenetic tempo was frequently both mind-boggling and exceptional in comparison to both popular music in general and the larger hardcore scene. Through the skill of speed and the authority of noise, "the guitar . . . is meant to sound like a spontaneous eruption of maverick psychic energy manifested in musical expression."[40] This technical virtuosity of pure speed, along with the sheer force of sound, acts as affirmation of the trope of hypermasculinized guitar sacredness.

Beyond the personification and subsequent gendering of instruments, the vocals of hardcore punk enact another form of power. Much as timbre helps us to immediately identify an individual instrument, even if multiple instruments have the same loudness and pitch, a person's voice stands out as both unique and emblematic. The voice "*is* the person, it is our means of representing our 'selves' to other people."[41] We understand the voice as a representation of the person from whom it comes. Even if we cannot physically see the person, we know it is mom, our professor, or our best friend, just by the voice. Not only that, the voice acts as our agent; as Simon Frith argues, it *is* the person. As surveyed in the previous section, the vocal stylings of Garfield, Stabb, and Alec MacKaye represented a bellicose violence that is aurally disquieting. It is this vehemence, this technique of screaming as voice-and-self, that contains the power of control by containing the power to disrupt. Think about this sonic effect in more familiar terms—the sound of a baby wailing at the top of her lungs:

> Babies are endowed with . . . inordinate lung power and vocal chords of
> steel, it seems, capable of producing high decibel and transient values,

cutting timbres and irregular phrase lengths. . . . A baby's yell is always upfront, foreground, urgent, of varying periodicity and quite clearly designed to shatter whatever else mother, father, big sister or big brother is doing . . . desires and needs must be fulfilled *now*, they cannot wait.[42]

If we simply replace the noun *baby* with *Garfield*, *Stabb*, or *Alec*, we can understand how their vocals can act as sonic statements of urgency and that this urgency is a function of power and control. Of course, these hardcore singers used this method deliberately; a baby lacks intentionality. But the effect is the same. Just as a drill sergeant, a sports coach, or an emergency worker yells to concentrate attention, emphasize authority, and command compliance, so too does the roughshod vocal gymnastics of these singers demolish tranquility and demand attention.[43]

Connected to this disruption and control model of singing, power is associated in the rebellion against and validation of this untraditional singing style. When *Billboard*'s top musicians of 1980–83 include Hall and Oates, Rick Springfield, Air Supply, and Foreigner, and the ostensible nonconformist Billboard chart toppers are John Cougar Mellencamp, Blondie, and Joan Jett, it takes an enormous amount of gall to reject the mainstream mandate of vocal melody. Garfield's undeveloped singing style, Stabb's "incoherent, incomprehensible vocals,"[44] and the way Alec MacKaye "sang so hard he'd pass out or hyperventilate"[45] acted as an assertion of power, a refusal to be silenced, literally and figuratively, by the cultural musical directive of what singing should, *must*, sound like. Agency, and the power that it allows for, emerges from a deliberate eschewal of musical norms. Rejecting the musical dictates of the majority offered S.O.A., Faith, and GI the ability to act independently, to self-represent. Of course, the structural paradigm in which this agency was enacted, including institutionalized gender coding, was the very foundation that made such agency possible.

In a similar way, the recording and performance of hardcore was an act of power, both in the ability to musically represent one's self and viewpoints and also in the presumption of value in such representations. Although mainstream culture and its accompanying musical culture rejected hardcore, its creation, production, and performance still acted as a form of male agency. In a rather Nietzschean way, these albums were a form of "will to power," a tactic of asserting one's self and dominating others as a form of life-affirming self-realization. As Garfield himself says, "All I had was attitude and a very intense need to be seen, a real I-need-attention thing."[46] The noise of hardcore, the intensity of vocals, the utter force of guitars and drums, the quashing of conventional musical aesthetics, and the exaltation of fervidness over technical aptitude expressed a power that was essential to maintaining the sonically coded male space of both music and society.

As suggested in the preceding paragraph, this sonic agency performed by S.O.A., Faith, and GI was inexorably entangled with sociocultural models of masculinity and their local manifestations in the space and place of Washington, DC. The religious, familial, cultural, and professional domination of males has a well recorded and nearly universally recognized history: as kings, prophets, and deities; as eligible dowry receivers, breadwinners, and fathers-know-best; as CEOs, scientists, politicians, and military personnel—men have traditionally been "socialized to think of themselves as all mighty and powerful, and, consequently, to feel entitled."[47] Even in the late '70s and early '80s, when feminism had begun to shift the sociocultural landscape and slowly alter the conventional markers and idealizations of gender, positions of authority and influence were still teeming with men virtually exclusively, affecting merely superficial fissures in the patriarchal hegemony. Notwithstanding the cultural advent of the so-called sensitive male, masculinity primarily still rested on the ability of a man to exert power and control.

Such nationwide fetishized masculine traits were not simply mirrored in Washington, DC, they were exaggerated and lionized amid the government-based economy, culture, and subsequent hierarchy of power and control in the city. As the seat of national and global power, DC epitomizes influence and control, as do the people who make up the three branches of government. And from 1978 to 1983, the exclusive positions of government were nearly the sole purview of men. The executive branch, including the most power-laden offices of the president and vice president, was obviously occupied by men,[48] and the Supreme Court had all-male appointees until Sandra Day O'Connor's somewhat contentious nomination in 1981, tipping the male-to-female ratio to a lopsided 8:1. Congress was similarly disproportionate in its gender distribution: the

Ninety-fifth Congress (1977–78) had eighteen women in the House and three in the Senate; the Ninety-sixth (1979–80) had even fewer, sixteen congresswomen and two female senators; there was a slight increase in the House of Representatives in the Ninety-seventh (1981–82) and the ninety-eighth (1982–83) with twenty-one and twenty-two, respectively, though the number in the Senate remained the same.[49] At most, then, there were scant 22 out of 435 members of the House of Representatives (5%) and 3 of 50 in the Senate (6%). Power, as demonstrated and flexed by Washingtonians, was decidedly male. Those who were allowed to speak for the US public, who made decisions premised on the betterment of society, whose moral and social beliefs were openly broadcast and frequently memorialized through speeches, legislation, and monuments, were male. Among them were the fathers of the band members and the DC hardcore community: military men, journalists, World Bank workers, professors, government employees, and, in one case, a US senator. In these examples of male power, in both the microcosm of DC and in their own families, was a tacit message of male privilege via male agency. Music, then, became the mode of power for Faith, GI, and S.O.A., an age-accessible form of agency that was, like their city's powerful, overtly male.

PART II

The DC Hardcore Scene

5

Do-It-Yourself Cultural Production

Arlington, Virginia, 25.8-square-mile county directly across from the southwestern bank of the Potomac River and Washington, DC, may seem a bit strange as a site to become the mecca of DC hardcore. Ceded back to Virginia by the federal government in 1847, Arlington grew to be a flourishing suburb and thanks to the installation of two Metro lines (the Orange in 1978 and Blue in 1977) and a major thoroughfare that paralleled the Orange Line in Interstate 66, boasting a population of 159,600 in 1980. The history of Arlington is contradictory and nuanced: it was named for General Lee's family home, but it also was the first school system to integrate. And ask anyone around the DC metropolitan area and they will tell you—Arlington is Virginia. And Virginia is not DC. Still, territorial pride aside, Arlington was pivotal to the powerhouse of cultural production for DC hardcore: the Dischord house.

In 1981, Ian MacKaye and Jeff Nelson moved into what would be named the Dischord house, a red bungalow-style house just off of Washington Boulevard in Arlington. The house has become famous, not only for the iconic photo of Minor Threat in front of it on the cover of *Salad Days*, but also as the place where Dischord as a label got its start (and continue to operate, across the street in a small, cramped space underneath a dry cleaner and 7-Eleven, behind an unmarked door) and where Minor Threat practiced in the low-ceilinged basement. Hordes of punk fans still pilgrimage to the now-overgrown front porch with the rusting chain-link fence and peeling exterior paint nestled between teardowns that now list for more than $1 million, housing families with Generation X parents who have never even heard of Ian. That house, in all its former and current glory, with its creaky wood floors, slanted ceilings, and exposed wire, now stores the largest single archive of Minor Threat recordings on the wooden shelves of an old bedroom on the second floor of the house and stands as a living memorial to the spirit, the ethos, and the attitude of DC hardcore: Do-It-Yourself.

The DIY Ethos

Consumption, as a model for happiness and a symbol of status and capitalism, as a political and economic inevitability and an altar at which to worship, emerged as a developed ideology by the 1920s, though its roots stem back to the expansion of US territories and the transportation revolution that accompanied it. By the second decade of the twentieth century, consumption had been transformed; what qualified as a necessity had shifted perilously close to what had formerly been seen as a luxury, and the newly booming advertising industry propagated the notion that consumption could be a panacea for any woe. At the onset of the 1950s and still today, the premium on consumption and the complicit role of capitalism have only grown more colossal and all-encompassing. Thorstein Veblen's nineteenth-century theory of conspicuous consumption has shaped the dominant sociological and psychological concept of consumerism, which posits the acquisition of material goods as a representation of social status.[1] That is, economic power connects to social power.[2] Consumption, therefore, is a performance, meant to assuage personal angst, reinforce community standing, and arouse jealousy in others. What you choose to buy shows your level of taste, your ability to be "in the know," and your financial footing for purchasing material goods. More than just a form of self-identification and satisfaction, consumerism in some ways became *the* fundamental way to relate socially, filling a void left by urbanization and massification and the ensuing collapse of conventional social relations.

DIY as a contrast asserts the role of the individual and extols the importance of autonomy, rebuffing the characteristically passive role of the consumer by promoting a hands-on philosophy of production. In America, the first DIY culture was connected to the Arts and Crafts movement of the 1900s. Reacting to the increasing modernization and industrialization occurring in urban centers, the arts DIY culture focused on handmade items, spurning mass-produced styles in favor of the middle-class aesthetics of personal craft. And although there was always a strain of DIY in US culture, particularly within the realm of home improvement in the 1940s and 1950s, the concept became a philosophical standard for the counterculture of the 1960s. Growing your own vegetables, sharing your living space in a communal style crafted from existing structures, and using secondhand clothing with hand-sewn repairs and alterations all became a way to revile not just the dictate of "keeping up with the Joneses" but also hippies' own largely middle-class, white, privileged background. Embedded in this DIY ethos was a particular set of preferences and choices—of how to use material resources, money, and even time—but also the privilege of having such a choice and exerting such a preference.

With no disrespect to the Arts and Crafts movement and the hippie subculture, it is no exaggeration to claim that DIY has become synonymous with punk, which was similarly premised on an anticonsumption dogma, a stance cultivated in reaction to the idolization of excess and wealth in both music and everyday life. Punks rebuffed mechanization and overindulgence in society by creating their own world: their music, their clothes (as will be discussed in chapter 7), their shows, their record labels, and their culture.

One key aspect of punk DIY was performance, and the bands of DC hardcore fully embraced this hands-on, lowbrow approach. Their performances were, both necessarily and proudly, unprofessional, eschewing the excess and glamor of traditional rock concerts. Their setups were slipshod, thrown together by communal effort, assembling whatever equipment could be found. At one Minor Threat show in 1981, the zine *Touch and Go* described the scene: there were "no mikes on the drum set but Jeff seem[ed] oblivious, pounding away—a mohawked madman. . . . Ian—screaming at a wall so to speak with an inferior PA."[3] Bands often shared equipment, with Bad Brains passing their instruments to Teen Idles between sets. The lack of professional equipment was consistent with DC hardcore's postmodern, DIY ideal of eschewing the differentiation between high and low culture at their shows. Abolishing the distinction between high and low art was also accomplished, in part, by the place where the shows took place.

Venues for performances were also frequently DIY, since bars and university spaces, if allowing DC hardcore bands to play at all, nearly uniformly never let them come back. Instead, shows happened in spaces that were not necessarily meant for performances—lofts in DC, pizza parlors, art galleries, the basement of parents' homes (one dubbed "The Shithole" was a basement in a house in Potomac), garages, local high schools, and recreation centers (the Wilson Center and a Latin American youth center, being two). The spaces were frequently in more dangerous neighborhoods and, as DC hardcore promoter and fan Steve Blush noted, "if the bathroom had a door, you were off to a good start," despite the fact that "when some idiots inevitably trashed the bathroom or tore out the plumbing, it was time to find a new venue."[4] Even the now-famous 9:30 club, which was originally named Atlantis (and was located across the street), was simply an underpatronized restaurant at the bottom of an office building with an owner who eventually barred minors from coming in, was "scared for his furniture," and even was known to screw bands out of their money.[5] The roadblocks to securing traditional venues seemed unending: bars such as the Bayou—a storied hard rock bar in Georgetown—refused to hold all-ages shows, and owners were inappreciative of low alcohol sales and wary of the liability of underage patrons; punk earned its (perhaps rightful) label of having destructive performances, with windows and chairs smashed at Georgetown University's Hall of Nations, and the near-collapse of a Civil War–era floor from the dancing;[6] and Prince George's County, where bars close to the University of Maryland hosted shows, issued a blanket ban on all "punk shows." Even those traditional venues that became hardcore stalwarts—Madam's Organ being one of the most prominent—was "creepy, smelly, and badly run," with "everyone always pissed off at how bad the sound was."[7] Madam's Organ still operates today in Adams Morgan as a blues bar, having eventually closed as a punk co-op when the landlords (perhaps intentionally) raised the rent to an untenable level.

Within these venues, none of the traditional logistics of concerts applied—no liquor licenses, no security that was bonded or insurance for liability, no sellers' licenses or W-4s for setting up and tearing down. Audience members were roped into acting as security, and the shows themselves were promoted and put on by the bands and their fans, with no outside money. As Blush recounted, "The promoters were kids—same as the bands and the fans."[8] These DIY shows also included elements that did not work: flash pots made out of coffee cans that produced smoke instead of light; tables collapsing when people stood on them for better views of the bands; Alec MacKaye getting the wind knocked out of him by the dance-floor chaos he sang amid a rowdy crowd at dc space; DC police on horseback breaking up a free Bad Brains show in Lincoln Park; brief bans on all hardcore shows at the 9:30 club. Reclaiming urban public space, playing outside the mainstream venues and performing shows in low-rent neighborhoods without the traditional use of a stage allowed DC hardcore bands to skew the lines between performer and spectator and open its arms to the unwashed masses.

The performance itself added to this flattening of the hierarchy between band and audience. Often playing on the same level as their fans, as opposed to a pedestal-like stage, hardcore bands attempted to erase the divide between producer and consumer, musician and fan. As Tom Lyle of Government Issue said, "One of the main reasons why hardcore was such a fantastic genre was that the division between the audience and the band was often nonexistent."[9] The erasure of division was reinforced by the audience's full-throated and full-throttled singing of the lyrics along with the bands. Audience members knew every single lyric to every single song. One night, when MacKaye blew out a vocal cord during a sound check, he wrote out the lyrics on signs and the whole crowd sang, one of the singer's favorite shows. MacKaye also made it a habit to pass the microphone around in the crowd, letting audience members sing songs and take ownership of the experience. Because the DC hardcore scene was so small, it was also tight-knit—the same people performing at the Chancery were the same people from high school or around the neighborhood. As a DC hardcore fan Greg noted, "John [Stabb] and Peter Murray [from Marginal Man] broke the fourth wall for me. I'd see GI and Marginal Man at the Wilson Center and then buy a ticket to a Bruce Lee matinee movie from Stabb or see Pete at the Safeway [grocery]."[10]

This realignment acted as a way to de-commodify hardcore as a music and the bands as a product. Rather than paying for a concert "experience" in the form of Pink Floyd or Cher, the members of S.O.A and Minor Threat and GI and Faith and Bad Brains, as well as their audiences, not only were the experience, but also *made* the experience themselves. They were not beholden, nor did they have access, to the money machine of the music industry. Band and scene members played the music, recorded the music, found the venues, acted as security, were the marketing team, sang the songs. Such a communal, rather than capital-based, approach acted to re-distribute agency (though not really any money). Rather than power being concentrated within the traditional triumvirate of band, industry, venue, it was rearranged between all those involved within the scene.

Two important notes. First, this redistribution of power allowed for a greater sense of agency for marginalized members of the scene—namely, woman. As music journalist Michael Azerrad noted, "Women assumed an auxiliary role, taking photographs, helping run Dischord, publishing fanzines, hosting shows in their parents' basements."[11] As has been explored in the pages of this book (and will be explored further in subsequent chapters), the DC hardcore scene was dominated not only by males, but also by masculinity: of sound, of band members, of audience. However, this DIY ethos transformed women and girls from the historical and traditional role of female-as-consumer in both the music and cultural realm to female-as-producer. Yes, this production was both disproportionate to that of the males and still firmly nestled within the conventional gender roles of women, but it was manifestly a power beyond buying concert tickets and buying posters of teenage heartthrobs to pin to their wall. Second, as was discussed in chapters 3 and 4, the ability to create a scene was itself a by-product of privilege born primarily of class. Like the hippies they so much hated, DC hardcore punks rejected the class-based model of production and consumption from the relatively safety of their middle-classdom. Scene members—band and audience alike—had, for the most part, comfortable homes to which to return, colleges to apply to, and opportunities to fall back on. DIY was a choice, not a demand.

"Here's What You Get": DC Hardcore Flyers

Handmade, cut-and-paste, decoupage, handwritten flyers announcing DC hardcore shows were one of the most visible artifacts of the DIY tenet and, as with so much else in the scene, were both a product of necessity and a statement of resistance and power. Flyers were, as UK fanzine editor Welly described, "one embodiment of the democratization of art that punk brought about."[12] As discussed in the previous section, the bands and larger scene members took on the roles typically assigned to the vast and well-paid marketing wing of the music industry. Flyers, painstakingly drawn, cut, and collaged, were photocopied by the dozens, wheat-pasted on lamp poles, fences, and walls around Georgetown. The flyers certainly offer a semiotic lens into the sociopolitical mindset of the DC hardcore scene (as will be explored in the paragraphs to follow), but they were also a practical way of advertising shows in a scene that had no conventional means of advertising and for an audience who recognized those flyers as part of that scene. As Brian Baker recalled, "After I went to that first Teen Idles show I went to everything with a handmade flyer."[13] The flyers themselves were a part of the experience of the show. Rather than a ticket stub, "collecting show posters was a part of the experience of being young and going to shows,"[14] according to one hardcore fan.

The flyers themselves were, like other street art before the commodification and idolization of the form (for which Banksy, perhaps the most notorious street artist, holds the dubious crown), a contradictory antiart that acted as "a slap in the face of public and aesthetic taste, a way to resist the gentrification of poster craft,"[15] and a meaning-laden graphic representation of the DC scene itself. And part of that representation is within the (anti)aesthetics of the flyers. Because scene members had to rely on the trusty photocopy machine, and because color paper costs more than plain white, the majority of the flyers were black and white. Again, this aesthetic is at a least a partial function of pragmatism—cost, time, and resources. At the same time, there is no denying that the stark binary of black and white coincides with the philosophical worldview of DC hardcore. It was one or the other: hardcore/not hardcore; straightedge/not straightedge; DC/ the rest of the country; with us/against us. Black and white also aligned with hardcore's rejection of culturally constructed labels of art with a capital A: "Theirs was an essentially undecorated, unadorned world. . . . Hardcore kids dismissed art as a bourgeois indulgence."[16] If art was what DC's National Gallery, the Hirschhorn, and the Corcoran displayed, oil paintings with textured, rich colors, neo-expressionism, and neo-pop, then hardcore was the opposite: flat, black and white, ransom-letter-type cut-out lettering, and scribbled hand-drawns.

The flyer for a Bad Brains/Minor Threat/SOA/Untouchables show in December 1980 embodies the binary between the functional and the symbolic. The flyer itself is divided: the bottom half shows a cut-out John Wayne, brandishing his gun, set in the forefront of a burned-out, seemingly bombed town, with smoke curling up to the second half of the flyer, which is blacked out but for the names of the bands. On the one hand, the flyer disseminates only the most important information: the top half of the flyer is black with only the logos of the bands performing outlined in white amid the smoke from the burning town. And the price ($2), date ("Sat. Dec. 13th"), and venue (1929 Calvert Street) are scrawled in the white space between two plumes of smoke. This utility and minimalism can be linked to the role of hardcore—the music, the sound, the bands, and their shows could all stand alone. Indeed, the bands' logos are proportionately the largest part of the flyer and their positioning in the top half constructs them as the looming and perhaps dangerous presence above the debris below. Moreover, the use of the branded font of each band (which corresponds to their albums and makes them identifiable) is in sharp focus and contrast to the blurred bricolage of the John-Wayne-town-destruction scene that they float above. The juxtaposition with the blurred destruction and band names reinforces the primacy of the music and the black-and-white binary of us versus them.

On the other hand, the ever-looming threat of Bad Brains, Minor Threat, S.O.A, and the Untouchables is created only because of its contrast with the bombed-out town and the archetypal cowboy aimed at the viewer. Clearly, these images have been reappropriated and reconstructed via collage; John Wayne doesn't quite fit in the scene of disaster surrounding him, and the decimated town seems to be cut from a history book on post–World War II Britain. Such reappropriation articulates a variety of meanings created by the flyer and, by extension, the DC hardcore scene. First, the postmodern use of bricolage expresses the theoretical underpinnings of postmodernism itself—skepticism about objective truth, heavy doses of irony and humor, and antiauthoritarian posture. These qualities mirror both the music and the DC hardcore scene. Second, postmodernism as a philosophical tenet, while not perhaps consciously imbued in the flyer, gains more meaning through its spatial positioning in DC. That is, this unreality or lack of truth that the flyer reflects is also a reflection of what DC is to hardcore: a city decimated not by John Wayne, but instead by the more modern cowboy—Ronald Reagan. The image of John Wayne-cum-Ronald Reagan pointing at the viewer, squeezed among the rubble of a town decimated—is the real threat. The bottom half of the flyer, then, expresses the alienation of the hardcore scene using a "new language of rupture and roughness" and "crude aesthetics"[17] that reposition the power structure of DC, inverting it so that DC hardcore stands atop that hierarchy, with the city and its symbolic authority blown to bits. And just to add the cherry on top of this sundae, the hardcore flag—the DC flag with the stars replaced with three straightedge "X's"—is planted at the bottom of the flyer, claiming the ruin of DC for the power of DC hardcore.

The elements of this flyer were not unique to the DC hardcore scene; they were emblematic. Flyers "emulated the music's immediacy with quick, sloppy, angry creations,"[18] including a utilitarian, mélange, minimalistic style that questioned not only the validity of culturally mandated aesthetics (also like hardcore itself) but also notions of authenticity, power, and agency. Handwritten dates, places, and names; ironically placed reappropriated cultural symbols and images; grainy black and white visuals; ransom-letter-like cut-and-paste lettering; the bands' proportionately domination of the composition—all these (anti)aesthetic choices worked to resignify both the act of creation itself and the content of what was bring created.

Cheap, Fast, and DC: Hardcore Zines

Although the origin of the term zine is typically attributed to the fan magazines created by science fiction devotees in the 1930s, the concept has evolved to include a wide spectrum of genres: literary, musical, and cultural. The thread linking all these zines is the DIY ethos embedded in their creation: zines are made by individuals, typically fans, and are stalwartly nonprofessional and noncommercial, distributed in small batches and necessarily to smaller audiences. Much like hardcore as a music, zines allowed for a certain demystification of the production process, opening up access to anyone to be a writer, an editor, and a publisher, which imparted an agency that was part and parcel of the hardcore ethos (and reality) of standing outside a music industry rife with hypocrisy, corruption, and bad taste. And like DIY as an ethos, the zine has, in many regards, also become synonymous with hardcore. The most famous of the zines throughout the national hardcore scene—*Touch and Go* (Lansing, Michigan), *Maximum Rocknroll* (San Francisco), *Profane Existence* (Minneapolis), *Suburban Voices* (Swampscott, Massachusetts), *Flipside* (Los Angeles), *New York Rocker* (New York), and *Search and Destroy* (San Francisco)—all represented a first-person record of hardcore through the lens of fans. By the 1980s, nearly all hardcore scenes across the country had some form of a zine .

And DC was no different. The number of zines produced during hardcore's heyday is somewhat difficult to document, what with the lack of mechanized distribution and preservation processes, as well as the somewhat ephemeral nature of the zines because of the materials and medium used. An at least partial list of DC zines during 1979–83 is informative in the sheer volume: *Capitol Crisis*, the *Infiltrator*, *DeScenes* (which evolved into *DisCords*), *Brand New Age*, *If This Goes On*, *Now What?*, *Critical List*, *Punk Is No Hobby*, *Thrillseeker*, *Truly Needy*, *Zone V*, *Most Things Suck*, *Hit and Run*, *Slickzine*, *For Those Concerned*, *Metrozine*, *WDC*. These zines, created by fans from the DC region—including Virginia and Maryland— were a critical aspect of the hardcore scene, producing an alternative creative space that not only shared practical information like schedules for shows but also created cultural narratives by publishing interviews with bands, fan-written reviews of albums, opinion pieces (or rants, as some may describe them), and space in which community could be fostered and individuals could communicate.

Zines acted as a physical manifestation of the metaphysical spirit of DC hardcore. Put less within the New Age lexicon, zines helped create the DC hardcore collective identity. One crucial aspect of this collective identity was through the construction of a placed self; that is, Washington, DC, as a geographic locale framed hardcore kids' sense of self. *Thrillseeker*, issue 2, announces itself as a "DC zine " on its cover and had a "Local's [sic] Only: News 'bout the Homeboys" section; *Metrozine*, issue 3, had a collage page called "HarD.C.ore" that featured pictures from DC bands and hardcore audience members at shows; *DisCords* (December 1981) dedicated a full page to upcoming shows in DC; *Brand New Age*, issue 2, reviewed local DC hardcore albums and advertised local hardcore albums; *Capitol Crisis*, issue 1, provided in-depth analyses of all the DC bars, venues, and spaces where hardcore shows occurred; *Zone V* (1983) was a photozine of local hardcore bands as they were performing. It is important to note that all this DC-specific content—reviews, photos, local show listings, interviews—was integrated into all local zines; although I gave specific examples of DC content from specific issues of specific DC zines, all these DC zines had some iteration of such content. It was this collectivity of DC zines' visual and written history and narrative of DC hardcore that helped contribute to the consolidation of the DC hardcore identity.

Of course, these zines were not exclusively DC-centric. They all also included "scene reports" from other hardcore cities, interviews with bands from other cities, reviews of other hardcore albums and other shows played in DC, and pictures of shows. Although such diverse geographic inclusion may seem contrary to the construction of a DC-centered identity, it was actually indispensable. As semiotics pioneer Ferdinand de Saussure posited, meaning is achieved only by reciprocal determination: what something *is* can be understood only by what it *is not*.[19] The concept is mutually dependent and constitutive; a DC hardcore identity is created in zines only in comparison and contradiction with the scenes, albums, and bands that are *not* DC. Just as the hegemonic understanding of "woman" includes an exhaustive list of socially constructed gender roles that are derived from *not* being roles for "men," so too is the DC hardcore individual understood as being *not* from Boston, *not* from New York, *not* from Los Angeles. Embedded in these binaries, de Saussure continues to explain, is an assumption of a value judgment, a hierarchy of one opposite over the other: historically, "man" is valued over "woman," "good" is better than "evil," and "white" is preferable to "black." In the same way, the DC identity is constructed by these zines as dominant over any other geographic scene. DC hardcore scene > LA hardcore scene; DC hardcore scene > Boston hardcore scene; DC hardcore scene > New York hardcore scene. Such binary opposition likewise contains secondary value-laden binaries—good/bad, liked/disliked, authentic/poser. Thus, the DC hardcore scene > equation implicitly argues that the greater than symbol includes a multitude of other dominant opposites that make its collective identity more valuable.

The construction of this DC hardcore collective identity should not be simply understood, however, as an outcome of the cultural production of zines. Instead, as collective identity theorist Alberto Melucci directs us, we should view collective identity as processual, a series of interactions between individuals who are able to define themselves, as well as their relationship to the environment around them, not in some linear fashion, but instead by interaction and negotiation.[20] Zines were critical to this interactive process, primarily through the inclusion of letters from those in the DC hardcore scene. Such letters were nearly monolithic throughout the local zines—within the first few pages, at least one page always was dedicated to local hardcore kids' opinions about the zine and the DC scene: praise, disgust, excitement, anger. In *Thrillseeker*, hardcore fan Thomas writes,

> Thanks for the Minor Threat and F.U.'s interviews. There is so much in-fighting on the "scene" these days that it was good to hear some positives. Lyle Preslar was correct when he said DC was spoiled. It appears a band is only perceived as serious or valid if they are poor and unpopular. When recognized, they have sold out and are trashed. There is a middle ground where it is possible to be professional yet fresh and vibrant. Listen up DC, it passes fast without support.

This letter allows for a negotiation between the zine itself (produced by a member of the DC hardcore scene) and scene members; by praising an interview that the zine published, the reader is promoting an identity grounded in positivity and unity. At the same time, the letter allows for (oppositional) interaction between Thomas (and Lyle Preslar, through its transitive properties) and the DC scene. Thomas is at once reinforcing the identity of the DC hardcore scene as spoiled but also contests its creation of authenticity within the DC identity (read: "poor and unpopular"). Collective identity is being negotiated through the back-and-forth interaction of zine and letter production and publication.

Capitol Crisis, created by musician and DJ Xyra Harper, took a satirical approach in "Ask Auntie Xyra" to the advice columnists in mainstream papers, providing a more explicitly documented interaction between zine creator, DC hardcore kid, and the DC hardcore scene itself. In issue 5, Sincerely Sickened from DC wrote in:

> What makes it so impossible to be honest in the music scene, without getting shit on? Why don't friends stick together and why are female fans such back-biting, self-centered bitches? As a female, I've noticed the same, tacky, groupie mentality creeping into the NEW music scene, as was prevalent in the Rock scene of the early 70's. (No savoir-faire?) It's nearly unbearable to see all this separatism & competitiveness taking place. . . . (Guys do it too; I guess you could just say I'm disappointed in human nature.)

Sincerely Sickened was negotiating two important elements of the DC hardcore identity with her letter. First was the visibility or inclusion of women within such an identity. As has been noted previously, there was a massive gender disparity in the DC hardcore scene, which was disproportionately populated by males. As one of my interviewees, Drew, remembers, there were "not many women [and] those who were involved seemed to stay more to the sidelines. I don't think the scene appealed to many women."[21] Both the writer to Auntie Xyra, and Auntie Xyra in her publication of the letter, attempts to renegotiate that male-dominated identity by recentering women within the scene. Second, *how* women are constructed as a part of the DC hardcore identity is even more significant. Sincerely Sickened contests the historical role of women in music (the "groupie mentality" of "the early 70's") that parallels the role of women in the DC hardcore scene ("back-biting, self-centered bitches"). The writer does parenthetically attribute the behavior to men as well, thus creating a collective trait for the scene, but it is clear her focus is on women. In this way, Sincerely Sickened reinforces the hegemonic construction of women in general, as well as the identity of women within the scene. As another interviewee of mine, Lars, recollected, there were "not many women, and, like in most social groups, they were embraced in direct proportion to their 1) attractiveness and 2) ability to fit in."[22] Yet the letter writer also displaces the responsibility or onus of the gender disparity and gender construction on women themselves.

Auntie Xyra's response works as another interaction, another bid at negotiating the collective DC hardcore identity. She reaffirms the writer's experience, writing "I have observed & been effected by the back-biting you refer to," likewise reinforcing the blame for such actions: "Perhaps we ALL should value our friends more, but a lot of us can be insensitive, at times. (I'm certainly guilty of that, myself.)" Then Auntie Xyra, like Thomas in *Thrillseeker,* calls for a reimagining of the DC hardcore collective identity: "There's GOT TO BE more caring (or consideration). . . . Be cautious, but not callous, & like me, continue to hope for the best—but DON'T *expect* it!!! What *you* do, is equally important!" (emphasis in the original). Harper's exhortation to the letter writer arbitrates the value system of the DC hardcore identity by demanding that it be more caring, or at a minimum, more considerate, and it similarly referees agency and power through the importance of the individual. If the DC scene was male-dominated and thus constructed as masculine, Harper intercedes in this identity by placing responsibility on the individual. This individual responsibility was of course gendered—she is writing back to a woman about women in the scene—but it was also gender-inclusive. Not only did Harper affirm in her reply to the reader that "Yes, guys DO do it too!!" but also the readership of *Capitol Crisis* reflected the larger DC scene, making it predominantly male. In this way, the responsibility for caring, for consideration, is for *all* members of the DC hardcore scene, and the interaction between participants is writer → responder, in addition to writer → responder → reader, and perhaps writer → responder → reader → responder.

It should also be noted that Harper's ownership and production of *Capitol Crisis* itself works as an interactive mode of negotiation, particularly within the framework of gendered cultural production. The gender disparity of the DC scene was twofold. First, it was visible in the composition of DC hardcore bands. While the proto-punk bands in DC had women in them—including the Slickee Boys, Tru Fac, the Urban Verbs, Tiny Desk Unit, and the Nurses—none were in the hardcore bands. And there would be none until 1986, when the all-girl group Fire Party debuted.[23] Second, as the previous paragraphs alluded, few females were involved in the scene, and those who were, according to the men and women I interviewed, often were relegated to subordinate roles. As Janelle Simmons recalled, "looking back now, women didn't really have a place."[24] Cynthia Connelly[25] reiterated this, saying, "From my perspective,

Hardcore discouraged women from doing things."[26] Harper's creation of this zine, then, worked to contest the dominant maleness of DC hardcore and its cultural production. Her zine came about because, as she said, "people were bursting to get out and be creative, and they had to create something because there wasn't anything."[27]

The production of DC hardcore zines, both as a part of and aside from the DC hardcore collective identity, also worked as a form of agency for a group of young people who, because of age and geographic location, often had none. Zines not only democratized one aspect of youth cultural production but also offered freedom: freedom from censorship; freedom from the confines of mainstream aesthetics, language, and composition; and freedom from the market demands of traditional periodicals. As the editorial on the first page of the first issue of *Capitol Crisis* inveighs, "we must evolve and be open to change, and not be dictated to by the commercial music industry and commercial media." But zines also afforded the freedom *to*: the freedom to construct their own version of DC hardcore without intermediaries, the freedom to create a new language, new images, new meanings. Also in the first issue *Capitol Crisis*, on the cover, is a cutout of a solider wearing a gas mask, casually sitting on the ground and gripping his assault rife with a white text box diagonally intersecting the image with the words "Only *YOU* can determine the outcome of your own destiny." Control, responsibility, power for self-narration, for one's destiny, was reassigned to the individual reading and creating the zine, rather than their parents, their school, the federal government, or the mainstream culture or media. In such a construction of their scene and their city, DC hardcore producers and readers were granted a certain element of autonomy and self-determination that comes with the power to produce any representation. The ability and opportunity to create a counternarrative allowed them, at least on a basic level, to question the relationship between DC, its inhabitants, and their sociocultural, political, and economic values.

Dischord Records

Perhaps the most celebrated and enduring aspect of DC hardcore's commitment to the DIY ethos was the creation of the independent,

DC-centered, punk-specific record label Dischord Records. The label started as so much of the DC hardcore scene did—under cultural and economic duress. As MacKaye recalled to *Flipside*, "In L.A. you hear 'record label' and 'getting signed.' You don't hear that in Washington." Without a label to put out their music, Teen Idles pooled together their funds from playing shows from the previous year to produce *Minor Disturbance* and create Dischord. MacKaye noted, "We could've split the money up and had $150 each or we could put out a record. Everyone said put out a record."[28]

The record label was born of necessity, but it quickly became MacKaye and Nelson's[29] sociopolitical and musical mouthpiece, a way to release DC hardcore albums that no other label would touch and, at the same time, deemphasize the monetary aspects of the music industry. This was perhaps the most radical aspect of the label: Dischord embraced[30] music as a decommodified form of art. With the consolidation of the music industry into only a handful of firms, and musical diversification permissible only at the whim of these companies, innovation was hamstrung by concerns about money and "sellability." Standardization and appropriation ran rampant in the industry, and "commercialization [wa]s seen to make it impossible to sustain authenticity and mean[t] that resistance is no sooner expressed than sold back to young people."[31] The history of the music and the culture of the 1960s, which began with the promise of revolution and upheaval, sonically and socially and transformed into a fashionable depoliticized trademark to sell nearly everything, made MacKaye and Nelson wary of mainstream society absorbing, commodifying, and ultimate neutering the oppositional sting of hardcore. As DC hardcore participant and author Steven Blush argued, Dischord Records "set into motion a mindset that created almost everything we now call hardcore. Ian's anti-industry, anti-star, pro-scene exhortations have become Rock Biz clichés. Hippies fired the first salvos in the battle for artistic independence, Punks espoused DIY, Ian and his DC crew codified the mindset."[32]

Their label was a personal, though ultimately political, tactic in the valuation of music over the valuation of profit. As MacKaye says, "we set up Dischord so we could put out music we liked by people we liked, and put it out cheap. Our goal was not to make lots of money, but rather to help out as many of our friends' bands as we could."[33] The record label shunned the normal division of labor of the music industry, distributing and selling its recordings solely through mail order or direct sales to record stores, in an effort to free bands in the production and content of their albums. Forming relationships with record-store owners across the country, MacKaye and Nelson would send out records in the mail and have faith that the owners would send money back through the mail. In the true spirit of the DIY ethos, each and every album was hand-created, with Dischord house members folding song lyric sheets, putting together album sleeves, taking mail-order sales, and shipping them out to individuals using cardboard salvaged from the next-door dumpster at 7-Eleven with handwritten addresses and decorations. All this production was in addition to the day jobs the label owners had: Nelson worked at 7-Eleven and MacKaye had three jobs—working at an ice cream shop in Georgetown, working at a movie theater during the weekends, and driving a newspaper delivery truck before dawn. Of course, both Nelson and MacKaye still came from a solidly middle-class background, a positionality that matters when discussing the agency not only to create but also to fail. The safety of their class allowed them to have the privilege to (attempt to) decommodify music from economics.

It should also be noted that Bad Brains were, in some ways, the exception to this DIY mode of cultural production. In 1980 the band was introduced to restaurateur and wannabe Brian Epstein to the Bad Brains' Beatles, in his own words. Mo Sussman not only gave the band a rehearsal space an hour outside of DC on a friend's farm (which was later raided by the police in a drug bust) but also financed recording sessions at Omega Studios, a professional studio in Maryland, and shopped the demo to major labels. However, the relationship with Sussman unraveled because HR, more deeply connected to his Rastafarian ideology, saw his financier as an evil capitalist and instead wanted the music to be free and for the people. After moving to New York and tearing up multiple contracts, Bad Brains finally released their first album with Reach Out International Records (ROIR), an independent label. Despite eventually signing a contract with ROIR, Bad Brains still had an anti-industry ethos. As the label's founder, Neil Cooper, recounts, "They were very suspicious of record companies, of contracts being meaningless, feeling that things should be done on a matter of trust. They didn't understand the commercial aspects of a record company or the need for a contract to protect both themselves and the record company."[34]

Even without Bad Brains, Dischord became the DC hardcore powerhouse. The label's second release was S.O.A's *No Policy* (paid for by Garfield himself) and, with the money coming in for that album, along with Teen Idles' *Minor Disturbance,* Dischord released singles by Minor Threat and GI in 1981, along with Minor Threat's EP *In My Eyes.* Since the first year of Dischord releases, the label has released albums by nearly all the titans of DC hardcore: Teen Idles, S.O.A, Minor Threat, GI,[35] Youth Brigade, Faith, and Void, as well as a compilation of DC hardcore bands that included Red C, Untouchables, Deadline, Iron Cross, and Artificial Peace. Starting in 1983–84, Dischord also released albums by DC hardcore and posthardcore legends discussed in chapter 9 of this book—Scream, Marginal Man, Embrace, Rites of Spring, Beefeater—and other DC-centered bands like Egghunt, Gray Matter, Dag Nasty, Snakes, and Soulside, among others.

The near monopoly on the production and dissemination of DC hardcore, regardless of the label's commitment to the DIY ethos and goal of decommodification, still performed a significant and inherent—if often invisible—privilege associated with the production of music for mass consumption. Consider the history of the phonograph, which was "conceived as a privileged vector for the dominant speech, as a tool reinforcing representative power and the entirety of its logic . . . to preserve a representation of power, to preserve itself."[36] Those who possess the ability to record are endowed with a unique form of power and control. The fact that their words, ideas, speeches, or sounds are considered by those seemingly omniscient and omnipotent cultural forces important enough to be recorded necessarily creates a power differential, a hierarchy based on those who are recorded and those who are not. The act of memorialization that is integral in recording, with its implicit value judgment, elevates both the content of the sound (whether it is music, comedy, or speeches) and the producers of that sound. In this way, recorded sound becomes an "essential symbol of a privileged relation to power . . . [of] social status, and order, a sign of one's relation to others."[37]

Contained within the control of production fundamental to recording is the implicit acknowledgment of and respect for the consumption-based tenet of ownership and the corollary privilege of agency. Proprietorship has always been a precept of the traditional American Dream—owning the house, the car, and the appropriate accoutrements. To own is to progress into a higher social status; possessions, both tangible and as cultural capital, act as a symbol not only of one's class but also of one's worth. This ownership equation had a particularly unpleasant history with musicians and the music industry. Black artists, particularly those early ones in the blues and R&B genre, were not only never paid for their original compositions and their subsequent records, but white record executives also frequently hijacked their songs, employing white musicians to cover them. Musicians were denied ownership both financially (often tragically leaving them in financial ruin) *and* culturally. Dischord, in an attempt to nullify the insidious effects of ownership industry practices, refused to either market its bands or sign contracts that would create intellectual property. If the traditional music industry and the corollary society demanded economic and cultural capital, Dischord embraced what sociologist Sarah Thornton famously dubbed "subcultural capital": values, norms, beliefs, and principles that reflected the hardcore scene. Hardcore's subcultural capital was created in opposition to dominant culture; the DIY ethos and accompanying attempt to decommodify hardcore music was a show of substantial subcultural capital force. And, certainly, it was an admirable and important approach, in light of the industry's history of commandeering music. However, it should also be understood within the context of social control—of power fashioned from freedom and the privilege of agency. MacKaye puts it this way:

> I think the reason we take the approach to music that we do is that then we ultimately have complete control over how we do our music and operate the band. We don't feel compelled by *anyone* to do *anything* that we don't want to do. We're not indebted to anyone. When a band signs to a major label, no matter how good a contract they think they have, no matter how much control they think their contract provides, it's unavoidable that you are conscious of being an investment. Somebody puts money into you and you have to pay off somehow. And you *want* to pay off.[38]

Dischord, then, acts as a tool of emancipation from the strict monetary and creative confines of the music industry. Yet that emancipation, that ability to control the creation, production, and distribution of one's own self and music, is in itself a privilege. As previous chapters have discussed, regulation is nearly ubiquitously used as a function of social control; thus, Dischord's assumption of the creative and financial processes of their own bands is a seizure of that privileged instrument of control. In doing so, the label and the bands that it represented enacted a curious paradox of the class-and-status formula. By destabilizing the conventional music industry practices, including the financial motive for music and the perilous battle for proprietary rights, Dischord actually reinforced the traditional capitalistic and consumption-driven ethos of ownership and, with it, the attending virtues of agency and control. Perhaps ironically, these qualities acted to propel MacKaye and Nelson and all of Dischord into an upper social echelon, one where ownership, the ability for self-representation, and freedom of creative control necessarily indicated a privilege the label and its owners were in no way seeking.

This status and hierarchy are complicated, however, by the other radical aspect of recording, mass distribution. Despite the seemingly hegemonic control of recordings, the phonograph, and its competitor, the gramophone, offered a revolutionary reimaging of cultural and public space. The capacity for reproduction and repetition of the recording of sound, specifically that of music, brought about significant alterations in the perpetuation of cultural systems of power. Recording artists, as they would come to be known, draw significant portions of their power from their sheer ability to reach and influence huge swaths of society. Of course, dissemination also affects the consumers of sound in profound and interrelated ways. The sharp lines of social class, particularly in musical consumption, which had previously been limited to (price- and class-exclusive) concerts and performances, were blurred and rearranged. A person who could not afford the expensive luxury of attending the symphony could now purchase that same performance for a fraction of the price. In this way, the recording of music helped democratize the consumption of sound. This democratization, then, led to a flattening of disparities in cultural capital, whereby musical knowledge and experience was, to a certain extent, not wholly contingent on class. The individual who listens to an opera on record could have the same understanding—the same appreciation, lexicon, and ability to enjoy—as the individual who attends the opera in box seats.

In turn, recorded music acts as a part of the function of the collective experience of listening to recorded music; no matter where in the country (or city or town or world) a person is, no matter what gender, race, sexuality, or age a person is, she is hearing the exact same sounds, the exact same tempos, timbres, pitches, and phrasings.[39] Such communality serves as a way of constructing a musical identity, which simultaneously links disparate fragments of society together and imbues the producers of the shared identities with an enormous amount of cultural power. The recording process is thus a necessarily cyclical and paradoxical process: it broadens the culturally constructed social class of musical consumers but also concentrates the number of people able to and responsible for the formation and content of this cultural capital. Dischord's capability and success with recording albums were, then, both signs of privilege and a meaningful expression of agency. And even more than DC hardcore flyers and zines, whose readership was limited by geographic space and mass production capabilities, Dischord acted as a mode of self-expression and a creation of self-narrative. Certainly, the label and the attending bands' construction of Washington's narrative was simply one of many rival narratives from many opposing forces, a semimarginalized effort in a sea of adversaries; however, it was still a pointed avenue for personal expression and agency, giving (recorded, memorialized, and distributable) voice—and the accompanying social power—to the bands, their members, and Dischord as a label. In one way, then, Dischord reclaims recording from the "institutionalization of bourgeois culture and its claim of universality, which includes taking possession of history."[40] Yet, in another way, they perpetuate such control, simply shifting the pattern of power. In their effort to subvert the elite's narrative command, the label serves, albeit perhaps unintentionally, to merely reallocate the power rather than upend it, bequeathing that control and privilege on the band and their music rather than on the music "industry."

Dischord encountered a number of other economic contradictions. The first is the paradoxical pride of economic "failure" as discussed by Stacy Thompson in her article on market failure and punk economics. As Thompson noted, a lack of mainstream popularity that typically connotes a form of failure in the business realm is re-formed as subcultural capital. Dischord Records, with its DIY approach to production, was not a traditional commercial sensation. They were unable to pose a threat to the dominance of the major labels' market share, and even within the relatively small, though growing, independent music market, Dischord had only a tiny market. As Vic Bondi, lead singer of Chicago hardcore band Articles of Faith, said, "Hardcore didn't change the rock business . . . against the competition, none of us destroyed the music business."[41] And although Dischord sold out 1982's compilation *Flex Your Head*'s four thousand copies and *Out of Step*'s three thousand copies in just a week, as MacKaye and Nelson wrote in their liner notes for 1984's *Four Old 7"s on a 12"*, "for at least two years the bands made no money off their records." Indeed, as Ken Inouye from Marginal Man recounted, "*Out of Step*—they lost a fortune, once you included shipping costs, production, this and that, they were losing 20 cents a record. . . . They wanted to sell the record for X amount. . . . In a sense, that's very cool and ideologically pure but you're not keeping in mind how much you're putting out to get it in." However, such a market failure was seen as a success. The lack of profit was understood as a by-product of the art/business divide and celebrated for avoiding such economic motivations. Making money on music falls outside the "authentic" punk collective identity, and so economic failure becomes subcultural capital.

At the same time, these tenets of decommodification and market failure were ultimately part of the tensions that foretold the demise of Minor Threat. Says MacKaye, "our last hurrah of honesty was to bow out before it became a dishonest situation, in the sense of being 'too big.' . . . You don't have to sell yourself."[42] Becoming a commodity was, to these bands, a cardinal sin. This growing disillusionment with the commodification of music, and the associated implications that Minor Threat was actively participating in such a transaction, spurred their satirical song "Cashing In":

> We don't care. We don't pose
> We'll steal your money. We'll steal your show
> I got your money and I feel fine
> A couple of dollars and really good time
> Well, you know I'm gonna be alright
> with the money I'm making off of you tonight/Sucker!
> Know something? The problem with money is I want more
> So let's, let's raise the price at the door

How much tonight, three thousand or four?
You know we'll make a million when we go on tour.

Underlying this parody, however, were feelings of hurt and betrayal, particularly from the DC scene who had embraced the band for the previous three years. Their popularity, within the subcultural capital values of the hardcore scene, was understood as a breach of identity, a selling out.[43] In an act of irony, underlining the betrayal the band felt from their DC community, Preslar and Baker showered the crowd with coins after their first reunion show. As MacKaye said, "It was our big fuck you to all the people who gave us shit when we got back together, telling us that we were cashing in on our popularity, that we were doing it for the money. . . . The lyrics are as ridiculous as the idea that we were actually doing it for the money."[44]

Dischord, and even the bands whose albums they released, were unable to fully extract themselves from the capitalist economic system, producing yet another fiscal paradox. More than the market failures seen as successes, DC hardcore became commodified by the bands themselves, as well as the audiences. Fans sold homemade band T-shirts at concerts; merchandise tables at shows sold CDs, LPs, stickers, patches, and zines, and the bands charged admission to their shows. Though the prices were significantly lower within this structure than within the mainstream music industry, an exchange value was still occurring, and the bands and Dischord as a label, try as they may, were never fully able to remove themselves from the system. Even the recording of the music itself—in the form of LPs and CDs—acts as a commodifying force. Recording music turns a performance—an ephemeral creation of art—into a material object, which can be bought and sold, changing the nature of the music. Despite the fact that MacKaye attempted to capture the "performance" or "realness" of the songs—that they were a moment in time, rather than a constructed, produced sort of song—the end result still produced a tangible commodity. MacKaye, Nelson, and Dischord Records, who clearly created their label in order to allow punk musicians to control and produce their own music, still acted as small-scale capitalists. The labor theory of value still stands.

6

Straightedge

A (White, Male, Middle-Classed)
Music-Based Social Movement

No exploration of DC hardcore can be complete without a discussion of straightedge, an individual philosophy that eschews drinking, drugs, and unrestrained sex, which became not only an emblem of the city's hardcore scene but also a national movement. The origins of straightedge are unvaryingly tied to Minor Threat, whose 1981 song "Straight Edge" declared the clean living ideology that rebelled against the youth-based and music-centric culture grounded in the consumption of drugs and alcohol, where sexual conquests were badges of honor and getting wasted was a nightly occurrence. Much academic and popular literature has been devoted to understanding straightedge,[1] and it would be nearly impossible, and even less desirable, to recite the history and transformations of the straightedge lifestyle within the confines of this chapter. However, many of the works tend to ignore the classed, raced, and gendered implications of straightedge. One straightedge author even claims in his introduction that "issues of class and race tend to assume little manifest prominence in defining the boundaries of straightedge culture and identity."[2] And if there is neither an overt nor comprehensive declaration of a class-, race-, or gender-centered dogma in the straightedge lifestyle,[3] clearly significant, sometimes contradictory sociopolitical assumptions and assertions are embedded in the straightedge ethos. Thus, the remainder of this chapter will focus on the way in which the straightedge ideology helped define the DC hardcore scene, but more precisely how this ideology at once reinforced and subverted cultural constructions of race, class, and gender.

In part, straightedge originated as a reaction to the emerging and past culture of alternative music scenes. The rock scenes of the 1960s and 1970s were nearly synonymous with drugs and alcohol. Songs glorifying, mystifying, and codifying their centrality in rock 'n' roll abounded: Jefferson Airplane's "White Rabbit," the Beatles' "Day Tripper," Dr. Feelgood's "Milk and Alcohol," Rolling Stones' "Mother's Little Helper," the Velvet Underground's "Heroin," George Thorogood's cover of "One Bourbon, One Scotch, One Beer," Eric Clapton's "Cocaine," the Doors' "Crystal Ship," Tom Waits's "Warm Beer and Cold Women"—just to name a select few. Drug-overdose-related deaths riddled rock—Jimi Hendrix, Janis Joplin, Brian Epstein, Keith Moon, Alan Wilson, Gram Parsons, Billy Murcia, Tim Buckley, Danny Whitten—yet the combination of drugs and alcohol remained a standard emblem not only for musicians but also for their audience members. As Henry Garfield recalled after he and Ian MacKaye went to a Led Zeppelin show, "We saw people passed out in their chairs. There's guys drooling on their leg, asleep, because they're 'luded out. We both said, 'Well, that will never be us.'"[4] Likewise, MacKaye described what he saw as the stupidity of drugs and music: "As a Hendrix fan, I'd talk to people who'd seen him play and they couldn't remember it because they were high. It doesn't make sense to me that you wouldn't want to remember your life."[5]

Even punk rock, with its promise of revolution, stopped short of resisting the allure of sex, drugs, and booze. The British and US punk scene both saw drugs and alcohol as part and parcel of their social and political revolution. The Ramones sang about sniffing glue, Sid Vicious died of a heroin overdose, Johnny Thunders sang about "Chinese Rocks," the New York Dolls had "Pills," and even the Dead Kennedys were "Too Drunk to Fuck." As MacKaye says, "You've got to remember that the older punk scene was really fashion-based, and kind of druggy. . . . It was really druggy and kind of, like, snotty."[6] At the same time, consumption in the form of drugs and alcohol were rampant in the local DC scene, both as a staple of Bad Brains–era punk and as the more general teenage mainstream culture. Bad Brains, and more specifically lead singer HR, became thoroughly enmeshed in the drug scene, going so far as to overdose one evening from heroin. He was known to pilfer the band's money from gigs for drugs and on numerous occasions was thrown off stage and getting kicked out of residences in DC for excessive use of drugs and alcohol.[7] MacKaye and Minor Threat, who admittedly would never have begun their own punk rock band without the influence of Bad Brains, encouraged their friends and fellow musicians to get clean and internalized the drug lessons for themselves. As Jeff Nelson argued, "I don't think that being punk includes, you know, hanging out at bars and drinking alcohol, you know, just like every other college kid and young adult does. . . . I think anything you do to separate yourself from what goes on in mainstream society is punk. And again, I think mainstream is definitely geared towards drugs and alcohol."[8] But it was not just Bad Brains who were ensnared admirers with this brand of consumption. Drugs, money, and sex were typical in both the high school scene from which DC hardcore emerged and the more general Washington, DC, area; straightedge was a direct rejoinder to that dominant social norm. MacKaye says,

> In the late seventies, I mean, everybody got high. I mean, in my high school, everybody got high or drank. . . . For me, it just seemed like a really stupid way to spend time. It just seemed like in the trajectory of life that, those years, it seemed such a waste of time to only think about medicating oneself.[9]

Henry Garfield agreed, recalling that "We'd go 'fuck it, we're straight' to set us off from the dopes, to set us off from the boring, dead alkie trip and the take-ludes-and-fall-asleep-in-the-parking-lot-of-White-Flint-mall thing."[10]

Even before the movement-forming musical declaration of abstinence by Minor Threat's "Straight Edge," MacKaye (and, to a lesser extent, Nelson) were laying the theoretical underpinnings for a no-drinking, no-drugs, no-meaningless-sex credo through their songs in Teen Idles. "Sneakers" laments the need to grow up too fast, upbraiding teens who are "sixteen going on thirty-two/Confusion of age surrounding you/Cigarette dangles from your painted lips/You wear the shoe because it fits," and "I Drink Milk" glibly announces, "I drink milk/I drink milk/I don't care what people say." If these musical declarations were in some way ambiguous or imprecise, Minor Threat clarified its position on drinking, smoking, drugs, and sex with "Straightedge" and cemented their stance in 1983's "Out of Step (with the World)," proclaiming "Don't smoke/Don't drink/ Don't fuck/At least I can fucking think." For MacKaye and large swaths of the DC hardcore scene,[11] "The structure of society is an oppressive concept. I don't see self-destruction as a valid form of rebellion."[12] Instead, straightedge became that rebellion.

The Intersectional Privilege of Straightedge

On its face, straightedge was simply a personal reaction to the mainstream cultural acceptance of and the countercultural near mandate to participate in the drinking, drug, tobacco, and sex lifestyle. But the adoption of a straightedge life also carried with it other crucial raced, gendered, and classed implications. Both the perception and realities of drinking, drug use, smoking, and having sex are clearly divided by categorizations of gender, class, and race. Most obviously, like the DC hardcore scene from which it sprang, straightedge was dominated by men. As one woman in the hardcore scene noted,

> Straightedge didn't involve me. The demographics of every single straightedge practitioner I knew were completely alien to me: they were all young white wealthy boys . . . trying to forge some other road to divert themselves from the ease and indulgences of their comfortable suburban realties. I think they wanted to try to understand their maleness, their humanness, in a different way.[13]

Blush also described the masculinity-laden nature of straightedge, saying, "The straight-edge scene was 100% testosterone-fueled—and the 'don't drink, don't smoke, don't fuck' ethos assured an all-male audience."[14] Even MacKaye has acknowledged that straightedge was "extremely 'boy' oriented. . . . I was trying to actually think of a single, straight edge woman singer. I couldn't think of one."[15] However, the lack of straightedge women, and even what straightedge author Robert Wood classifies as a scene "embedded with a latent male-oriented bias" including "discursive examples of gender bias,"[16] can be understood as a result of the highly masculinized ideology of straightedge. That is, the resistance grounded in the tenets of straightedge was a resistance to a culturally constructed understanding of masculinity. And such a masculinity was, of course, defined in large part by its difference from femininity.

Example A is the straightedge practice of abstinence from meaningless sex. First and foremost, such a dictate has been and still is always mandated for women; television, magazines, music, parents, peers—all have reinforced and reproduced the construction of "good" womanhood as viewing one's body as a temple, saving oneself for marriage, not "giving away the milk" so that he will "buy the cow," and constructing virginity as a precious gift. Women historically and contemporaneously have been assigned the role of being responsible simultaneously for controlling the "natural" uncontrollability of young male desire and for fulfilling those men's desires and needs. Such constraints on female sexuality stem in part from our personal and cultural socialization that not only reinforces differential and preferential gender roles but also constructs those female (sexual) roles by rewarding emotional expressiveness and submissiveness.

Such a construction is significantly power-laden, with men atop the hierarchy. Indeed, it was such a construction of conventional masculinity as it pertained to sex that straightedge sought to subvert. The history of Western civilization is replete with narratives of male power being intertwined with male sexuality, a description that excludes those men *not* exerting such (sexual) power. Society rewards the culturally masculinized traits of aggression, competition, autonomy, and emotional distancing in pursuit of that (sexual) power. Men must be virile, sexually dominant, independent, and goal-oriented, valuing emotional control over emotional attachment and internalizing desires or feelings, which frequently conditions them to feel they have the right to women's bodies.[17] The straightedge ethos works to undercut this construction of masculinity, defining masculinity aside from, as MacKaye said, "boys trying to fuck every girl they could because they had issues."[18]

Subversion of hegemonic masculinity is still a choice. It is still an assertion of power that allows them to maintain their credibility and authority as men, "claim[ing] heterosexual desire in the absence of heterosexual practice."[19] And, as the aforementioned quote indicates, this authority and power lies not just at the altar of gender but also of sexuality—the ability of straightedge men to maintain their hegemonic masculinity is partly a strategy that reinforces their heterosexuality. The control, though in a slightly different context, is the same power and authority that men have before, during, and after sex. As one female member of the hardcore scene recalled in *Maximum Rocknroll*, straightedge implied "a super-hero aspect, a secret knowledge or concept that mere mortals could not grasp. And hard, needless to say, related to maleness. Male genitals. Male behavior. Male minds."[20] This "superpower" of abstinence is reinforced by the agency and accompanying power embedded in the act of gender reconstruction, a rewriting of the culturally determined narrative of masculinity and the assertion of oneself as a "sexual activist."[21] Straightedge promulgates the fluid sociocultural understanding of sexuality, redefining it as not solely a physical act for satisfying sexual impulse but instead as an instrument of control for defining when, where, and how a man should be sexual. By continually demarcating sexual definition through their straightedge identity, DC hardcore males reaffirmed an alternative construction of masculinity that contested the performance of gender replicated by mainstream institutions and social actors.

The authority to rewrite masculine narratives about sex was also a function of the whiteness of straightedge. Men of color, particularly black and Latino men, have been culturally constructed as hypersexual, endowed with cartoonish sexual prowess, ability, and desire. And white men, of course, have been positioned in contrast to this construction, bestowed with the responsibility and power—and thus control—over white women in an attempt to fend off uncontrollable nonwhite sexual desire and save those women (for themselves). This power dynamic, in which white men dominate both another group of men (of color) and women, accounts for the ability of straightedge men to renegotiate this aspect of masculinity. Their racial privilege not only gives them the legitimacy to reinscribe masculinity but also affords them the privilege to think about such aspects of their identity. That is, free from the daily physical, emotional, and spiritual burdens of racism and sexism, white (heterosexual) male straightedge members are free to contest this aspect of hegemonic masculinity.

Similar threads of power, privilege, and hegemonic masculinity are found in the cultural construction of drinking. And, as MacKaye notes, drinking and sex are often linked together, particularly within the context of youth:

"What it all boils down to is sex. It's all a social thing and for people to loosen up, to drink a little alcohol to loosen up their sexual organs or whatever, to get the nerve to do what everyone wants to do anyway. It seems pretty stupid."[22] Like sex, drinking has historically been reserved for men. It was women who had the responsibility to take care of the home; it was women who frequently organized temperance movements; and it was women who were almost completely excluded from male spaces for drinking (the exception being women there for male pleasure, including brothels, saloons, and strip clubs). In this way, male drinking was created as a homosocial event, creating a cemented gender identity through the ritual of imbibing alcohol and as a distinct protest against and contrast with womanhood. Being a man was and is defined, in part, by drinking. Drinking is a rite of passage, a ritual of young men in high school, in fraternities, in the armed forces, for Friday and Saturday nights, for premarriage traditions, for football watching on Sundays, for any event where masculinity is centered. Drinking rituals reinforce the already conventional traits of masculinity: competition (Who can drink more? Who can win at beer pong? Who is going to puke first?), aggression (fights are a frequent outcome of overindulgence in booze, particularly if one's masculinity is threatened), and sexuality ("liquid courage" to hit on women, get the girl, and engage in nearly compulsory one-night stands). Drinking rituals also often reinforce gender segregation, reinforcing male bonding and group cohesion, which is reproduced throughout our social and cultural institutions.[23]

Straightedge contests these rites of passages, these signifiers of masculinity in their abstention of drinking. But, in one way, such rites of passages merely changed and were not eliminated. As Minor Threat guitarist Brian Baker said, "The reason I didn't drink was because I missed that period where kids break into their parents' liquor cabinets. It wasn't a huge statement; I just didn't drink."[24] Instead of drinking, the homosocial ritual was going to hardcore shows. And these new rituals were still heavily steeped in hegemonic norms of masculinity other than drinking (and sex); as explored in previous chapters, and will be explored in subsequent chapters, conventional masculinity in the form of anger, aggression, violence, power, and control were integral to both the sound and the scene of hardcore. And, despite a handful of women in the scene, the gender segregation of the sports team, the military base, and the fraternity still stood. The boys' club remained; only its location changed. And just as drinking was often a result of peer scrutiny and pressure, a way of proving one's self and one's masculinity to other boys, so too did *not* drinking become a way to gauge one's commitment to straightedge. As DC hardcore fan Tom Berrard recalled, "When I was in high school, I drank with my friends and smoked pot. But in the DC hardcore scene the peer pressure was to not drink, so I said, 'Fuck it,' and stopped. It wasn't like people were giving you a real hard time; it just was not cool to be drinking."[25] Being a (straightedge) male meant *not* drinking, which aligned with the traditional masculine directive of doing your own thing, being an "inner-directed male" instead of the less manly "other-directed" approval-seeking male.[26] The point is not to undercut the significance of straightedge's no-drinking practice. As I hope the previous paragraph makes clear, such temperance was a meaningful and perhaps even risky choice to make as a young man being constantly regulated and measured for one's manhood. But it is equally important to note the ways in which one form of hegemonic masculinity is traded for another form.

In addition to abstaining from alcohol and casual sex, people who are straightedge eschewed drugs. And their music reflected the stance. Government Issue is less than subtle in their 1981 track "Asshole," charging "Asshole, Asshole/look at me I'm as drugged as I can be/ Asshole, Asshole/ Can't you see I'm so drugged that I can't see" and making a grislier pronouncement on their 1982 "Teenager in a Box" ("Doing drugs and booze everyday/driving your car in a psychotic rage/you don't hear what anyone says/I'll read about you in the obituary page"). S.O.A dedicates one of their ten songs to slamming those who use drugs, offering a similarly lethal prognostication for those peers:

> Up in smoke, I laugh in your face/Fucked on drugs, lost in space/See your friends they laugh at you/But don't get mad 'cause they're drugged too/ You spend your time on the floor/Go throw up, come back for more/Eat those pills, take those thrills/Who's gonna wind up dead? You!/Snort that coke, what a joke/Who's gonna wind up dead? You!

Faith bemoans those choices in "Another Victim" ("It's not too late to make a change/Who cares if they don't understand/It's better if they think you're strange/Than dying to prove you're a real man/Live fast, die young, you're full of shit") and are even more overtly hostile in "You're X'ed," a play on the straightedge signifier ("You drink, you fuck behind my back/You're not my friend, I don't need your crap"). And, of course, Minor Threat's soon-to-be anthem, "Straight Edge," laid the foundation for morality-centered abstinence:

> I'm a person just like you/But I've got better things to do
> Than sit around and fuck my head/Hang out with the living dead
> Snort white shit up my nose/Pass out at the shows
> I don't even think about speed/That's just something I don't need
> I've got the Straight Edge!
> I'm a person just like you/But I've got better things to do
> Than sit around and smoke dope/'Cause I know that I can cope
> Laugh at the thought at eating ludes/Laugh at the thought of sniffing
>   glue

Two years later, Minor Threat's "Out of Step" laments that they "can't keep up/can't keep up . . . with the world," directed at their classmates who saw substance use as an accessible avenue of rebellion. Drugs and booze as a form of leisure were reproached, contrasting those who used with themselves—"at least I can fucking think."

The intersectional implications of straightedge are magnified with DC hardcore's no-drugs ethos. For the working class, intoxicants are often seen as an escape from the mundane everyday and the burdens of poverty; similarly, drug (and alcohol) use frequently associated with this class implies abuse rather than leisure use. Rooted in this reading is an assumption that there is no choice involved, that socioeconomic factors predetermine the way that drugs are consumed. Many state and federally sponsored studies tend to support this view. According to the National Institutes of Health, "research has shown persons at high risk for drug abuse often are those whose lives are marked by poverty, illiteracy, malnutrition, and other unhealthy environmental conditions."[27] Furthermore, drug abuse is habitually connected to place, perceived as an outcome of city decay and labeled an urban scourge. In this construction, the poor, who are often simultaneously racial and ethnic minority city dwellers, abuse drugs not as a personal choice but as a somewhat inevitable outcome of their socioeconomic class and as a (raced) cultural outgrowth of their demographics. On the other hand, the upper-class use of drugs is understood as a symbol of status, as a demonstration of both wealth and leisure. Disposable incomes allow for the choice, the preference, of buying and consuming drugs; affluence provides the resources (to buy fake identification, to procure drugs, to pay for lawyers if they are arrested) and the perception of recreational, rather than addictive, use. If one is rich, there is no reason to use drugs except for the pleasure of it. Rather than to escape mechanized routine, as the motivation for working-class use of drugs is conceived, upper-class use is seen as a sign of leisure, a sign of money, time, and lack of run-of-the-mill concerns. Indeed, research indicates that young people in a higher socioeconomic status engage in more frequent episodic heavy drinking and recreational drug use, perhaps because there is less supervision and more exposure to peers who are also using illegal substances.[28]

Having choice in drug use is tantamount to two race- and class-based forms of privileges: control and agency. An essential aspect of the adoption of straightedge was the veneration of both mental and physical control. Imbibing drugs and alcohol muddles thinking and can lead to addictive practices that negate the freedom of self-control and self-made decisions. As MacKaye says, "someone who is a junkie or an alcoholic is not entirely in control. They're somewhat at the mercy of their habit."[29] Brian Baker made a similar characterization of straightedge, saying it was "an outlook on life. In the sense that you want to be in control of your body and yourself, you want to have a clear view of what's going on."[30] Not taking drugs (or drinking alcohol or smoking) empowers straightedge participants, giving them discipline over their own bodies, reclaiming self-discipline through sobriety as an act of enfranchisement. By refusing to ingest anything that would, either cerebrally or materially, impinge on their ability to make rational, self-possessed decisions, hardcore participants sanctify the body and mind as a place devoid of the outside influence. The ability to choose, the assertion of self-as-free-agent, is itself a performance of agency. The ability to control choice, that is, to have a choice amid the often seemingly will-less mire of social and cultural dictates, is a privilege. Indeed, choice is nearly unilaterally understood as an instrument of privilege, the ability to choose what clothes to wear, what school to attend, what kinds of food to eat, where to live, what job to have—choice is a luxury not afforded to all. To be able to make these sorts of choices, some of which may even seem banal, is not only a consequence of socioeconomic class and race but also a reinforcement of that class and race, a sign of status. MacKaye's stated goal of "controlling things and not letting them control you" is itself a signifier of privilege, reinforcing sociological and psychological research that has found those with higher socioeconomic statuses reject a situation that limits personal choice and instead transform it into a situation in which they can choose.[31] Having access to resources—whether they be material, emotional, social, or psychological—implies higher levels of control and power, including the power to reject culturally mandated behaviors for young people. Such control and power were even more significant in Washington, DC, where the racial and economic disparities were (and still are) monumental, and home rule had just been established a handful of years before, in 1973.

But the concept of control and power within straightedge itself was somewhat paradoxical, insofar as one form of authority—adults, mainstream culture—was traded for another. Namely, Ian MacKaye. In part, this had to do with the obsession of national zines with MacKaye and straightedge—interviews with him and Minor Threat were never solely about their music but always talked about his straightedge philosophy. The decision was not MacKaye's. As he noted, "I stand behind the song, but it wasn't intended to be a movement."[32] Intentional or not, straightedge became a movement, with MacKaye its unanointed leader. At the same time, Minor Threat's music, specifically the lines from "Out of Step" that commanded "Don't smoke/don't drink/don't fuck" seemed to indicate a mandate rather than a description of personal preference. And although MacKaye explained the *I* was missing from those lines because the extra syllable did not fit, the implication was that such behavior was obligatory. The tension between the band and fans resulted in a parenthetical *I* in the lyric sheet and an introduction in the rerecording of the song in 1983 with MacKaye saying, "Listen, this is no set of rules. I'm not telling you what to do." As with his unsolicited leadership position, MacKaye's personal interpretation of straightedge was less important than the perception of straightedge to its followers. As one woman in the hardcore scene noted, "I don't mean that these were membership rules explicitly set forth; in fact, I don't think that the boys could even comprehend how exclusive their straightedge 'movement' was. But I certainly had no thread there to grab hold of."[33]

Thus, a new form of hierarchy within an alternative form of hegemony was born. Proceeding from sociologists R. W. Connell and James Messerschmidt's concept of hegemonic masculinity, I posit that straightedge produced a hegemonic identity—one grounded in alternative forms of masculinity and class but still framed within whiteness. As Connell and Messerschmidt describe it, in order to maintain dominant social control, masculinity is subjective and normative, adjusting to certain sociopolitical and historical milieus, and retaining power by (socially) punishing those subordinate or marginalized masculinities that deviate from the norm. This leads to complex "levels" of hegemonic masculinity—local, regional, and global, all with their slightly different standards of masculinity, all with their slightly different hierarchies and social penalties.[34] Straightedge did the same. It did not dismantle any single hegemonic vector of identity—dominant modes of masculinity, race, and class remained—but instead refashioned a new system. Straightedge participants sought to reinscribe the implications of excess. Overindulgence in violence, music, or attitude (staples of hardcore) were not frowned on, but instead drugs, booze, and what MacKaye derisively labeled "following your penis around" were. Being straightedge was understood as an advantage, a privilege over others. The term itself implies that those who are "straight" (in the drug and alcohol context, rather than as a sexuality identifier) have an "edge" over those who are not. And it was an intentional descriptor. As MacKaye explains, "OK, fine, you take drugs, you drink . . . but obviously I have the edge on you because I'm sober; I'm in control of what I'm doing."[35] However, as with any system that is formed and maintained, the rules and regulations of straightedge often favor and serve the needs of some while ostracizing, ignoring, or denigrating others. The ruling class has changed while remaining the same: white, middle- to upper-class class males. Straightedge's alternative local system of identity indeed subverted many of the regional and global systems of masculinity and class, but it also merely rearranged such power and left in place hegemonic male whiteness. Moreover, the local straightedge system still depended on the same problematic social processes embedded in regional and local systems of hegemony, creating hierarchies based on authenticity and salience to the local system hegemonic standards and marginalizing those who did not achieve such standards. As social theorists have noted, reinforcement of hierarchies with a concomitant system of reward and punishment ultimately reproduces regional and global hegemonic systems of power, reentrenching dominant modes of race, class, and gender.[36]

Straightedge as Both Subculture and Social Movement

Straightedge has, with good reason, frequently been written about through the lens of subcultural theory. Robert T. Wood's 2006 book on straightedge has as its subtitle "complexity and contradictions of a subculture" and theoretically frames straightedge through the near deities of subcultural theory past: Albert Cohen, Dick Hebidge, David Matza, the Birmingham School, and Mike Brake. The association between straightedge and subcultural theory and frameworks continues, both titular- and content-based, in a vast majority of studies on straightedge in the past twenty years.[37] The concepts grounding this subcultural framework within this literature are both logical and useful for understanding straightedge: the lived experiences of the individuals in the subculture; the ways in which youth react to and are influenced by mainstream culture; the symbolic rejoinders to this mainstream culture using, as per the Birmingham School, rituals, consumption, and performative practices; the ways in which these practices and rituals are infused with ideological assumptions and hegemonic underpinnings; the semiotic encoding and decoding of resistant and reinforcing meanings; and how the conceptual scaffolding of identity, the more contemporary lynchpin of subcultural theory, works to create meaning and resist dominant forms of representation. It makes academic sense that straightedge, from its position within the subculture of punk, and then within the subculture of hardcore, is primarily understood as a subculture, with all the attending theoretical and conceptual keystones.

Less frequently has straightedge been conceptualized as a social movement. The crucial exception is Ross Haenfler's excellent work, *Straightedge: Clean-Living Youth, Hardcore Punk, and Social Change*, which, while predominantly concerned with subcultural theory (identity, culture, and symbolic ritual and performative practices), has a chapter dedicated to straightedge as a social movement. And although Haenfler's focus is primarily external to Washington, DC, and on a period much later than the origins of the movement (situating his research in the 1990s and early 2000s), he reframes aspects of straightedge as a social movement. In part, Haenfler's more overt politically tinged examination can be tied to straightedge's post-1980s subcultural identity. As straightedge crept from its DC hardcore-based womb and made its way around the country (and world), the values, beliefs, and norms changed, transformed, and expanded as well. While the no-drinking, no-drugs, no-promiscuity tenets remained, other explicitly political values emerged: animal rights and veganism, environmentalism, human rights, and in some cases, Krishna-core. In this way, the more contemporary straightedge identity is, on its face, more concretely political. Even so, Haenfler describes straightedge's forms of resistance as "primarily cultural, rather than political, in nature" in its use of collective action, creation of ideology and identity, and participation.[38]

What I argue in this section is that straightedge, from its inception in the heart and soul of Ian MacKaye and its infancy years in the DC hardcore scene, was always-already both a subculture and a social movement. What is the difference? Why does that matter? Who cares if we label it one or the other? To put it simply, what is at stake—as with many a semantic struggle over labelling—is power, agency, and legitimacy. Subcultures are frequently relegated to the realm of youth, and in doing so, afforded with less social and political legitimacy and therefore power. They are just kids. Resisting. Rebelling. They'll grow up, become adults and change their identity. And if these subcultures *do* pose a threat to the status quo and to hegemonic norms in some way, those threatening subcultures will be culturally neutered by either commercialization and commodification— what I call, tongue-in-cheek, the Hot Topic-ization of subcultures[39]—or delegitimized by the media, politicians, or adults in general[40]—or both. Social movements, on the other hand, are more often understood as the purview of adults. They are constructed as formal organizations with formal political goals and thus represent a more formal and legitimate type of power. They can still be neutered by the dilution of their values and beliefs into political platforms,[41] but they are still imagined having more (direct) influence on sociopolitical outcome through their use of more institutional means. Yet, to use a good ole cliché, subcultures and social movements are different sides of the same coin. By understanding subcultural practices as a part of social movements, we can include noninstitutional arenas in which loosely connected individuals enact social change and recognize the resistance of personal value identities connected to collective identities.

The DC straightedge scene is both subculture and social movement. Certainly, the origins of straightedge and its intersection with hardcore come from a form of class-based grievance, located within social movement's theoretical history. Grievance theory argues that the structural strain on the individual prompts collective action. That is, the promises at the societal level filter down and affect how the individual processes her needs; if particular social structures are inherently inadequate, or if there is insufficient regulation, there will be a change in the individual's perceptions of means and opportunities. Discontented individuals without other avenues of redress form groups to challenge their suffering and press for change. As the previous chapter explored, the cultural production surrounding DC hardcore was, at its core, a reaction against the commodification of music and the embedded status-based hierarchy of control and power that accompanied such commodification. From flyers to zines to the creation, production, recording, and dissemination of music, DC hardcore worked as a form of collective action against the corporate interests that had overtaken music and the accompanying star system. Straightedge, in perhaps a more direct fashion, mobilized around and because of another economic dictate: the business of booze. Their grievance was clear: young people should be able to hear music and not be denied entrance to a venue because they could not buy alcohol. As MacKaye explained it,

> It was a real slap in the face that all these bands that we invested our beliefs in, that bands that really spoke for you, that they would come to your town and you couldn't see them because you weren't born in the right year. When you realize that this is a situation that was really predicated on the sale of alcohol it really aggravated us because we didn't even buy alcohol. It was ridiculous, the fact that we weren't going to buy alcohol made us not welcome at these music events, it was fucked, it was totally the wrong thing.[42]

Grievance was primarily grounded in a violation of procedural justice insofar as the ideal (fairness and equality as seen through entrance into a venue) does not match the reality (denied entrance). What makes the situation a breach of procedural justice was not only the lack of fairness because of age but more specifically because of the mismatch between DC law and venue policy. DC regulations required that all venues serving alcohol also serve food; in this way, there were no bars in the traditional sense. In theory, then, anyone should be able to come into the venue. The reason underage DC hardcore kids were denied entrance was simple, according to MacKaye—money: "Venues, by and large, are bars and their economy is based on the sales of alcohol. . . . At the end of the day that is their economy so what they are interested in is selling alcohol and therefore they need clientele."[43] In this way, their grievance, grounded in procedural justice, was the disparity in the way they were treated in trying to gain entrance to a venue, which itself was grounded in the capitalist system entrenched in the music industry.

It should be noted, however, that grievance theory within the social movement pantheon focuses primarily on the structural inequalities that spur collective strain. In this understanding, it is the ever-growing economic gap between what individuals are told to have/achieve/be and the reality of everyday achievability. For the civil-rights movement, it was the ideal of "All men are created equal" next to the reality of the legacy of slavery, redlining, Jim Crow, segregation, and separate but equal; for Occupy Wall Street it was the promise of the American Dream and the myth of a system of meritocracy versus the 1 percent who hold more wealth than the entire 99 percent below. But in the case of DC hardcore and straightedge, grievances were not born of necessity. As has been discussed throughout this book, there was a conscious and intentional *choice* in participating both in the hardcore scene and the straightedge lifestyle. Such choice is frequently a delineating factor between subcultures, a form nonnormativity that includes the agency to be viewed as different as opposed to marginalization, which implies structural, dictated difference without the privilege of self-definition. I don't dispute this difference. The ability to self-name is tantamount to self-efficacy and sociopolitical agency. However, nonnormativity does not, I believe, exclude the scene from enacting the social and political action that constitutes both a subculture and a social movement.

Political opportunity theory emerged in the 1980s as a reaction to the gaps in grievance theory. Academics argued that although grievance theory offered an explanation of *why* a movement mobilized, it could not account for *when* and *how* it did so. Political opportunity provided that when and how, arguing that state structures and political cleavages create stable opportunities for collective action. As Sidney Tarrow, social movement theorist behemoth, explained, political opportunity can be understood as "consistent—but not necessarily formal or permanent—dimensions of the political environment that provide incentives for people to undertake collective action by affecting their expectations for success or failure."[44] Expanding on this definition, Jack Goldstone added seven more factors, which he termed external relational fields, that are necessary in creating a political opportunity for a social movement to mobilize and succeed. Some of Goldstone's factors are "political and economic institutions (and their history) that provide the framework in which movements recruit, act, and seek responses" and political actors, religious and economic elites, and various public communities whose responses to the movement help shape the claims and dynamics of that movement, among which are "symbolic and value orientations available in society that condition the reception and response to movement claims and actions."[45]

For DC straightedge, political opportunity was aligned with both Tarrow's "consistent . . . dimensions of the political environment" and Goldstone's external relational fields, primarily within the context of place and social space. More precisely, Washington, DC, afforded an inherently sociopolitically charged framework for everyday action and explicit politically directed acts. Because of its brimming symbolic power—of sovereignty, politics, and authority—as well as its functional, everyday power—to create law, to enact change, to alter the course of history—DC has historically provided structure for social movements. From the suffragettes (1913) to the Hunger March (1932) to the Rabbis' March (1943) to the March on Washington (1963) to the Poor People's Campaign (1963) to the protest of the Kent State shootings (1970), the Women's Strike for Equality (1970), and numerous marches to end the war on Vietnam (1965–72), DC offered and continues to offer figurative and literal visibility to sociopolitical issues and the people who take action about them. MacKaye himself remembers "being brought to antiwar rallies by his parents, fascinated by that period's counterculture." Indeed, being in a city nationally and globally defined *as* a political opportunity structure

and entrenched with a tradition of social movements offered the possibility of mobilization and change, though straightedge ideals were clearly
divergent. As posthardcore DC punk Bubba Dupree of the band Void
acknowledges, although many in the hardcore scene had "parents [who]
were ex-Hippies . . . it wasn't the same set of morals that inspired it."[46]

Straightedge shunned the rampant drug use of the 1960s counterculture, which had killed so many of the musical icons of that era and seemed
to be counterproductive for the social-justice goals of the hippies. Teen
Idles documented their sometimes-vicious loathing of the drug-fueled
music and political scene in "Dead Head":

> Deadhead, deadhead, take another toke/Deadhead, deadhead, you're a
> lousy joke/Friend of the devil, who you trying to kid/Friends of the devil
> are dead like Sid/I'll be grateful when you're dead. . . . Riding that train
> high on cocaine/The music is really lousy, the fans are a pain/Troubles
> behind, troubles ahead/The only good deadhead is one that's dead.

Clearly alluding to fans of the Grateful Dead, but also the drug-infected
punk scene (and the death of Sex Pistol Sid Vicious), the band attempted to
"distance leftist punk from its psychedelic political parallel, the hippie movement."[47] Their distancing, however, still benefited from what Goldstone
called the "symbolic and value orientations available in society." Though
the expression of this subculture and social movement took a new and different form, it was the hippies, the counterculture, the political movements
of DC's past that allowed for the construction of straightedge. As MacKaye
recalls, such a history, and the symbolism and power rooted in that history, was critical to his understanding of the ability to enact social change:

> I was born in 1962 and I was here in Washington right through the civil
> rights stuff, the anti-war stuff, gay rights. My parents and I went to a
> church that was radical liberation—very, very left, it had a woman say-
> ing mass in 1972, gay marriage in 1974, the Black Panthers spoke there,
> rock bands played there—it was radical. I was raised in that environment
> so I thought that's how society would be. Then the '70s came along and
> you had this period of people partying and disco music and such obso-
> lescence, it was such a bummer and I felt so disconnected from it. I was
> like, 'where's the counter-culture?' It seemed so real to me as a child but
> as a teenager it was gone.[48]

Deriving from a storied, but drug-addled, musically and politically infused countercultural history, as well as going to high school with the rich children of senators, cabinet members, policymakers, and political powerhouses, DC hardcore and straightedge became a substance-free "portal to the counter-culture," as MacKaye describes it. The straightedge philosophy acted as an unconventional form of resistance. As MacKaye notes,

> We felt as if we were deviant. I mean, there was all these other people who were challenging all these conventions. Sexual conventions, political conventions, sociological conventions, philosophical conventions—every kind of convention, musical and artistic . . . and so were we. We were challenging social conventions too.[49]

Straightedge, then, not only operated within the sociopolitical framework of the '60s and '70s countercultures and social movements, but perhaps more meaningfully *because of* its spatial and symbolic location in DC.

Beyond a theoretical framework in which to understand the structural and social conditions that afforded straightedge a way to mobilize and communicate their message, both social movement and subcultural theory aid in understanding the effects of DC straightedge. Traditionally, social movements are thought to transform marginal subcultures into real choices by offering models of alternative forms of meaning; yet that unduly separates the two ideas. In the DC straightedge subculture and social movement, the lifestyle and music conventionally associated solely with subcultures is merged with the political resistance often linked exclusively to social movements. Straightedge as a subculture and a social movement (re)constructs meaning and identity that draws on both the dominant and the residual cultures in creating alternatives to both.

One such reconstruction is found in the reappropriation of the signifier of abstinence. Straightedge in DC was occurring down the road from Pennsylvania Avenue as President Ronald Reagan was once again declaring a War on Drugs. At the same time, the First Lady was visiting elementary schools around the country, publicizing her husband's anti-drug campaign and touting her newly coined phrase, "Just Say No." With these sociocultural frames came policies and regulations. The Reagan administration oversaw the implementation of zero-tolerance policies in schools, DARE programs (Drug Abuse Resistance Education), and simultaneously expanding law enforcement capacity and the creation of a federal task force, one that was militarized in its technology and efforts to combat even casual drug use. Arrests skyrocketed, as did the prison population. Drug users of any stripe were constructed as criminals, deviants, and dangers to society. These ideological positions aligned with the Republican party as a whole—drugs and drug users were immoral and wrong.

Straightedge, on the other hand, worked to resignify those who did not do drugs, much like those who did not drink, smoke, or engage in casual sex. Rather than connoting conservatism, grounded in either a religious fervor or a political ideology, straightedge abstention from drugs was about self-control, the reclamation of power for young people, and personal responsibility. "There's nothing I hate more than hearing people use that shit as an excuse," MacKaye explains. "Too many times it's, 'I'm sorry what happened last night, I was fucked up.' Well, fuck that shit, man."[50] In this way, straightedge as both a subculture and a social movement worked to reinscribe not only what it meant to not imbibe (drugs, alcohol, cigarettes) but also what it meant to be a teenager. The cultural narrative of coming of age and the concurrent expectation of rebellion via excess, the rituals and rules ascribed to high school, were subverted and reworked by straightedge. As Nelson described MacKaye's script-flipping adoption of straightedge, "His thing was 'I don't need drugs, I'm not going to take them.' A very unusual strength of will. A very tiny percentage of the population has anything like that kind of willpower and determination and self-control and resistance to peer pressure."[51] At the same time, and as discussed earlier in this chapter, straightedge also worked to resignify hardcore as a music. No longer was hardcore simply Black Flag's "Wasted" ("I was a hippie/I was a burnout/I was a dropout/I was out of my head. . . . I was so jacked up/I was so drugged up/I was so nebbed out/I was out of my head") or Circle Jerk's "Group Sex" ("Group sex! Group sex! Group sex!") or even their mentors and friends Bad Brains, with HR stealing money for drugs. Instead, hardcore started to be synonymous with straightedge. As Haenfler writes, "Straightedge remains nearly inseparable from the hardcore music scene."[52] What started in DC with MacKaye and Minor Threat diffused to Boston, New York, California, and, eventually, around the world. Straightedge was hardcore and hardcore was youth and youth were in control of their minds, bodies, and perhaps even souls.

The outward manifestation of this resignification of youth, hardcore, and clean living was itself another reappropriation of a cultural sign: the X. Originally, this X was a necessary practicality. As described in earlier sections, DC hardcore bands and their fan base were mainly underage and unable to get into clubs and bars to perform and watch other hardcore bands. In order to admit minors and avoid the fines that came with serving underage youths, MacKaye and others convinced bar and club owners to mark those under twenty-one as a warning not to serve them alcohol, a practice they had seen at clubs and bars while touring in California. Business motivations prevailed and the X was born—a large, ineradicable magic-markered symbol on the hands of underage hardcore kids, enabling a significant expansion of places for hardcore shows to happen, many of which were indeed in bars: the Bayou, the 9:30 club, the Chancery. In this way, the X first signified age. It was a forced identity that marked individuals as underage and unable to drink legally. As MacKaye noted, "It represents youth. The markings on the hands were just what kids in Washington, DC had to deal with just to see music, to be free."[53] Quickly, however, these Xs transformed from an expediency to a symbol of pride. The X emerged as a symbol of straightedge—a physical marking out, a *self*-labeling, of identity. No longer was the X a way of crossing out their agency—a signal or stigma that broadcasted they were not able to drink, were not allowed to drink. Instead, the X was reframed as a choice, announcing a conscious and identity-forming decision, constructed as a stark binary to the adult world trying to label them. As Nathan Strejcek, lead singer of Teen Idles, said, "Since we weren't allowed to legally drink we said, 'Fine, we don't want to,' just to piss the lawmakers off. This is where we established a new place in modern society for ourselves . . . clear-minded thinking against the most evil of all, the adults."[54]

Finally, DC hardcore as a music acts not only as a form of cultural change tied to the subculture and social movement of straightedge but also as an ideology itself. Providing a means of explaining why things are as they are, complete with images and symbols that provoke an emotional response (albeit a more abstract response than overt political rhetoric), the sound and production of hardcore voiced both an opposition to the massification of society and domination of commercial values and a chaotic, dissonant noise meant to parallel sociopolitical feelings of unrest. As previously discussed in this book, the sounds and lyrics of DC hardcore, in addition to their DIY musical ethos, all act as politically laden expressions. Hardcore and straightedge used the politics of the everyday in order to enact an oppositional consciousness. What transformed this opposition from a personal articulation[55] to a subculture and social movement was the way in which individuals, bands and fans alike, also adopted this identity. In doing so, individual inequality became subjectively experienced dissatisfaction, and the "I" became "we," the basis of collective identity. Of course, as music and social movement scholars Ron Eyerman and Andrew Jamison argued, there is a significant dialectic between the music and the movement—they are mutually constitutive and work to frame each other to insiders as well as outsiders.[56] Hardcore inspired youth to become straightedge and straightedge offered a collective identity that framed not only those youth but also came to frame the music itself.

Resistance in general, and that of DC straightedge specifically, was contextual and multilayered rather than static and uniform. It often centered on individual opposition to domination and the subjective redefinition of societal norms, so that "to an increasing degree, problems of individual identity and collective action become meshed together: the solidarity of the group is inseparable from the personal quest."[57] Unlike most subcultures and social movements, however, hardcore and straightedge did not attempt to naturalize, and therefore legitimize, their subculture or social movement and their associated actions and symbols but instead gained political value in their ability to frustrate and provoke the expectations of most of society. The meaning of DC hardcore to its members was as a transgressive experience—a subculture and a social movement that crossed (or at least straddled) the traditional binaries of social realities such as good versus evil, or even melodic versus dissonant. In doing so, DC hardcore offered individual control and the concurrent opportunity of losing oneself to a greater cause.

7

Embodying (White, Middle-Class) Masculinity

Fighting, Fashion, and Slam Dancing

The last show S.O.A. performed was opening for Black Flag in South Philly in 1981, with about thirty DC hardcore kids in the crowd, including Ian MacKaye. As Henry Garfield recalled, "We really didn't come up to beat up Philly punks, but I guess we came up to fight for something."[1] The fight came to them. As John Stabb from Government Issue recalled in the punk zine *Now What*, "When everyone was inside the club, that's when the Philly freak show began," first in the form of fights on the dance floor, followed by a free-for-all melee on the streets with local Philly kids wielding baseball bats and sticks. Even with police lined up around the block, one DC punk had his head split open, another was sliced in the nose by a lead pipe, and the night crawled to an end with everyone from DC "covered in blood,"[2] taking off for the local emergency room. Philly attendees not associated with the riot didn't fare much better. As Philadelphia music promoter Nancy Petriello-Baril pronounced, "We were lucky to get out alive." She got out with a pair of black eyes instead. Bryan Lathrop, whose Philly hardcore band Sadistic Exploits also opened for Black Flag that night, ended up with a fractured skull.

Such outbursts of violence were not all that unusual for the DC hardcore scene. Not only was their music infused with it, as explored in chapter 4, but so too was the scene itself. Whether it was fights in a club or on a stage, fights against outsiders in the form of punks from a different city or, as Garfield describes them, suburban "young wise-asses . . . fucking with our little piece of the world,"[3] slam dancing or the inherent threat of chains and spikes draped on coats and used as belts, DC hardcore's violence manifested through the bodies of those in the scene. As a site of control and self-agency, the body worked as a powerful channel through which DC hardcore punks could perform and negotiate difference. This chapter explores the ways in which such performances of difference—through clothes, through hair, through dance—signaled a (white, classed, masculinized) DC hardcore identity, at once challenging and reinforcing the ways in which vectors of identity are organized and naturalized through the body.

"A Warning to Enemies": DC Hardcore Hair and Fashion

The body as a site of power and struggle has a long theoretical history and is most contemporaneously linked to Michel Foucault's argument of discipline and punishment. In what is admittedly a vast oversimplification of a nuanced, complex, and dense argument, Foucault asserts that the modern body has become "normalized" by social, scientific, and economic surveillance in order to bring it under control by hegemonic forces. In this way, individual aspects of the body are differentiated through "the principle of elementary location or partitioning. Each individual has his own place; and each place its individual."[4] Social locations work to reinforce specific ideologies and thus relations of power in everyday and often invisible ways. At the same time, these micro-level power relations allow for the body to act as a site of resistance, a way to use personal choices about one's body to perform political functions. Just as powerful forces "inscribe" the body as they "invest it, mark it, train it, torture it, force it to carry out tasks, to perform ceremonies, to emit signs,"[5] so too does the resistant body.

The history of subcultures is rife with examples of how deliberate choices in outward physical appearance have been not only a method of creating difference from hegemonic and authoritative forces but also a way in which to self-identify and form a collective identity with other like-minded people. Haircuts, shoes, jewelry, fashion—all these work as explicit and important signifiers, producing overt signifieds that were invaluable in the public and private formation of resistant identities. Mods, the post–World War

II British subculture, relied on expensive high fashion and the sporting of custom-made suits with skinny ties and narrow lapels, along with Beatle boots and scooters, as their subcultural calling card. Besides subculture membership, their dress expressed their fealty to the modernist lifestyle and post–World War II conspicuous consumption, the emerging jazz scene, and an existentialist philosophy. Hippies adopted the uniform of long, unkempt hair and beards, tie-dye psychedelia, bell bottoms, and flowing, peasant-style shirts, which performed their subcultural values of nonconformity from standard beauty norms, sexual and personal freedom, and an eschewal of rampant consumption. And greasers sported fitted tees with rolled cuffs, denim and leather jackets, motorcycle boots, and a pompadour hairstyle in an effort to represent their adherence to a working-class ethos, including a passion for hot rods and motorcycles and an affinity for rockabilly and rock 'n' roll. In each of these instances dress and accoutrements function threefold: as a mode of differentiation (from the hegemonic culture), as a mode of association (with members of the same subculture), and as a mode of identification (connoting sociopolitical values through the symbols of clothes, hair, and adornment). What's more, these subcultures were nearly unilaterally represented by men,[6] thereby promulgating a specific and sometimes marginalized depiction of (white) masculinity within that subculture. For mods, the message included a repudiation of the proto-typical working-class male ethos of London in favor of a more feminized polish of dress and attention to style; for hippies, conventional masculinity was inverted by redefining masculine coding with previously established feminine markers and middle-class conspicuous consumption was traded for DIY aesthetics; and greasers fashioned their notion of masculinity as a reaction to the so-called feminization of popular culture in search of a form of nostalgic manhood, as well as a form of masculine power in frequently marginalized ethnic and classed communities. In the same way, then, the DC hardcore scene forged their communal and subcultural identity—one premised on a specific type of corporeality linked to race, class, and gender, grounded in both a reaction to popular culture and an assertion of agency in the specific sociohistorical context of Washington, DC, in the late '70s and '80s—through their appearance.

Hair in and of itself is a culturally neutral manifestation of biology. But we humans have imbued these protein filaments, particularly the ones on top of our heads, with personal, social, ethnic, religious, historical, and even economic meanings and, in doing so, we "socialize hair, making it the medium of significant 'statements' about self and society."[7] Hair as a symbol classifies and categorizes along racial, gendered, classed, and aged identities, working to signify specific sociocultural and political locations. Think of the afro, the pompadour, dreadlocks, or the mop top. Each one signals not just different vectors of one's identity (gender, class, race) but also one's social positioning because of those vectors of identity. Hair in hardcore accomplished analogous performances of self and social location. Before the evolution of punk to hardcore, when the musicians of DC's most influential and prominent hardcore bands were merely fans in their early teens, their hair was still a signifier of difference, a sociopolitical statement of male identity. Henry Garfield sported a mohawk, pledging his follicle allegiance to the shocking, avant-garde British punk style, and Ian MacKaye wore a shaggy, longer hairstyle associated with the skater subculture of which he and his friends were a part. These hairstyles were already an embodied aesthetic adherence to countercultural symbolism, delineating their white, male, middle-class bodies as nonmainstream. In a curious way, both these prehardcore hairstyles were a more feminized version of traditionally constructed masculinity and simultaneously reinforced class privilege. The mohawk involved (in part) the growing out of the male's hair, in addition to the exorbitant amount of time and commitment to both hair products and the actual process of grooming, both purviews previously ceded to women. The skater 'do was similarly associated with the longer locks of females, and both hairstyles scorned the very specific white, male, professional-class mandate of the 1980s: short, clean-cut, naturally colored hair.

These marginally feminized hairstyles were soon radically eliminated with the rise of hardcore. Instead, the symbol of DC hardcore became the complete antithesis of longer hair—it was the shaved head. Nearly every lead singer had one: Ian and Alec MacKaye (Teen Idles and Minor Threat, and Faith, respectively), Henry Garfield (S.O.A.), and John Stabb (GI), who actually had his head shaved on stage. The research on the sociology of hair is sparse, but, such as it exists, it indicates that men who shave their heads are thought of as more virile and commanding, in part because of their choice to subvert societal norms that equates a thick, lush mane with sexuality. That is, in order to buck social dictates, men with their shaved heads must be confident and dominant—able and willing to ignore conventions. The uniform of a sheared head as a unifying, collective symbol of hardcore was, at the same time, a unifying and collective symbol of a hypermasculinity that paralleled the aggression and vehemence of the bands' music. In some measure, a shaved-head hypermasculinity was inextricably linked to the aesthetic connotations of the military buzz cut, which itself signaled discipline, fierceness, and severity. DC hardcore's style of the shaved head, then, acted as a more extreme version of the militarized (and concurrently socially constructed hypermasculinity) haircut. If the buzz cut designated the military, with its accompanying masculinized characteristics, then the punks' shaved heads amplified and exaggerated that. Such a relationship was by no means coincidental. Georgetown was full of marines who lived at nearby bases and who frequently attacked—both verbally and physically—DC hardcore punks. By reappropriating the sign of a shaved head from the military and resignifying it as a symbol of rebellion and resistance, the DC punks were capitalizing on the already embedded hypermasculinity of that haircut and simultaneously reinscribed masculinity on their own defiant bodies. When Garfield and MacKaye were "frequently stopped and asked if they're Marines,"[8] they were at once subverting the traditional sign of buzz cut = military = masculinity: actively participating in that equation by retaining the signifier and simply readjusting the signified. The power—both in its physical and cultural manifestations—of the military was deflected and redirected by DC hardcore's assumption of the shaved head.

The respect that came with the threat of danger was more than just an aesthetic found in hardcore punk hair; it was the primary signifier entrenched in the clothes and fashion of hardcore. Traditional symbols of violence were detached from their typical context and reassigned meaning. Among them were the pervasive style of combat boots, chains, and spiked leather cuffs that members of Minor Threat, Faith, S.O.A., and GI wore, which their fans also adopted. As sociologist Dick Hebdige explains it, these mundane, often practical objects of everyday life contain a double meaning, at once threatening the "normal" world and also offering an alternative identity to "deviants." By employing bricolage, that is, decontextualizing these objects and using them in new and unconventional ways, those in the DC hardcore scene were able to create new meanings. No longer were combat boots merely a practical footwear for a military that needed ankle stability, grip, and foot protection in rugged and sometimes treacherous terrain; no more were chains simply a tool for lifting, pulling, securing, or connecting heavy machinery or subjugating and containing prisoners, criminals, or slaves; nor were spikes and leather cuffs deployed in their historical use as torture devices or trappings for cowboys. MacKaye explains, "Our appearance was so offensive to people that it made us realize how disgusting the mainstream was, and we were glad to be outside of it. The violence was born of what was going on in this country."[9] Objects like the shaved head were reimagined as a symbol of hardcore while retaining their implicit (and sometimes explicit) threat of violence. As Blush asserts, "Hardcore fashion constituted a defensive posture: a warning to enemies and an effort to look tough. Such displays are common in the animal kingdom, where creatures make them look larger and meaner."[10]

The pragmatic and historical denotations of these objects, which meaningfully include overt expressions of power, domination, and violence, were merely re-formed to define hardcore masculinity[11]—a masculinity that was, by its very nature, white. Indeed, it is important to note that the ability to perform such symbolic violence and pose this sort of cultural threat was permitted in large part because of the DC hardcore scene's overwhelming whiteness. A hoard of black males sporting chains, spikes, and combat boots would signal a perceived threat to the hegemonic dominance of whiteness and male whiteness; when young, white (middle-class) males engage in such performances, however, they are merely threatening cultural conventions, not structural, systematic relations of power. The analogy may not be perfect, but consider the Black Panthers' custom of carrying guns on their persons. All of a sudden the police, the FBI, the larger white media community were terrified of US citizens engaging in what these same individuals had once vigorously defended as God-given constitutional rights to bear arms. Arming one's (white) self against the amorphous tyranny of the overbearing government did nothing to disrupt or even threaten the raced, classed, and gendered hierarchy structurally embedded in the United States. Black men and women doing so most certainly did. In a comparable way, the threat of DC hardcore's material violence was a threat contained by their whiteness.

This contained (white male) threat was also performed by the lack of clothing worn, most often by the lead singers, who would be bare-chested while performing. This was frequently the case with Henry Garfield, whose "imposing physical presence"[12] was on display in the form of well-built biceps, sinewy abs, and a muscular bare chest performing with S.O.A. at the Wilson Center. The same goes for Artificial Peace's[13] lead singer, Steve Polcari, and bassist Rob Moss at a show at the Wilson Center in 1982, a wiry and shirtless Jeff Nelson drumming for Minor Threat in the summer and winter of 1982, and Faith's Alec MacKaye at Space Arcade II in early 1983. This tendency toward displaying their muscular, exposed physiques was even noted by journalists; in Richard Harrington's 1981 *Washington Post* article on DC hardcore, he refers to, as a descriptive term, the musicians and fans as "muscleheads" no fewer than three times.[14] This assertion of masculine corporeality, these performances of manhood as an embodied physicality and muscularity, were within the same performative vein as the more traditional white, working-class masculinity. As sociologists Karen Bettez Hanlon and Saundra Cohen explain, this kind of affirmation of conventional masculinity was, in part, a reaction to the flagging authority of this kind of manhood and its accompanying marginalization. Historically, "muscles were strong distinguishing markers of lower-class men [and] symbolic indicators of more marginalized men . . . and [the] tough guise via muscular strength, the ability to inflict and endure pain . . . served as alternative forms of status enhancement."[15] As inhabitants in DC, a city where power was analogous to political and economic capital, which in turn was nearly exclusively the territory of men, hardcore punks were in some ways excluded from the DC-centric formula of masculinity. Their assertion of traditional masculine signifiers then (i.e., bare-chested, muscular), and its relationship to working-class masculinity, can be understood as a way to reclaim and redefine powerful masculinity.

In a similar way, the omnipresent leather jacket or military coat as an accessory acted as a sign of a specific performance of conventional rough and menacing classed masculinity. Worn by fans and band members like Teen Idle and Youth Brigade's Nathan Strejcek, Teen Idles' Jeff Nelson and Ian MacKaye, and many others,[16] the leather jacket was prominently and culturally linked to hypermasculinity. Indeed, the history of this piece of clothing is grounded in the (white) military. German fighter pilots began wearing the brown leather jacket, which spread to the US Army Air Corps in World War II and slightly mutated in Germany, where high-ranking officers began wearing it as a symbol of power. By the 1950s, the black leather jacket was linked with a more marginalized masculinity, particularly within the biker and greaser subculture, which connotated both a working-class ethos and often an ethnic identity outside assumed whiteness. The leather jacket as symbol of Other was popularized and whitewashed by Hollywood with outsider icons like Marlon Brando, James Dean, and even the Fonz of *Happy Days*. Yet, by the late 1960s and early 1970s, the power of the leather jacket was reappropriated by the Black Panthers, with the jacket signifying the force, threat, and danger bestowed by its sociocultural past. By reimagining the "solace, strength, power and equality" that socioeconomically and racially marginalized men of the 1950s, '60s, and '70s found in the leather jacket, men of the DC hardcore scene wore it as an overt marker to "proudly and defiantly distinguish themselves" as a rebellious, fairly dangerous type of classed manhood.[17] It was one premised on freedom (from convention) but also on an underlying threat (of violence, of sexuality, of aggression, potency, and disruption). It was also a look that was easily achieved and, with the exception of designer editions, not incredibly expensive to buy.

The other near-universal outwear in the scene was the military coat, which performed a similar powerful masculinity, though within the confines of mainstream culture. Preferred by Bad Brains, worn by Teen Idles, and taken up by a profusion of other fans and lesser-known DC hardcore bands, the military jacket reinforced DC hardcore's shaved-head aesthetic, signifying a masculinity characteristically associated with the dominance, strength, and contained threat of aggression the armed forces represent. At the same time, the resignification of the military coat within the hippie subculture, a cultural appropriation meant to neuter and delegitimize the threat of a military that represented war and destruction (primarily as a reaction to the Vietnam War), imbued the fashion piece with countercultural capital. In this way, the style of DC hardcore performed two comparable forms of traditional masculinity: (1) the leather jackets and the military coats evoked the long-established male qualities of power and hostility, reinforcing such constructions through both the marginalized signifier borrowed from historical subcultures, social movements, and the mainstream connotation derived from the military, and (2) still associating themselves with the counterculturally rich symbols of greasers, bikers, and hippies.

The wearing of the leather jacket and the military coat also have class-based implications. Not only do those two pieces of clothing have links to working-class masculinity as just elaborated, but also the connotations of those pieces of outerwear in the early 1980s displayed an alternatively classed male identity. Middle-class and upper-class masculinity, and their accompanying sense of identity, was frequently associated with occupation, and that occupation demanded suits. Indeed, as middle-class men flocked to corporations, and those corporations demanded customer and client interaction, hiring and firing were based in large part on appearance. In this way, how a man should look, and the value of that man, was constructed by capitalist ideas of a successful businessman; the male body, and the accompanying personality, was to be packaged for economic material success.[18] DC hardcore males rejected this class-based aesthetic dictate. Wearing leather jackets and military jackets, particularly modified in the ways to be discussed later, showed a lack of concern about professional standards embraced by the middle and upper class. Young men in the hardcore scene were not concerned about being hired and fired by corporations demanding a different kind of jacket, nor were they attempting to represent their primarily middle-class backgrounds. If anything, they blatantly rejected their class-based habiliment by wearing leather jackets and military coats, engaging in another form of downward passing as discussed previously in these pages.

This construction of a DC hardcore (raced and classed) masculinity, however, was complicated by the Do-It-Yourself (DIY) ethos. As HR recounted, we "designed many of our own clothes, our friends helped out with the sewing. That was the thing that was so great about punk when we first discovered it. You made your music, you made your clothes, you created your whole thing."[19] The incorporation of DIY into DC hardcore clothing was most conspicuously a function of transforming, defacing, supplementing, and generally reimagining the fashion-based signifiers of traditional masculinity—the leather jacket, the military coat, and denim jeans and jackets.[20] These alterations (or mutilations, in some points of view) generally assumed a number of comparable configurations, often in the form of accessories. Homemade buttons, hand-painted tags and crudely sewn-on patches festooned band members' and fans' outerwear, reassembling and reimagining the style and thus meanings of the jackets they wore. Often in the same space and on the same material, safety pins, binder clips, and straight pins, stripped of their utilitarian purpose, were refashioned and affixed as decorative regalia on jackets. The Untouchables' Eddie Janney's military jacket was replete with pins, forming metal patchworks in seemingly random ways, aluminum patch outlines, and hanging chains of safety pins for even more dangling safety pins; Alec MacKaye's military coat sleeves were adorned with safety pins that seemed to hold together rips in the fabric and binder clips and pins lined the jacket's lapels; and Bad Brains' HR's military jacket had spike-bejeweled epaulets with DIY safety-pin-and-chain straps. Vests were fashioned from button-down denim and cloth shirts with the sleeves tore off, revealing the ragged strands of remaining fabric like the ligaments from a muscle, as seen on Faith's Chris Bald at the Wilson Center in 1982 and GI's John Stabb at the Chancery in 1981.[21] As John Stabb said, "I wore goofy and wacky clothes and I was the self-proclaimed clown prince of hardcore, but I was doing it just to be different. . . . Anything that would blind or sear the human eye, I would wear it so people would be 'man, turn that thing off.'"[22] Jeans were annihilated either through purposeful obliteration or indifference: bleach-splattered blotches up and down the legs, and rips, tears, and holes were scattershot throughout the knees, back pockets, and front legs of the jeans of fans and musicians, and, in the case of Minor Threat's Ian MacKaye and S.O.A.'s Henry Garfield, gaping voids in the crotch of jeans they wore while they performed.

These DIY stylistic modifications enact a dual, and somewhat paradoxical, representation of masculinity and class. In certain ways, DC hardcore's DIY clothing performs quite a traditional function of masculinity, validating the trope of manual labor as a form and function of masculinity. That is, there is a value—and a specifically masculine value—in being able to make things with one's hands. This theme is amplified by the fairly aggressive way this labor is created—the stabbing of countless safety pins, the physical act of tearing and ripping jeans and vests, the vandalism of a painting a jacket, all present a marked threat of violence or at least the

exaltation of destruction. The cyclical power of creation and destruction has, historically and culturally, been the purview of conventional
masculinity: from empires to companies to political administrations to
material structures, it is men who have been bestowed with the authority
and the right to build and demolish them. DC hardcore punks, with their
concomitant creation and destruction of clothing, seem to bolster this
masculinized construct. Similarly, the use of DIY aligns with the masculinized attribute of control that is grounded in a middle-class privilege.
That is, DIY has been theorized as the Marxian outcome of an alienated
workforce whose economic needs may be fulfilled but not their emotional
needs.[23] In this way, the act of creation works to take back control from
capitalism but also is enabled by having both leisure time and resources.
At the same time, the ability to make and create sets these men apart from
other men, both in DC and the larger national culture of masculinity.
In their resistance to middle-class aesthetics and culture is, thus, still a
reinforcement of social class-based status and traditional masculinity.

At the same time, the DIY clothing culture performed a subversion of
such a conventional masculinity. Primarily, gender disruption was waged
by the blurring of what constitutes "women's work." Crafts, sewing, and
fashion design were typically relegated to the realm of womanhood, and
even the Arts and Crafts movement in Victorian England (led and influenced principally by men) focused on the male-centric fields of architec-
ture and furniture design, domains of masculinized manual labor rather
than feminized domestic labor. By reconstituting the standard domestic
sphere of clothing and crafting to include men, while still presenting a
quasi-tough-guy masculinity typically performed by their gender, DC
hardcore was able to help blur gender lines. The DIY anticonsumption
ethos embraced and performed by these hardcore punks also acted to
undercut the traditional assumption of masculine earning power, that
one's masculinity is judged, in part, by one's wealth and ability to buy—
and display—that wealth. DC punks did not perform middle-classdom or
upper-classdom through their clothing. If Georgetown was, as described
earlier in the book, a place where one's status can be confirmed by the
shopping bags one carries and the designer labels on one's clothes, DC
hardcore ripped that equation to shreds, literally and figuratively. They
destabilized the conspicuous consumption mandate that was inexorably

linked to the exhibition of class-based gender. Finally, in an almost para-doxical tactic, DC punks upset the explicit expression of conventional masculinity in their defacement of those traditional masculine signifiers. In one way, the denim, leather jackets, and military coats are clearly an indication of powerful, pungent masculinity; however, by destroying and mutilating the denim, leather, and military coats, DC hardcore seemed to be simultaneously defacing, or at least complicating, the idea of tra-ditional masculinity and the accompanying class-based assessments of that masculinity. Their DIY treatment of clothes performed an ambiguity and ambivalence about their gendered and classed roles.

Masculinity and/as (Violent) Performance and Dance

Dance, as a corporeal social practice, can be a site of control for individu-als, allowing the dancer to operate outside the sociopolitical mandates of when, how, and where the body should be used. In doing so, dance allows for a contestation, reinforcement, or reformation of specific discourses and accompanying ideologies. In ways different from fashion, but within the same framework, the dancing body is heavy in its metaphysical and corporeal symbolism, conveying personal and social identities, forms of power, and structures of relations.[24] Whether krumping in the southern United States, youth dance troupes in Cameroon, Balinese Arja dancers in Indonesia, or Alvin Ailey's modern dance company in New York City, dance often works in seemingly innocuous ways to reclaim narratives, memory, and identity. Some may jokingly contest the label of DC hard-core slam dancing *as* dancing, but the use of the body at hardcore shows most assuredly constructs personal and social identities rooted in a form of violent masculinity.

DC hardcore dancing was "a full contact sport,"[25] a practice inspired by the burgeoning hardcore scene in Los Angeles and San Francisco and adopted and transformed by DC, which came to symbolize the tough, ferocious, and often vicious reputation of its hardcore scene. In slam dancing, audience members "danced" by violently hurling their bodies toward one another, swinging their arms frenetically, pogoing up and down, and flinging themselves off the stage into the waiting crowd. Slam dancing occurred in the pit, a term suggesting a dark, dank, and brutal

space, the area near the stage where the crowd convened in a disorga-
nized, spontaneous outburst of appreciation for the band. Certainly,
DC's pit was known as particularly unforgiving and was described by
the *Washington Post*'s Richard Harrington as

> Ferocious and frightening: Young men's bodies slam into each other, arms
> and elbows out, fists flailing, like razor-edged Mexican jumping beans
> popping madly on the dance floor. Mayhem is played out against relent-
> less, primitive, over-amped rock. The lead singer does combat with the
> instrumental backing. Occasionally a dancer will leap to the stage and
> execute a swan dive back onto the floor; sometimes, it's the band mem-
> bers who fly into the audience without a trapeze or a net to catch them.[26]

The bands themselves, while not directly participating in slam dancing,
were no less physically aggressive, as Harrington alludes to. Dodging the
fans who were onstage slam dancing and leaping into the pit below, Minor
Threat's Ian MacKaye, Bad Brains' HR, Faith's Alec MacKaye, GI's John
Stabb, and S.O.A.'s Henry Garfield leapt, quivered, quaked, screamed,
reeled, and contorted their bodies while they sang, using their bodies as
a physical manifestation of the anger and anguish in their lyrics. Such
performances, by the bands and the audience members, portrayed once
again a traditional type of violent masculinity. The all-male slam dancing
fans and band members at once asserted their individual, exclusionary
masculinity while reaffirming their collective identities as males.

Before slam dancing had become a semi-institutionalized aspect of DC
hardcore, Bad Brains' HR was already an intense, ferocious front man.
In Philadelphia hardcore promoter Steve Eye's video footage of "Right
Brigade," HR is stooped forward, as if in pain, mercilessly spitting lyrics
into the microphone as his head shudders vehemently until the guitar
solo, when he convulses around the stage with the mike, lurching his
body up and down in time with the drum beat; all the while, fans are
climbing onto the stage and somersaulting off into the crowd, bodies
angled in apparently unnatural positions. Bad Brains' 1979 performance
of "Pay to Cum" provoked the same sort of destructive, bellicose bodily
performance, with HR jittering and jarring as if he's having a grand mal
seizure, mouth agape, shoulders quaking, hips jerking between chucking
his lyrics into the microphone, which he grasps with two intertwined,

fisted hands and fiercely shakes. As music producer Jerry Williams describes him, he was "the maniac vocalist dancing across the stage and screaming and whooping and hollering and just singing his soul out in the microphone."[27] The cross between acrobatics and lethal spasms is again on display in HR's 1979 performance of "Attitude," as HR rolls, spins, and whirls around his bandmates in a less graceful, more uncontrollable expression of emotion, jumping up and down, shoving away and then dragging back the microphone to his mouth. During a short guitar solo, he breaks away from the microphone, performing a sort of feral, rowdy incarnation of the twist, legs cockeyed, body brutally forcing itself back and forth to the ground before hopping back up to the microphone stand.

The meanings constructed by this form of performance and audience dancing will be explored in much more detail later in this chapter, but for now it is crucial to pause to unpack the unique racialized implications of HR's black body performing, particularly within a nearly uniform white scene. Historically, the black body has acted as a spectacle for the pleasure of the white audience, harkening back to the days of slavery:

> A brief delineation of that history must include the demands that kidnapped Africans dance on board slave ships during the transatlantic passage from Africa to the New World. Such performances not only provided a way for the human cargo to remain agile and fit, but also transformed the ship deck into "a stage upon which race and gender roles were prescribed and performed." As a result, the ritual purposes of African dance in such contexts were subsumed by the violent, dehumanizing project of commodification, thus rendering the performance of black dance for white onlookers into enactments of white dominance and black subjugation.[28]

Entertainment, including the relationship between the performer and the audience, is always already embedded in raced and classed structures of power, and, for HR and Bad Brains, the violence of the history of slavery and the commodification of bodies are manifest in his performance. And even though white audiences were the norm in DC hardcore, as they were around the country, the band clearly felt the implications of race. As HR said, "In the early days, we faced a lot of racists. Sometimes they'd throw beer bottles and do a little spitting. They'd yell racial slurs."[29] And at the clubs in DC "they were harassed and called 'nigger' by some in the crowd

. . . [and] in a Baltimore suburb the band was greeted by racial epithets and threats."[30] At the same time, HR reformulates this violent racial history by appropriating the violence for himself; it is his body that is the threat, not the white owners. As the lead singer of Bad Brains, he is certainly a spectacle, but the white audience is subjugated to *his* performance, *his* voice and *his* body. Even within more recent performance history, as in the advent of rock 'n' roll, blackness became a stand-in for the emotions and rebellions that a white body would not or could not perform, "a means for the public expression of normally private sensations for white teenagers in the 1950s."[31] This proxying was premised, as chapter 2 discussed, on the sociopolitical constructed binary and accompanying hierarchy of white/intellectual and black/emotional. In this configuration, blackness is equated with the body, the physicality of emotion in which "the sound and beat are *felt* rather than interpreted,"[32] while whiteness is the cool, detached interpretation, rooted in formality and logic. Although Bad Brains' and HR's performance should not be completely isolated from the larger DC hardcore scene, it would be just as oblivious to pretend that their black bodies performing with and for "fucked-up but smart white kids" who were steeped in racial turmoil and "resented their own socioeconomic status or harbored guilt over their forbearers' [*sic*] racism"[33] had no racial implications. HR's visceral, emotional, physical performance aligns with the culturally constructed notion of blackness, but it simultaneously extends that anger, passion, and threat to those white teenagers dancing around them. The performance, then, works to both propagate and subvert racialized (and gendered) social norms and behaviors.

Minor Threat, disciples of Bad Brains, similarly perform with corporeal force and belligerence, albeit with the white privilege afforded to them. With the most video-documented shows, it is clear that both MacKaye and his audience took immense pleasure in the fierce physicality of performing and slam dancing. During MacKaye's 1982 performance of "Seeing Red," bodies are flying from stage to audience, limbs thrashing and battering those around them; the crowd is an indistinguishable pulp of arms and heads squashed into a single brutal mass, pushing and pulling bodies up and down and side to side. MacKaye sings like a boxer in the ring, crunching his body into forceful contortions and swinging the microphone like punches, to and from his mouth, out to the audience and back to himself. In a 1982 Minor Threat performance at New York's CBGB, the same spectacle ensues. As the band breaks into their opening song, "Stepping Stone," fans are hauling themselves onto the stage one second, just to heave themselves into the arms of the pack below the next. In the pit, fans explode up and down, pogoing and smashing their bodies into one another. Throughout their thirty-seven-minute set, Minor Threat at once operates as individual cyclones of energy and ferocity, playing their instruments as if they were opponents in a fight, pulsating their heads in time to the beat they are keeping, and also avoiding the throng of fans who have ambushed the stage to dart back and forth, brandishing their fists in pumps of exaltation, and flinging themselves into the slam dancing crowd. In fact, it's difficult to differentiate between band and audience,[34] the bodies are so intertwined and knotted by arms and legs, a sea of shaved heads and the deafening roar of the crowd singing with MacKaye, every word of every song, unifying their voices into one booming, uncompromising scream. Similarly, Minor Threat's 1980 show at d.c. space is a muddled melee of MacKaye shrieking his songs as he wrings the neck of his microphone stand and the fans—all men—thrusting elbows, hips, heads, and the full force of their bodies against one another in orgiastic dance.

Of all the DC hardcore bands, however, State of Alert was known as the epitome of savage, untamable rage. In part, the reason is that lead singer Henry Garfield was one of the first hardcore fans (before forming his own band) to bring back the California-informed style of violent dance. He recalls coming back to DC and "mowing through people, elbows into heads . . . within two weeks every male hitting puberty was in that crowd like aghhhh and every bouncer is getting swung at."[35] That sense of rebellion-based hostility translated in S.O.A.'s shows, which, according to fan Tom Berrard, were always "more violent—the slamdancing during S.O.A. was way more intense. . . . You just went at it harder during S.O.A."[36] Richmond hardcore fan (and future lead singer of the infamous metal band Gwar) David Brockie agrees, recollecting when he came to an S.O.A. show, "I just walked in there and was like 'Oh my God! These people are killing each other!' You know, it kind of frightened me but it was kind of fun at the same time."[37] Garfield embodied this violent masculinity; he would "do this pacing thing, he was all pumped up, and he would exercise like crazy before a show, doing chin-ups and pull ups."[38] As one male hardcore fan says, "Henry Rollins was one of the most dangerous of the dancers and I saw him take a few people out. . . . The hardcore kids meant business." In his performance of "Draw Blank" at d.c. space's Unheard Music Festival in 1980, his aggressive physicality was on display. Hunched over with his sleeveless arms, and noticeably beefy biceps flexed, Garfield roars into the mike, exerting so much effort the veins visibly pop from his neck. In the two-second lull between singing, he paces and spins like a caged animal until the audience rushes the stage, slamming into Garfield and each other with abandoned frenzy, even as he continues to sing.

Faith and GI also performed with raging force and a physicality that resembled violence. Living up to his "reputation for intense, confrontational performances,"[39] Alec MacKaye aggressively swings the microphone down to the audience during a performance of "Face to Face"; some in the front row indecipherably yell the lyrics while thrusting their fists into the air while the surrounding audience (again, all men) slam into each other and launch themselves onto the backs, heads, and hands of the people around them. Similarly, GI's John Stabb's brutal performance at the Wilson Center in September 1982 was "the highlight of the evening," according to *Maximum Rocknroll*,[40] and at one point his head slam sent him to the hospital, only weeks after taking eight stitches in the nose from a microphone stand at a show at the University of Maryland.

Such violence on the stage and in the audience is clearly meaningful beyond its functional adolescent release of frustration. The choice to dance, the choice of this particular type of dance, was an investment of their bodies in a specific practice, one that asserted and explored a countercultural idea under the pretext of entertainment. For these bands and their fans, violence evolved into a potent symbol of the DC scene; bruises and blood were battle wounds, signs of violent revolution, and an assertion of masculinity in a town where power was defined by political and cultural strength. And although clearly violence cannot, and should not, be associated with a certain gender, the pride with which slam dancing was engaged in and the badges of bruises afterward did point to a specific construction of masculinity. The body, rather than the consumption and spectacle of other material goods, was the sole representation of masculinity, and strength—the ability to dominate over others—became a way to establish an individual statement of manhood. At the same time, such individualistic masculinity was premised on the collective audience, along with the bands, performing this same type of manhood. The threat of mayhem and disorder slam dancing portended was also a unifying bond with their fellow hardcore men. In this way, violent slam dancing "mirror[ed] the ideologies of rebellion that exist[ed] . . . by emphasizing individual and communal motion."[41]

Crucially, both this individual and communal identity born from slam dancing was an exclusionary one. Slam dancing, and its construction of masculinity, fashioned its meaning from who did *not* participate—namely, women. This sentiment was echoed repeatedly by both women and men in the DC hardcore scene in my interviews. According to Malcom, "the guys definitely controlled the dance floor. I don't think the guys intentionally pushed the women to the side, it was just a very physical scene and when push came to shove, the guys had the physical advantage. . . . It was aggressive and sometimes bloody."[42] Intentional or not, Brian reiterates that "the mosh pit was male-only . . . a boys club," which led to the practical exclusion of females.[43] Another participant adds, "The scene was inherently violent (though often in a good-natured sort of way), which I guess kept some women away. . . . Without a lot of females around I felt more freed up to delve into the music . . . and the oh-so liberating aggression and physical exertion."[44] The absence of women in the pit allowed for the construction of a specific form of manhood, a masculinity grounded in the expression of hostility and violence. Indeed, as Scott, another interviewee and both a hardcore fan and later guitarist in postpunk bands, explains, "Of the mostly male audience members a great many of them seemed to be working out their 'manliness' issues, and slam dancing was an integral part of that 'work.'"[45] Women also felt the alienating effects of the aggressive atmosphere. Amy Pickering, a devoted hardcore fan, "began to feel excluded—by force. . . . Slam dancing and stage-diving were separating the boys from the girls."[46] Sharon Cheslow, another hardcore fan, saw the changing hardcore scene and, by 1981, "started looking at the scene and asking myself, 'Am I really with a group of friends? A lot of the girls felt the way I did and started dropping out."[47] Slam dancing, and the accompanying bodily violence it produced, worked as a way of erecting both a physical and metaphysical binary between men and women. Gender was, then, delineated in part through violent materiality and identity formed individually and communally through this bifurcation.

Slam dancing also provided a representation of freedom, of control, that those in the DC hardcore scene had found lacking at home, in school, and in the surrounding community. As performance scholar Joseph Roach notes, "Violence in human culture always serves, one way or the other, to make a point. . . . All violence is excessive, because to be fully demonstrative, to make its point, it must *spend* things—material objects, blood, environments . . . [and] all violence is performative."[48] Using their thrashing limbs, hunched over and battered bodies, and contact with one another through slamming, DC punks employed their bodies in a violent and purposeful way to react to and take control of their current social and political situation. An ideology of violence already dominated the landscape of Washington, DC—that of the state against other countries, and the state against minorities. This included US foreign policy decisions such as Reagan's authorization of the largest military increase in US history, including new missiles and bombers, funding so-called freedom fighters in communist countries, and military action in Libya, Sinai, and Lebanon. At the same time, both federal and local ordinances attempted to metaphorically kill the hardcore scene. For example, with the federal establishment of the Noise Pollution and Abatement Act in 1972 (42 U.S. Code § 4905), the government legislated the concept of sound, arguing that citizens consider street noise "disturbing, harmful or dangerous."[49] In particular, DC's Noise Control Act of 1977 banned "any sound which is loud and raucous or loud and unseemly and unreasonably disturbs the peace and quiet of a reasonable person of ordinary sensibilities,"[50] rhetorically embodying the spirit of hardcore. These two laws exemplify the way in which noise, music, and the concurrent message contained within those sounds is controlled, ignored, and imbued with authority. Socially, the delineation of sound "effectively define[s] which type of people are acceptable . . . and which are not";[51] that is, the intolerance for and rejection of hardcore by mainstream society acts as intolerance for and rejection of their specific social positions and political opinions. The lawful renunciation of "noise" that did not conform to the majority's evaluation of music, which often included hardcore performances, was part of what the DC hardcore scene was reacting to.

Rather than violence on behalf of authority, slam dancing and hardcore was violence in reaction to authority, violence *instead* and *as* their own authority. And that violence did not remain within the realm of dancing— it was often a reality both within the performance spaces, as discussed in the opening of this chapter, as well as in the streets. As music journalist Michael Azerrad noted, "When it started, hardcore was *stylized* violence, an expression of the clamor and aggression of the music, and of the participants' adolescent inner tumult . . . but as time went on, the difference between fighting and dancing became extremely hard to discern."[52] The targets—and often the perpetrators—of these fights varied. Bouncers were viewed as potential threats to be eliminated, and outsiders to the scene were viewed just as apprehensively. As Henry Garfield explains, "just imagine all your life you've been hounded by jocks, cops; all of a sudden, you're charging one with a chair; eighteen years of rage just comes out on some stranger."[53] The men of DC hardcore were also physically and psychologically threatened through the derogatory and aggressive use of "fag" thrown at them by other men on the streets of Georgetown. Such language was a way of invalidating their masculinity, of using an offensive epitaph about sexuality to label them as outsiders, someone less than the reviler. As Teen Idles' Mark Sullivan recounts, "We were walking down M Street or something and somebody says, 'Hey, fag!' and six lightbulbs went on over six little heads and six little guys trounced somebody. It was a very powerful feeling."[54] Violence was a defense mechanism and a way to assert power. It was a way to construct themselves and their scene. And as MacKaye described in *Maximum Rocknroll*, it was nearly a philosophical stance:

> It may be violent or animal or brutish or whatever but I believe in violence as much as I believe in sex or anything else. If it's done purely, I think it's a fine thing, a natural thing. It's not like I want to break people's nose or poke out their eyes, but as a form of communication, violence is really good.[55]

This form of communication, and its grounding as "natural thing," is constructed as a form of masculinity. Kicking someone's ass is a way to perform one's dominance by showing one's worth in comparison to and with other men while still sustaining one's place in the social hierarchy. Engaging in the trope of the "angry white man," the men of DC hardcore were able to retain mastery over themselves and establish symbolic possession of the space and place of the city as well. Aligned with the long historical leitmotif of white men as the chief controlling force of civilization, fighting for the "real" American way and against the forces of evil, DC hardcore engaged in violence in order to sustain their territory and the values and mores contained in that symbolic space. At the same time, their reputation as fighters, both within the city and within the country's larger hardcore scene, served as a convincing and deliberate paradox to the restraint, conformity, and respect for authority that DC, as the symbolic nucleus of national politics, was seen as. In doing so, the hardcore scene began the process of contesting physical space and claiming cultural landscape in a city they believed had run amok with men of the wrong stripe.

8

The Transformation of Hardcore

DC Posthardcore, after 1983

The collapse of the original DC hardcore scene was the outcome of a number of interrelated personal, sociopolitical, media-induced, and cultural changes. Some band members grew out of adolescence and went to college and others moved to other states or joined other bands. At the same time, the local and national media coverage of punk had reached a boiling point; no longer was punk seen as a threatening act of deviance by an underground few. Punk's representation in the public eye, primarily as a function of style, neutered the revolutionary foundations it had been built on. To still others, hardcore had become simply an outlet for violence, rather than for music and rebellion. Kids flocked to DC shows for the express purpose of getting into fights. And in their city, original hardcore punks saw politics becoming both more relevant and more untenable as Reagan took office for a second term. The original DC hardcore scene was crumbling. As Ian MacKaye notes, "By 1984, DC was in a depressing situation. There was intense friction within the Dischord scene, the shows sucked, and violence was so prevalent."[1] Brian Baker of Minor Threat (and, later, Government Issue), agreed: "A lot of the people who had started this local music scene in 1979 and '80 had become a little bit disillusioned; the baby was no longer cute."[2]

By 1984, the original DC hardcore bands had dissolved. Minor Threat had broken up over creative differences. So had Faith. Henry Garfield had left State of Alert for southern California's iconic punk band Black Flag and become Henry Rollins. GI was still kicking, but had, by 1984, already changed lineups multiple times, changed labels multiple times, and changed their sound and core audience. Bad Brains was in splinters. After joining with strange bedfellow Ric Ocasek of the Cars and producing a flop album, *Rock for Light*, HR formed the all-reggae Zion Train, and then a self-titled band, HR, while the remaining members unsuccessfully tried to carry on as Bad Brains sans their front man. The band briefly reunited for *I against I*, a heavy rock album that strayed from their reggae and punk roots on SST records, but with the band's financial troubles and loud Rastafarian belief system, including a quite public and offensive vendetta against homosexuality, Bad Brains' zenith had already been in rapid descent.

Before these paradigmatic DC hardcore bands had dissolved, however, they had begun to receive a significant amount of media coverage. The *Washington Tribune* put John Stabb and GI on its front page in a cover story; the paper consistently covered DC hardcore shows and wrote album reviews; so did the *Washington City Paper*; even *Playboy* covered the DC hardcore scene. In part, coverage of the scene led to the commodification of one element of hardcore—fashion. Boutique shops started popping up selling "punk fashion" in DC; for example, Georgetown's Commander Salamander. DC punk was starting to turn into a distinct product, defined by a specific sound and visual aesthetic, allowing anyone to copy it. As William Dagher, a part of the original DC scene, argues, hardcore had become "an establishment. It consists of conformists conforming to a nonconformist movement."[3]

At the same time as the local media was covering the DC hardcore scene, so too were the national zines. Articles, interviews, scene reports, and record reviews on Faith, Minor Threat, Bad Brains, GI, S.O.A, and other DC hardcore bands appeared in *Touch and Go* (Lansing, Michigan), *Forced Exposure* (Boston), *Ripper* (San Francisco), *Brand New Age* (Arlington, Virginia), *Suburban Voice* (Boston), *Inside View* (Detroit), *Maximum Rocknroll* (San Francisco), and *Damaged Goods* (New York). The national attention triggered not only more exposure for these bands but also a wider and larger audience. Most bands would welcome such an increase in fans, but the *type* of fans who began flocking to the DC shows was quite different from the type in the original scene. Vandalism and random bloodshed were rampant from a deluge of violence-prone

THE TRANSFORMATION OF HARDCORE
...

outsiders, so-called drunk punks, who were more interested in fighting than in listening to hardcore music. As Dischord house member Alec Bourgeois remembers, hardcore shows had "degenerated into huge mosh pits of mostly ex-jocks and skinheads."[4] Converting the violent undertones of hardcore into an excuse for violence under any circumstances, these new fans "were becoming increasingly, moronically violent and a lot of people were like: 'fuck it, I'll drop out, I don't want to be a part of this anymore,'" according to Ian MacKaye.[5] The close-knit community of DC hardcore had devolved into a free-for-all. As Henry Garfield notes, "today's music [scene] is not responsible, people aren't saying the real thing. It was do or die then. Now it's a casual attitude—casual youth casually shitting where they live because there's always some kind of Mom to clean up for them."[6]

The changes within the DC hardcore scene cannot be isolated from the changes that were occurring within the scene's city itself. The Reagan revolution was in full effect as Reagan took his second term in 1985, and with it arrived a myriad of national policy changes swept up in the riptide of conservatism. The country was already amid a recession caused by Reagan's tax policies; unemployment skyrocketed to 10 percent,[7] even as the president pursued his four pillars of Reaganomics: shrinking the marginal tax rates on income from capital and labor; cutting regulation; controlling the money supply to reduce inflation; and slashing the growth of government spending. The effects were clear, both socially and economically. Poverty increased, and the number of people in the United States below the poverty level jumped from 29.272 million in 1980 to 31.745 million in 1988; at the same time, however, the share of total income received by the 5 percent highest-income households grew from 16.5 percent to 18.3 percent.[8] Reagan cut funding for the Environmental Protection Agency, engorged the military's budget, and ramped up the War on Drugs. He also opposed the Civil Rights Act of 1964 and the Voting Rights Act of 1965, initially resisted a holiday for Martin Luther King Jr., supported prayer in school, and had a hardline foreign policy, advocating anticommunism coups in Central America, Angola, and Afghanistan.

The original DC hardcore scene took note. Former DC hardcore participants I interviewed were highly conscious of this social and political landscape. As one said, "We were rebelling against our government employee parents and the values of the people in DC. . . . When I told my mother about some of the horrible things our government has done or is doing she would reply, 'Michael, we don't want to know that.'"[9] Another, Bernie, saw DC as a socioeconomic contrast: "Government, monuments, museums, universities and a huge ghetto,"[10] and Tim "saw Reagan creating a poor class in America and so there was a lot to protest."[11] According to Lars, the Reagan "establishment definitely prized financial gain over integrity."[12] Mike agreed, saying that "the politics of the time—Ronald Reagan for example—naturally fed into our anger and sense of rebellion."[13]

The turning point was the summer of 1985, when the DC hardcore scene consciously and conscientiously reimagined what DC, and its punk community, could and should be. They called it Revolution Summer. Named by hardcore fan and Dischord House regular Amy Pickering,[14] during her internship at the Tenleytown (DC) Neighborhood Planning office, the concept embodied the initial rebellious spirit of hardcore but was redirected toward a more overtly political center. In a scene that once disdained politics, by Revolution Summer "art and politics suddenly made sense to us and we ran with it,"[15] according to MacKaye. Apartheid, homelessness, and women's issues became just as important as espousing a straightedge lifestyle. Says Thomas Squib of the next generation DC hardcore band Beefeater, "The original punk philosophy was 'fight bullshit' and 'do something real.' The punk scene was doing neither of those things. Revolution Summer was about getting back into fighting bullshit again."[16] What's more, this reinvigoration and revisualization of politics were instilled and suffused into the new sound of hardcore. As the sociopolitical and cultural context of Washington, DC, shifted, so too did the music. Within this milieu, these newly formed DC hardcore bands found themselves in a battle to redefine what it meant to be, and to sound, punk. As Rites of Spring's Guy Picciotto puts it, "who represents the ideal of punk more?"[17]

Hardcore, Revisited:
The (Sociopolitical) Evolution of Sound

Despite the many fragmentations, dissolutions, implosions, and sonic makeovers of the early DC hardcore scene, new bands and new music were constantly emerging from the city's musical murk. Fusing the hallmark elements of DC hardcore with a burgeoning sense of political and personal epiphany and urgency, a handful of hardcore punks challenged the musical status quo and unwittingly created a new genre: emocore[18] or posthardcore. This sound revamped the two major foundations (some would argue rules or regulations) of DC hardcore—form and content. And within this new iteration of hardcore in DC were five noteworthy bands—at least for the purposes of this author and this book— Scream, Marginal Man, Rites of Spring, Beefeater, and Embrace.

Scream originated in Bailey's Crossroads, an unincorporated area between Arlington and Falls Church. As a band, Scream also stood between DC hardcore in its heyday and its subsequent emocore germination, first playing shows together in 1982 and putting out its two seminal albums in the years following. Composed of brothers Franz (vocals) and Pete (guitar) Stahl, drummer Kent Stax, and bassist Skeeter Thompson, Scream was eventually signed by Ian MacKaye's Dischord label, releasing *Still Screaming* in 1983 and *This End Up* in 1985.

Marginal Man emerged as a patchwork group stitched together from the remaining stuff of the pre-1983 DC hardcore scene: Mike Manos (drums), Pete Murray (guitar), and Steve Polcari (vocals) came from the short-lived, though extremely popular, band Artificial Peace; Andre Lee (bass) played in Toasterheads, a one-off hardcore band with Kenny Inouye (guitar), who also happened to be the son of Hawaii senator Daniel Inouye. Credited as the first DC hardcore band to incorporate two guitars in their sound, they released only one album with Dischord Records, 1984's *Identity*, before switching to a California label, but their debut nine-song LP instigated the shift toward the new simple, melodious DC (post)hardcore.

Rites of Spring, perhaps more than any other band in Washington, DC, or anywhere in the country, is known as the paradigmatic emocore innovators. Playing only fifteen shows together, the band's influence greatly outlasted its time together. With Guy Picciotto on vocals and guitar, Mike Fellows on bass, Eddie Janney on guitar, and Brendan Canty on drums, Rites of Spring infused conventional hardcore with nuanced emotion, releasing only one album—1985's *Rites of Spring*.

Beefeater, who played their first show in 1984, was truly the post-'83 hardcore vanguard, pioneering a funk-infused punk sound and pushing

an explicit liberal political agenda through their music. Another multiracial band, Beefeater boasted Thomas Squib on vocals, a Caucasian male
who sometimes would play nude and had a "hippyrasta vibe," bassist Dug
"Bird" Birdzell, an "owl-glassed floppy funky bass player with the v[ery]
serious studious respect-all-life PETA attitude," African American guitarist Fred Smith, who brought the funk and metal sound to the group,
and drummer Bruce Taylor, previously from DC hardcore bands Hate
from Ignorance and Subtle Oppression.[19] Releasing two albums, *Plays for
Lovers* (1985) and *House Burning Down* (1986), Beefeater's music has the
rage and power of hardcore but channels it through the groove-heavy,
melodic, bass-centric feel of funk and jazz.

Finally, there was Embrace. Antithetical to what one might expect, it
was Ian MacKaye's new band that was the last on the new posthardcore
scene. Formed in 1985, Embrace released only one record, the eponymous
1987 album, which also breaks the mold from traditional hardcore. Singer
MacKaye and three former members of Faith—bassist Chris Bald, drummer Ivor Hanson, and guitarist Mike Hampton—fuse the tight, loud, and
technically adept aesthetic of their original hardcore sound with slowed-
down tempos, metal-steeped timbres, jangly pop melodies, emotionally
diverse lyrics of the new scene, and politics.

These five posthardcore bands represent not only the sonic evolution
of the DC hardcore scene but also how and why that sonic evolution happened. That is, this new music reflected the new sociopolitical milieu of
Washington, DC, and the band members themselves. The undercurrents
of hardcore's political aesthetics discussed in the previous chapters no
doubt still existed within the sound and content of posthardcore, but its
meanings and connotations changed. For these five bands, masculinity,
race, and class have been redefined sociopolitically—and therefore sonically as well.

TEMPO

Perhaps the most conspicuous and comprehensive development in hardcore's musical transformation was the nearly ubiquitous slowdown of
tempo. Certainly, the traditional DC hardcore sonic underpinning remained. Lyrics were shouted, shrieked, and squawked. The music's tone
was hard-driving, strident, and raucous. The guitars, bass, and drums

crashed, seethed, and wailed. But the roiling temperament of the new crop of DC hardcore was more restrained in its monolithic resentment and rage and more uninhibited in its compositional expression. Unlike the trademark chaotic, mind-dizzying speed of Bad Brains, Minor Threat, and their brethren, hardcore moderates the pace after 1983 and in doing so mitigates the aggression and violence of the previous years.

Embrace exemplifies this tempo switch in its self-named 1987 album. Moving away from a chainsaw-like charge of aggression that defined Teen Idles and Minor Threat, the album's sixteen songs have a significantly slower tempo. The album opener "Give Me Back" sets the pace for the majority of the songs, with Hampton's guitar playing crisper and pointedly gentler than nearly any song on his previous Faith album in the eight-second intro. After the twice-played guitar riff, Hanson's drums crash in, along with MacKaye's singing, just as loudly as years past but without any of the amphetamine-like velocity. Devoid of any drumrolls, Hanson trades speed for volume, focusing on a steady backbeat and even an almost-ten-second drum break (1:50–1:59), where his contribution is simply a constant pitter-patter of hi-hat shimmy. The opening track is emblematic of the tempo change of the rest of the album. As MacKaye sings in the second track, "Dance of Days," "Maybe we went a little too fast." Surely, he is referring to the meteoric rise of the DC hardcore scene, but the notion of speed must also be understood as a parallel to the nonstop, insanely wild tempo of the music in that scene. The same speed that defined the sound of hardcore also portended the haste with which the scene burned out. The music of Embrace, then, aims to slow down. The decelerated, nearly drowned-out guitar lines in "I Wish I," the flickering guitar whammy of "Do Not Consider Yourself Free," Bald's leisurely bass line of "Spoke" and the ominous, almost sluggish bass in "No More Pain," and the jangly mid-tempo drums of "Said Gun" embody the downturn of tempo. This is not to say that Embrace completely reject high-velocity tempo altogether. The interspersed bursts of guitar riffs of "Building," the undulating drumroll intro of "Past" and the erupting guitar solo of "If I Never Thought about It" all allude to the power and force that the blistering tempos of Faith and Minor Threat displayed, but these songs merely hint, sniff at, the underlying rage that was so prominent previously. Tempo changed from a blunt hammer of destruction to a thoughtful and moderated instrument.

As the only band that had direct sonic lineage (not to mention hardcore royal bloodlines in the form of Ian MacKaye) to the original DC hardcore scene, Embrace's album was by far the most conspicuous and most consistent in its use of slackened tempo; however, such decelerated velocity was also quickly becoming a tool in the arsenal of other more recent hardcore bands, including Beefeater and Marginal Man. By mixing songs with more measured, relaxed tempos in with the more traditional ferociously fast cadences, these bands at once consciously diverge from Hardcore's First Commandment (thou shalt play as fast as humanly possible) and simultaneously draw flagrant attention to that divergence. That is, the juxtaposition of the two tempos make the discrepancy in tempo—and what that discrepancy means—even clearer. For instance, Beefeater's *Play for Lovers/House* opens with the upbeat, funk-imbued "Trash Funk," with midtempo guitar and drums, a slap bass, and an onbeat/offbeat structure and the next song, "Reaganomix," displays the more archetypal hardcore tempo with a hard-driving drum beat, high-speed guitar riffs, and a steady bass line. It is interesting that "Reaganomix" is actually not that fast, comparatively speaking; in fact, the song is nowhere in the vicinity of the brutally aggressive, staggeringly blurry speed of bands like Minor Threat and Bad Brains. Yet, in contrast with the almost placid "Trash Funk," the song roars like a locomotive. By highlighting how slow they can go, Beefeater also emphasizes their speed.

Marginal Man's *Identity* performs the same high-wire act of offsetting tempos. Songs like "Pandora's Box" and "Emotional Scars" resume the hardcore mantle of earnest speed and urgency, although, like Beefeater, the playing is in a different league than that of their musical forefathers Minor Threat and Bad Brains. Yet the tempo is significantly slowed down in "Fallen Pieces" and is flat-out sluggish in "Torn Apart," which, with its slow, burning guitars and gradually crescendoing drums and hi-hat, understandably could be mistaken for the opening of nearly any Metallica song. Two of their songs synthesize speeds as well. The seventh track, "Identity," starts with forty-three seconds of an unhurried, twisting river of dueling guitars and the intermittent shimmering tremble of the hi-hat until it abruptly shifts into the customarily quick-and-dirty hardcore tempo. "Missing Rungs," the album's first song, mimics the partial structure of a Bad Brains song, beginning at a hard-driving pace with domineering drums and sustained, dynamic guitar riffs, until 1:25, when the pace stops on a dime, changing into a breakdown that lasts until the end of the song.

These modifications of tempo in hardcore represent, if not the dilution of, then at least the complication of, the explicit and unvarying representation of aggression and violence that typified not only DC hardcore but also masculinity. In no way was this sonic alteration a complete repudiation of bellicosity or its culturally mandated connection to manhood. Speed did not go away; instead, it was tempered, opening up the possibilities for multiple, sometimes simultaneous and sometimes seemingly contradictory forms of masculinity. Power need not be absolute, exploding in a two-minute hailstorm of ungodly speed and proving its dominance, its overwhelming hegemony, second after second, song after song. Yes, it *could* and often *was* a furious, violent barrage of velocity, but this new hardcore sound promised that manhood could also be soft and slow, thoughtful and measured. MacKaye, particularly, was unambiguous about what this new scene was about: "We fought for our community. . . . Revolution Summer was to re-involve everybody and remove the parade of macho behavior."[20]

MELODIES, COMPLEXITY, AND GENRE-CROSSING

More than just a near-tectonic shift in tempo, this post-'83 hardcore sound instigated a discrete sonic color influenced heavily by melody and a turning away from the strictly minimalistic, strident sound of previous years. Rites of Spring and their eponymous album encompass this seeming contradiction of melody and violence. The album's seventeen songs still display speed and the fervid thirst of earlier hardcore, except that they are not only softer but also made more meaningful by the "starling melody [and] stark expressions of vulnerability."[21] "For Want Of" opens with a choppy guitar line and jittery drumbeat that blend together for an unwavering, high-speed, yet still harmonious upbeat riff. Throughout the song, Janney and Picciotto trade guitar lines, interlacing their sound until it's impossible to distinguish which is a lead and which is a rhythm guitar, giving the song a warmer, fuller tone. Clocking in at 3:10, a near feat of impossibility for previous hardcore songs, "For Want Of" avoids the confining rigidness of preceding song structure, releasing their guitars and drums in a twenty-two-second instrumental harmony (2:15–2:37) and then ending in the last thirty seconds with a recurring call-and-answer catchy guitar, bass, and drum riff, with the final seconds mellifluously shifting into an ornamental guitar riff. Even when Rites of Spring is fully engaged with the fury and sonic onslaught of hardcore convention, they merge the assault of sound with earnest, catchy melodies to augment and alter the character of the music. "Theme" contains the roiling exigency of hardcore imbued with melodious flights of guitar riffs, producing a sound that was somewhat paradoxically "simultaneously pulverizing and delicate."[22] "Remainder" loops in pop-friendly background singers, at first crooning "ohhhs" and "ahhhs" and then shouting almost indistinct echoes of Picciotto, while the hard-driving drums and piercing guitars radically shift in the last thirty seconds of the song, metamorphosing from a seismic eruption to a funk-inflected jam session, with bass slapping and jerky guitar rhythms, backed by a decidedly rock 'n' roll thumping of tom-tom and snares on the drums.

Likewise, Marginal Man's *Identity* modifies the conventional hardcore sound through their use of heavier, thicker sonic color, instrumental introductions, and catchy melodic phrasing, while frequently also adhering to the hard/fast/loud trifecta. The album's second track, "Friend," predates the enormous pop-punk movement of the 1990s with an immediate launch into the song's punchy, energetic melody, which with its pitch movement climbing and descending provides a fluctuating contour. With short, bright melodic phrases, the sing-along tune maintains and repeats its motif for nearly forty-five seconds, when a three-second drum fill leads into an ornamental guitar solo before returning to the original melody. A bit fuzzy, a bit raw, and utterly hummable, "Friend" is reminiscent of a '60s garage rock jewel of a song contextualized within a posthardcore musical context. Muddying this crystalline pop sound with undertones of heavy metal and a wallop of hardcore's noisy chaos is "Mental Picture." The album's fourth song opens with three seconds of sonic distortion before the portentous sound of the bass enters; seven seconds later, the drums pound out a backbeat, and six seconds after that guitars rip out a jagged riff as hand claps erupt in a percussive backup to the drums. This propulsive fifty-three-second musical introduction is a mélange of genres: the bass and drums threaten in the troubled vein of heavy metal, the guitar shreds in a streak of hardcore and rock 'n' roll, and the claps twinkle and shine à la the Cars' "Best Friend's Girl" or Queen's "Another One Bites the Dust." With an abrupt shift, the song breaks into the song's melody, with a rollicking, vivid guitar trill and accompanying vocals that induce involuntary foot tapping until, once again, the song descends back to a moody, slow tempo with just the drums and bass for the last twenty-two seconds. The songs eschew the chaotic discordance of hardcore and do so intentionally. As Scream noted in *Flipside*, "we've always tried to be more melodic and tried to put more harmony in," and in doing so were "shooting for different styles and a variety of audiences."[23]

The transformation of sound acted as a parallel to the transformation of self and scene. Using melody, which is typically associated with the expression of emotion,[24] bands like Rites of Spring and Marginal Man sidelined the sonic and material place of violence, "revitalize[ing] and extend[ing] the music by rescuing it from codification."[25] By incorporating poppier melodies—one might dare to say catchy hooks—the post-'83 hardcore sound contained an emotional spectrum, decentralizing the monochromatic sentiment of anger, hostility, and pugnaciousness. That is not to say, of course, that these new bands pushed tuneful rainbows, sunshine, and puppy dogs; undeniably, the underlying—and sometimes outright—feeling of violence was still there in the composition of the music. But it was purposeful and less encompassing. Unlike the existing scene's penchant for indiscriminate and prolific violence, the aggression of these new bands was more frequently directed inward, personal rather than a public display.

In addition to changes in melody and overall sonic color, this new DC sound was similarly unconfined to the strict scripture of hardcore as a genre. Whereas the definitive DC hardcore of bands like Minor Threat, State of Alert, and even Bad Brains celebrated minimalism, a nod to punk's highly egalitarian form of music, this new, post-'83 sound was different. The combining of genres and the adding of musical complexity created a tension between loyalty to the tenets of hardcore and the desire for innovation and exploration of new sounds. Perhaps the most genre-crossing of these bands was Beefeater, who reimagined blackness and whiteness in punk by incorporating and reinventing funk and blues music. Much as Bad Brains did with jazz and blues, Beefeater reconceived traditional black funk and blues in a synthesis of white and black hardcore. Funk was an omnipresent and quite unique feature of this DC posthardcore band. With its insistent syncopated rhythm and outrageous groove of bass line, the unrelenting guitar riffs, and the demolishing drums, "Trash Funk," the first track on *Beefeater*, sounds like Parliament Funkadelics dosed with a heavy prescription of Minor Threat—funk and hardcore at its finest. The same sonic union is glorified in the twenty-second instrumental opening of "Mr. Silverbird," with funk's interlocking rhythmic drums and hardcore's squealing, squawking guitar solo. The rest of the song is predominantly funk-tinged, built around one primary riff and featuring the unwavering bass-slap drives of Bird with hardcore rearing its head again a minute and twelve seconds in, with the tempo zipping and zooming, guitars wailing, and drums hammering until 1:47, when the song backslides into funk territory, the bass reemerging and the tempo slowing to groove time.

"A Dog Day," on the other hand, is completely spoken-word, backed by the funk-driven groove of the bass, the jazz-tinged jangle of the hi-hat and percussive drums, and the blues-soaked impulsion of the rhythm guitar. Repeating the same riff over and over again, the music blends the aggressive rhythms of funk and the simple and heartfelt texture of soul music and the blues. Shading even closer to the blues is "Fred's Song," an acoustic ditty that is simply guitar and vocals drolly relating the woes of slam dancing. A complete sonic departure from hardcore, "Fred's Song" merges the form of the blues with the content of hardcore—singing the blues about hardcore. Even songs that tend toward the purer hardcore sound, like "Mourning," the sixth track on *Plays for Lovers*, infuse some funk elements, with the wah-wah pedal to up the groove factor and the slap-bass technique, and "One Soul Down," which opens with the indisputable funk glow of the bass and its clean, foot-tappable propulsion.

The genre-crossing was not just funk. Sonically, one of the greatest influences on these new bands was the epitome of not just technical genius but also racial musical blending—Jimi Hendrix. In Scream's "Your Wars/Killer," Franz's guitar is faster and more frenetic than Hendrix's, but the gut-wrenching, loud, wah-wah-pedal-thrashing guitar work evokes the mind-blowing electric blues of Jimi. The last eleven seconds of "Piece of Her Time" is another throwback to the Hendrix-heavy midsixties electric blues and jazz revival, with a piercing, hard-driving but clearly still rock 'n' roll riff, almost like a sped-up version of Hendrix's guitar in "Fire." The guitar solo and subsequent phrasing in "New Song" could have been an outtake from "Crosstown Traffic." Even the explosive-but-short-lived bursts of guitar in "Total Mash" (1:20–1:30) and "Who Knows? Who Cares?" (1:44–1:52) are conspicuous for their Hendrix-like twisted, flamboyant, outlandishly long guitar notes.

For Beefeater, the connection is even more obvious—they cover Hendrix's "Manic Depression" on the original pressing of *Plays for Lovers*. It's a fairly straight-ahead cover, copying the 3/4 tempo, the reverberating psychedelic energy, and even the midsong guitar solo of the original; however, Beefeater's version is clearly more stripped down, with an added sheen of distortion over the guitars and nearly a full minute bonus of music at the end of the song, replete with squealing guitar feedback, whammy bar warping, and an overlay of a female singing "Amazing Grace" over the last thirty seconds. This version acts in two interrelated ways. First as homage to Hendrix, a half-black, half-Native American guitar genius whose violent, searing interpretation of the blues brought black music to the white hippies. In this way, Hendrix performed a duality of race, an enactment inherent to the mixed-race musicians of Beefeater. Hendrix's racial dichotomy was a function of his own racially and ethnically blended heritage, expressed in music, but Beefeater performs this duality in the multiple bodies of the band—Franz, who is white, on guitar, mimicking Hendrix while his (white) brother Pete sings in an eerily faithful rendering of Hendrix's voice, and Smith, who is black and the "black leather potential Jimi [Hendrix]"[26] on bass—as well as through their sound. This racialized comingling of sound is the second implication of Beefeater's cover. By recording "Manic Depression" without any significant deviations from the original and putting it on their hardcore punk album, Hendrix serves as a de facto punk. That is, the sound of Hendrix, unaltered, was already punk; therefore, Beefeater's version becomes another racial bridge of sound—the black blues-rock with the white punk rock. This is the same racial and sonic hinterlands where Scream lived. Bassist Skeeter Thompson acknowledges the huge impact of Jimi Hendrix on their sound but recognizes "the hippies didn't like us because we were too fast and the punks didn't like us because . . . we weren't total thrash we were like melodic trash."[27] Like Beefeater, Scream's Hendrix influence acts as a racial channel between musics and races, reinforcing the hippie punk motif and its accompanying racial undertones.

It is this same duality of race and music that impels Scream's inclusion of reggae on a number of their tracks. In an effect much like Hendrix's, however, the reggae is offset, or perhaps complemented, by a hardcore and metal sound, diffusing or complicating the racial representation of its sound. A minute and fifteen seconds into "Fight/American Justice," which starts out as a traditional hardcore song with speed, vicious guitars, and a raging chorus of "fight," a reggae breakdown intercedes, with a staccato guitar, slower tempo, and a heavy, dense bass. Anger and force are sonically represented in the first half of the song ("Fight") by hardcore, but the second half of the song, concerned with the justice system, is signified by reggae. In this sonic way, Scream aptly suggests the tension and fusion of not only racial dynamics but also of the concomitant cultural view of blackness and whiteness. Aggressive white hardcore is welded with mellow black reggae; the combination of the two is a struggle, as much sonically as it is politically.

A similar musical vibe happens in "Hygiene," though on this track their sound is reggae-inflected with a side of heavy metal. "Hygiene" begins with the propulsive kick and snarl of a repeated guitar-and-drum riff before breaking into fifteen seconds of hand-clapping, introducing the slow, relaxed ambiance of reggae with the clipped guitar chords and dominant bass line. By the time the chorus arrives, though, the traces of heavy metal come with it—the onerous, dark bass line, along with the low, fuzzed-out guitar licks, speed metal solos, and the drubbing thump of drums. The instrumental after the chorus reverts to the reggae feel, with the addition of bongo drums and the repetitive but catchy bass groove and a sweltering guitar solo. In this genre-bending use of funk, heavy metal, reggae, and hardcore, Scream and Beefeater refer directly not only back to the legacy of Bad Brains but also more generally to the sociopolitical and racialized history of music, recreating a contemporary version of both race and hardcore. Both bands' own multifaceted racial makeup and outlook was represented by its sound, merging the cultural histories of music and race.

This interplay of genres epitomizes a larger, and possibly more significant change in the hardcore sound—musical complexity. Whereas the previous standard of punk in general and hardcore specifically had proudly been its simplicity, advocating for a kind of musical democracy, DC's evolving sound proudly paraded not only musical chops, which had differentiated Bad Brains and later Minor Threat from every other punk band, but also musical intricacy, merging technical prowess with a decadence of sound. Rites of Spring's Mike Fellows executes striking, almost delicate, bass lines in songs like "Theme" and "All There Is," Eddie Janney's guitar is blistering in "Hain's Point," and Brendan Canty rockets past the more one-dimensional bass-snare-bass-snare-end rhythm into more expert terrain throughout the album. With precisely fashioned nuggets of song craft, and two rapid-fire guitar players, Rites of Spring creates a lusher, denser wall of sound in their album, and if the guitars and bass often interact, each instrument is also distinct, adding a thickness of jangle and throb to the songs. Adding to the richness of sound is the frequent use of background vocals, particularly those in songs like "Drink Deep," "Deeper Than Inside," and "The Other Way Around," which act not as an echo of Picciotto but almost as another instrument, deepening and strengthening the viscosity of sound.

The two-guitar sound is also vital to the fullness of Marginal Man's sonic color. As Kenny Inouye says, "the DC hardcore thing was very straightforward. . . . About the most complex or technical it would get was the Bad Brains. But even then, in all those configurations, you're talking about one guitar."[28] More than simply adding to the texture, although the two guitars did do so, Marginal Man focused on the arrangement of their songs, imbuing them with melodic and catchy guitar lines and adding a sprinkling of surf rock backup vocals. The tracks are varied, intentionally so,[29] often dramatically shifting tempo, genre, and mood, making each song quite differentiable from one another, as opposed to the more conventional hardcore's formula of power chords, speed, and volume in every song. Marginal Man also tweaks the conventional hardcore song structure. "Mainstream" has only two verses and no chorus, highly unusual not just for punk but nearly any kind of music, and songs like "Torn Apart," "Fallen Pieces," and "Marginal Man" employ genre-bending extended instrumentals.

Beefeater also adds to the new gold standard of technical expertise, particularly in the form of guitarist Fred Smith, who rips and shreds solos and riffs alike. The opening of "Mr. Silverbird" has Smith burning through a whammy-bar happy solo, while his incendiary, thrusting riffs cut and slash in "Red Carpet" and pierce, rumble, and ricochet in the blaze of "Out of the Woods" until, in a chaotic distorted frenzy, his guitar (along with the furious drumming of Taylor) closes out the last thirty seconds of the song. But Smith isn't the only stringed specialist; Bird's bass adds both a depth of sound and a distinctive vibration to Beefeater's musical texture. Using his slap-bass technique, Bird mixes in a jazz and funk staple, intensifying the downbeat and contributing the band's strong percussive sound. His technique, highlighted in the bass solo of "Just Things" and "One Soul Down," contributes to a louder and more distinct sound of the bass, highlighting a typically background instrument and snapping and popping the strings to provide a lower, denser, reverb-soaked sound. The band is also unafraid to change the sonic landscape with snippets of other instruments—a short sax blast makes its way into "War in Space" with a longer tenor sax solo in "Song for Lucky"; bells chime in "Just Things," and African drums dominate in "Bedlam Rainforest."

(EMO)TIONAL VOCALS AND LYRICS

The posthardcore sound also opened and expanded the definition of manhood to include the theretofore feminine characteristic of emotional vulnerability, primarily through the expressive shifts in vocal delivery and the lyrical content of songs. Take Embrace and MacKaye, whose voice has always been distinctive. Even when he was shouting at nearly indecipherable levels in Minor Threat, his rough and impassioned vocals were consequential—the only difference being that in Minor Threat his vocals emoted anger and frustration, but in Embrace they contain a nearly full gamut of feelings. Yes, the album opening "Give Me Back" starts with MacKaye's characteristic barking style of vocals, but by the end of the first verse, ten seconds after he begins singing, his voice is transformed almost into a croon. Pleading "What can I do?" his voice is imbued with weariness and a trace of confusion; this sadly sung rhetorical question follows every verse, each of which enumerates the ways that MacKaye is disappointed. And although the pain in the first chorus lines is disguised with the standard hardcore anger via shouted vocals, MacKaye lets his emotional guard down in the answer portion of the song's call and answer. How does one react to the anger of disenchantment and disillusionment? According to MacKaye's vocals, with feeling those actual emotions and letting the melancholy seep in. A revelation of hurt rather than unremitting anger emerges in "Building" as well, where the song begins with MacKaye's slightly distant, resonant sounding lilt, singing in the traditional sense, but chock-full of resignation and defeat. In his low, reverberating delivery, MacKaye intones "I'm a failure" throughout the song's chorus. His bandmates join him in background vocals, singing slightly off-key in the bridge "nothing seems to work out right," at once expressing that something is emotional amiss—it is off-key, after all—but also hopeful, in the harmonious voices coming together and reaching the higher, tougher notes.

This sonic freedom correlated with the new music's content. Indeed, the oft-disparaged label *emocore* that arose from this innovative era of DC hardcore stems principally from the contemplative, introspective lyrics and the purgative, emotionally charged singing style that diverged from the virtually uniform emotion of anger in previous hardcore. From disavowing violence to self-discovery to love and relationships, posthardcore bands' words attempted to encapsulate emotion in a new way and inspire empathy in their listeners. As Marginal Man's Lee says in the zine *Inside View*, "we're trying to say something that's pertinent and interesting that everyone can relate to, something where people will say 'Hey, I've felt that way before."[30] Overtly rejecting the machismo pose rampant in the contemporary scene, Embrace pleads for "no more tough guy stance" in their "No More Pain" and rails against suicide in the same song ("no more suicide/it kills everyone"), as well as in "Past" ("I suppose I'm naïve/ But I find it hard to believe/A person could make/Life so cheap"). And although MacKaye's anger bleeds through in "Said Gun"—"Sometimes I'd like to/kick your fucking head in"—the next line adds nuance to that explosive assertion, saying, "But I guess/you're just a human too." By a subsequent verse MacKaye is even more conciliatory, proclaiming "there is no courage in hatred/only in love." Again, it is not that the intensity or anger has completely dissipated from either the bands' lyrics or their projection of masculinity, but that these emotions are counterbalanced or diminished by other sentiments, or else rerecognized.

Love, and its less romantic sibling, lust, was, for nearly the first time in DC hardcore lyrical history, discussed and considered in emocore. Scream spotlights the joys of the one-night stand in "Piece of Her Time" ("Don't know her name, she don't know mine/All I want is a piece of her time/I know what I want/You know they all need it too") and simultaneously reassigns the typically exclusive male trait of desire to women as well. This yearning, both physical and emotional, is also in Scream's "Human Behavior," where Peter asks, "Why is it every time I see you, I can't help myself/There's something inside me that draws my stares on you. . . . An impulse, instinct, reaction behavior." In "Emotional Scars," Marginal Man shows the vulnerability of heartbreak, declaring, "I'll never open my heart again like I did with you/I've been hurt once before/it won't happen again" and evokes the memory of love gone in another song, "Mental Picture": "Your mental picture I try to recall/But the more you're away the hazier it gets. . . . I never forget your face at night/I stood in shadows and you in the light." Even Beefeater, after declaring in the opening line of "Trash Funk" that "This aint a love song/just singing the blues/this aint a romance," he's actually bewailing romance gone bad, recalling that his lady, "when the morning begins/slips through my arms like a mannequin" and out the door.

Unlike most hardcore lyricists, Rites of Spring's Picciotto wrote extensively about love, though often in oblique and somewhat opaque ways that allowed and even encouraged wider interpretation. Faith, S.O.A, and GI had had perhaps two songs that even *mentioned* the opposite sex, whereas "in place of unfocused anger, [Rites of Spring] had a soulful passion that suggested that any given song could be about the end of a relationship—or the beginning of a new world."[31] Picciotto voices the wonder of love in "All There Is" ("It's more than love. . . . It's what I give to you/All there is in the knowing that this never had to end") but also the aching hurt of love lost in "Spring" ("Caught in a time so far away from where our hearts really wanted to be/reaching out to find a way back to where we'd been"). He opines how the pain of a broken heart leaks into any new relationship in "For Want Of" ("I bled/I tried to hide the heart from the head/And I/I said I bled/In the arms of a girl I'd barely met") and laments the inconsolability of the love in "Hain's Point" ("But it feels like I'm falling through a hole in my heart. . . . I could walk around fall in love with a face or two/but it wouldn't be you/no it wouldn't be you").

Rites of Spring's Guy Picciotto is often cited as the patriarch of emo singing, not because he reinvented an innovative melodic singing style, but because he merged the traditional hardcore vocal delivery of inflamed shouting with an authentic-feeling outpouring of varied emotion. Yelling became a vehicle for Picciotto's feelings, rather than merely an end in and of itself; volume and timbre articulated the intensity with which he felt. *Rites of Spring*'s opener, "Spring," displays this unification of hardcore and soft rock sentiment. His vocals rage with speed and fervor, but there's a lightness to his tone, as the last word of every line lilts upward, signaling a buoyancy that undercuts his howls. By 0:24, a desperation enters his voice as he growls "What could I do?/What could I do?" Much like MacKaye, Picciotto isn't angrily spitting out a facetious rhetorical; he's exposing his vulnerability. His voice, gravely and damaged, aches; he really wants to know what he could have done. Even when his singing verges on a nearly perfect reproduction of hardcore's vicious vocals à la Henry Garfield, the wild, high-speed strained delivery deviates from hardcore's playbook of anger and hostility. "Hain's Point," the album's fourth track, has Picciotto squawking and baying, his voice nearly hoarse with his effort and force. But those yelps and cries are not of attack but of anguish and fear, evoking a sort of catharsis that merges turmoil with suffering. When Picciotto drones "I'm not who I thought I was," followed immediately by a grunting, grating moan of "And I can't explain" with "ain" drawn out as if it were being hanged on the gallows, the pain you feel is pangs of empathy and of identification. The juxtaposition of hardness (of speed and tone) with softness (of emotional rawness) of his voice produce a jumbled, unruly feel—mirroring the disorder and confusion the singer is feeling.

These bands' lyrics on lust and love more explicitly demonstrate and perpetuate the heteronormativity of masculinity that was merely hinted at in hardcore, but they also reinforce the dominant stereotype of not only manhood but also of male pop and rock singers. By readjusting the DC hardcore representation of masculinity, particularly by controlling and renouncing aggression and introducing themes of love and sex, the lyrics, somewhat paradoxically, act to preserve archetypes of men. However, by focusing their emotional lyrics on more than simply the opposite sex, posthardcore bands broaden both the emotional and masculine spectrum. Sometimes the emotion is empathy and is directed toward friends, in the soft-rock vein of James Taylor, Carole King, or Ben E. King, as when Marginal Man avers "I'm here to help you when things go wrong/

Lean on my shoulder my friend" in "Friend," or when Scream declares in "Still Screaming," "Don't hide alone/in the unknown." At other times, the sentiment is self-reflection and emotional authenticity, as in Marginal Man's "Identity" ("I don't regret/who I am and what I've done. . . . but now things have changed/it's just not the same/there's a part of me that just can't let go/it's from my heart, these things that I feel/nothing is fake, it's all for real") or Embrace's "Building" ("I can't get what I want/I'm a failure/nothing seems to work/the way I plan/I can't express the way I feel/without fucking up something else"). Sadness and regret are not off limits, and one of the chief male taboos—crying—is shattered by both Rites of Spring ("And if I started crying, would you start crying?/Now I started crying, why are you not crying?") and Embrace ("You know I thought that my eyes they would be dry"). As in the sonic color and vocal stylings of these new bands, their new kind of DC hardcore lyrics react to the violence of the scene and the refiguration of what hardcore was supposed to mean. Conceiving music as "a play of mirrors in which every activity is reflected, defined, [and] recorded,"[32] the sound and content of posthardcore balanced the anger and aggression of the scene and the progressing vulnerability and openness of a new form of masculinity. Beefeater's Squib explains this new punk as "a heartfelt thing. This is a movement where the whole emotional aspect is brought in, which I don't think punk ever had."[33] Picciotto agrees: "It wasn't spikes and bloody meat and skulls with hammers in the head and the violent bloody macho thing. It was more open-ended."[34]

OVERT POLITICS

Love, romance, and sex added a new dimension to DC posthardcore lyrical content, and so too did the scene's newfound allegiance to the expressly political side of the capital city. In reaction to the second term of Reagan, the ever-growing conservativism of the Supreme Court, and the constant and consistent barrage on social, individual, and political freedoms, lyrics turned political proudly and explicitly. This is not to say that the personal was discarded in favor of monolithic anti-Reagan screeds. Instead, as with many of the sonic evolutions within the DC scene, the balance between "traditional" hardcore and this newer posthardcore social and sonic ethos was delicate and constantly being recalibrated. For instance, *Still Screaming* veers from the manifestly political (with songs about the atomic bomb, war, freedom, jingoism, and justice in the United States) to the more emocore-inflected personal on *This Side Up* (including themes of daily ennui, aging, friendship, and self-destruction), bridging the gap between the bubbling resentment of DC youth and the expanse of feeling that comes with getting older. Likewise, Beefeater's lyrics are just as polemical and act as the bridge between personal and social politics; their songs focus on issues like peaceful social activism, vegetarianism, apartheid, the sins of Ronald Reagan, and race and class relations in the United States. Front man Squib and the band's blatant political ideals frequently rubbed some audience members the wrong way, but their integration of lyrical liberal dogma, along with their expansion of the definition of hardcore sound, paved the way for new understandings of what hardcore could and should be.

At the same time, these bands continued hardcore's lyrical battle of class warfare, advocating an anticommercialist, anticapitalist stance. Indeed, MacKaye revisits his anticommercialist concept clearly in "Money" ("I can truly say/I don't give a fuck about your money. . . . Why does it mean it so much to you . . . money has nothing to do with the value of life/but that's just commonsense") and his anticonsumption position more indirectly in "If I Never Thought about It" ("I did my shopping alone this year/It revealed my loneliness"). Marginal Man continues the same theme of class division in "Missing Rungs," addressing the loaded dice that is the American class system and the inevitable failure of anyone to climb any higher—"The social ladder/Is incomplete/It's missing rungs/To protect the elite/So why is that they'll stand in line/To try that ladder one more time"—before the song slows down considerably and condemns the entire system, in unison and distorted, reverb S.O.A-like echo chanting "Rat race." Even in a song primarily about a broken heart, "Torn Apart" asserts that "The two most important things in life can't be bought," reinforcing the anticonsumption message before finishing the album with the outsiders' anthem, "Marginal Man," which expresses the feeling of never quite fitting into the rules and expectations of society: "Allergic to the outside world/On the outside look-ing in. . . . Out in the cold/Ain't life grand?"

This condemnation for society, particularly as a function of a distorted sense of the American Dream, is addressed bluntly and harshly in two of Scream's songs. In "Bedlam," Peter Stahl sings, "Looking through the headlines/Sheltered from what's real/There's a heat in the street/that you can't feel/You think we got the great society/The cities will snap before they bury me. . . . Social disintegration is paving the way/The next generation, just like yesterday," and "U. Suck A./We're Fed Up" seethes "Oh, say can you see/Through intellectual poverty/At your suburban luxuries/ From slimy sea to sea," correlating the country with the glut, excess, and machinations that are required to acquire such extravagance. And Beefeater takes direct aim at Reagan and his so-called trickle-down economics in "Reaganomix," fuming, "we get poor while the rich get fatter/Reaganomix, isn't it wonderful?" and accusing the president of not caring about war because he's "too busy worrying" about "national profit" in "Wars in Space."

Scream was perhaps the most prolific in their lyrical political awareness, particularly when discussing the issue of racial (in)justice. Their song "Solidarity" could almost be mistaken for folk lyrics of the 1960s, pledging their commitment to the struggle of freedom: "We don't know what it's like not to be free/Like when you've lost your sight you cannot see. . . . Do you know what this song's about? It's just a love story/About a people just trying to break out/Solidarity." Similarly, "Stand" challenges their audience to think about the social issues that were occurring in the world around them and join the band in their sociopolitical fight: "It's time to take a stand, are you there?/Or if you see a change now will you stare?/Or if I ask you to use your mind, do you dare? . . . Listen to what we got to say/Here are the screams of today/We're not telling you what to do/We're just asking questions of you." Scream even evokes the subcultural capital of Bad Brains in "Amerarockers" to persuade listeners of the need for social justice ("We must look to the other side/So we can tell what's wrong from what is right. . . . And when I look around/I see all wearing frowns/I know HR would say this is a real shame"), while arousing disgust for the hypocrisy of the American ideals of equality in "American Justice" ("No matter what's the truth, they're gonna put you away/Push you around, no matter just what you say. . . . And it's called American justice/but we know the truth").

Beefeater also lyrically emphasizes race but does so in an array of ways. In "Fred's Song," a ditty primarily about the violence of slam dancing, it's as an ironic aside, as Squib sardonically warbles about how "skinhead guys just turn me on," a phrase that gains even more satirical bite from the song's name, which is for the band's black guitarist, Fred Smith. Race moves beyond the black/white racial binary into the historical injustice inflicted on Native Americans in "Red Carpet," which opens with a spoken-word monologue: "White men made many promises, more than I can remember, never kept but one/promised to take our land/and he took it." Squib then launches into the vocals, singing, "Just so you never think you walk alone/ Just so never feel at ease/So you never call this country home/Just don't let our history be forgot/How much was stolen, how much was bought?" Spoken technique occurs again in the sermonlike opening of "Move Me Strong," when a preacher-type voice emotes, "Echoes and screams always returning, shadowing of long-forgotten folks reminding us that the struggle must continue if we are to be free. We are/we are/we are to be free. Oh Lord, can't give in now," which conjures shades of Martin Luther King's "I Have a Dream" speech. Indeed, another song, "Satyagraha," directly references the civil-rights leader, saying, "Heard the words of MLK/tell me what's your conscious say?" Even the name of the song itself, "Satyagraha," is a reference to the toil for racial and social justice; the term means "insistence on truth" or "soul force," a concept that was widely used in both Mahatma Gandhi's and MLK's fight for civil rights. Even Embrace, whose lyrics primarily focused on nonviolence in the hardcore scene, rather than on the larger political scale, called for solidarity in the fight for racial justice with their song "Do Not Consider Yourself Free": "So you can stay cool behind/ Your window and choose the view you want to see/But as long as there are others held captive/Do not consider yourself free."

This lyrical pivot was a function of the many changes occurring on the local, national, and international stage. In the local scene, as discussed previously, the rebellious origins of DC hardcore had patently shifted from insurgence against the mainstream to revolt against anything and everybody. As the originators of DC hardcore saw the banner of rebellion being flown as a justification for meaningless violence, they sought to refocus their struggle, and, as (relatively) older members of the punk scene, their focus shifted to the politics that were occurring all around them in DC. And as Ronald Reagan finished his first term and starting his second, race and social inequality were unavoidable issues. Reagan attempted to curtail landmark civil-rights legislation such as affirmative action and antidiscriminatory business regulations; the national trends for blacks were also disturbing, with unemployment skyrocketing, a housing crisis, a decline in college population rates, and a vast reduction in health and social services. At the same time, South Africa was experiencing a groundswell of antiapartheid activism, a large portion of which was led by people of the same age as the posthardcore punks. This racial cross-roads—of discrimination within their own city, across the country, and in countries far away—offered a rallying point for some of the posthardcore bands. The impetus was to address racial inequality through lyrics as well as through more overt activism such as drum protests outside the South African embassy on DC's Embassy Row. Such attention was by no means thoroughgoing in the new DC hardcore scene; many of the hardcore bands tackled personal rather than political agendas. However, it is important to note that the hardcore ethos did, in fact, change. Rather than simply looking inward, the new music demanded that the listener look outward as well.

The Last Days of (Revolution) Summer: The Remnants of DC Hardcore

Much as the first wave of DC hardcore did, the newer, second-wave emo-core or posthardcore genre soon found itself splintered, and by 1987 it had completely transformed. Nearly all the post-'83 hardcore bands had split up. In January 1986, Rites of Spring disbanded after Mike Fellows quit. Embrace also separated in 1986, amid tensions between Chris Bald and Mike Hampton. The year 1986 was also when Beefeater broke up, following disagreements about the political nature of the music and per-sonal politics. Scream went through lineup changes, as drummer Kent Stax left in 1986 (replaced by Dave Grohl, of latter-day Nirvana and Foo Fighters fame), Thompson battled a drug habit, and the group added and subtracted musicians and altered their sound. By 1987, none of the post-'83 hardcore bands remained in their original form. Revolution Summer had truly ended. The hardcore implosion was not just local; scene members, and authors recalling the scene, pronounced it dead nationwide in 1986.[35] The causes of death were nearly identical: the original members of the scene dispersed without anyone to take their place, the musical straitjacket of hardcore limited bands who wanted to expand musically, the rebellious, revolutionary ethos of hardcore lost its target objective, and the sound transformed into something only tangentially related to the original hardcore music.

Despite the dissolution of the new hardcore bands, many of its members remained on the scene, forming new bands and, as the sociopolitical and cultural landscape of DC shifted, creating an even more altered and reimagined (punk) sound. Most famous was the union of punk royalty Ian MacKaye with Rites of Spring's Guy Picciotto and Brendan Canty, along with bassist Joe Lally, in the band Fugazi. Perhaps the most iconic DC band (despite the influence of MacKaye in the hardcore scene), Fugazi transmogrified hardcore into a more palatable, mainstream sound, springing from the emocore sound—with slower tempos and more emphasis on heavy-metal-like aesthetic underpinnings. Their songs even included hardcore taboos like singalong and anthemic choruses, combining the power riffs of punk with sounds of funk and reggae and interruptions of sheer noise and screams. Remaining true to the DIY hardcore ethos, Fugazi released eight albums between 1989 and 2001, with four albums—*In on the Kill Taker* (1993), *Red Medicine* (1995), *End Hits* (1998), and *The Argument* (2001)—on Dischord, rejecting the ever-flowing offers from major labels and even still entering the Billboard 200. Perhaps even more significant and long-lasting was Fugazi's commitment to activism and dedication to independent music. MacKaye no longer embraced the personal over the political, instead conflating the two and lending his substantial cultural capital to causes like apartheid, hunger, and poverty, AIDS, gun control, violence, and women's rights. The lyrics of Fugazi also reflected their overt political stance with songs like "Suggestion" about rape and "Five Corporations" about the monopolization of industry. MacKaye and the rest of the band still played all-ages shows with low ticket prices, frequently playing benefit shows for favorite causes and free shows when they could, often partnering with Positive Force, an activist collective that emerged from the hardcore scene. At shows, the band discouraged violent dancing (even stopping shows if the violence got excessive), invited local activists up onto the stage, refused to sell merchandise, and passed out free lyric sheets. If hardcore embodied white, middle-class teenaged masculinity—with all its accompanying hormones, privilege, alienation, and power—Fugazi embodied the college-age progressive who has opened himself to be a free-thinking, tolerant, and sensitive man.

Fugazi and the DC posthardcore sound was also the breeding ground for proto-indie DC (and Dischord) bands, including the influential-though-underground Nation of Ulysses, Q and Not U, the Dismemberment Plan, Jawbox, and Shudder to Think in the early 1990s. Drawing on the hardcore sound, these bands fused dissonant punk with art, dance, and a sprinkling of '90s irony and slacker detachment. Another direct descendent of DC hardcore was Riot Grrrl, a female-centric punk movement that began in the District, as well as the other Washington—Olympia. In the early 1990s, a group of girls set out to abolish the males-only club of the punk rock scene, using the punk sound to demand attention and point out the hypocrisies in our social norms, particularly exposing the social and personal concerns of girls that were habitually excluded from the mainstream—notions of sexual abuse, anorexia, and body image. It is no exaggeration to say that Riot Grrrl would not have existed in its same form without (DC) hardcore.[36] The music was a direct reclamation of hardcore as a nongendered sound. Riot Grrrl sonically argued that hardcore did not have to be, and was not intrinsically, masculine despite its timbre, tempo, and volume. Women in the movement were not appropriating the sounds of anger, control, agency, and thus hypermasculinity; they were women who demanded that the arbitrariness of such sound be seen and then destroyed. It was DC as a place and space that offered the breeding ground for Riot Grrrl as a music and as a scene to germinate. Bikini Kill, without a doubt the most legendry Riot Grrrl band, and its front woman Kathleen Hanna and drummer Tobi Vail first listened to—and then played with—DC's Nation of Ulysses. Along with fellow Washington State Riot Grrrl band Bratmobile, DC became the adopted home of the Revolution girl-style NOW calling card of Riot Grrrl. It was within the city that Hanna and Vail, as well as Bratmobile's Molly Neuman and Allison Wolfe, felt a political energy and urgency, and they relocated to the city, playing with Fugazi and Nation of Ulysses, simultaneously churning out *Riot Grrrl*, a zine that was part activism, part gossip, and part forum for women and girls who had not had a voice in both punk and in culture more generally.

Indeed, it was MacKaye who worked with Bikini Kill at Inner Ear studio, arranged early shows for Bratmobile, and worked to give space and voice to not only women (and the women of these bands) but also the issues at the heart of Riot Grrrl—violence against women, rape, oppression. Perhaps the pinnacle of this DC–Washington State posthardcore love affair was the International Pop Underground festival, where Fugazi played alongside L7, Bikini Kill, Bratmobile, the Melvins, Kurt Cobain's one-off band Israeli Donkeys, Nation of Ulysses, Built to Spill, and the Spinanes. Showcasing the transformation of the punk sound alongside its progressive politics and youth rebellion, the festival epitomized the evolution, influence, and importance of hardcore.

The Evolution of Hardcore Nationwide

The sonic changes occurring in the DC posthardcore scene were by no means exclusive to the area, nor were the transformations in sound limited to one genre. And even though these sonic transformations were occurring in hardcore scenes across the country, I argue that DC hardcore was integral to those changes and to those sounds. In the most clear-cut case, post-'83 saw a massive proliferation of straightedge-saturated hardcore bands, modeled initially on Minor Threat but morphing into a militant straightedge ethos and music. New York and Boston were the two primary hotbeds of this new formulation of straightedge, and no other band represented this new sound and philosophy more than Youth of Today. Founding members Ray Cappo and John Porcelly consciously tried to elevate the straightedge philosophy and the hardcore sound, making both more formal and, some would argue, radical. As Porcelly said,

> We had a very defined idea of what we wanted to do with the band. Here was our mission statement: 1. Resurrect hardcore from the lame ass rock/metal direction it was heading in. 2. Bring back straight edge, in a new way, where the whole band walked the talk and believed in it wholeheartedly. We wanted to prove that it's not just a passing fad but a legitimate alternative to a self-destructive drug culture. 3. Take the positivity and hopefulness of bands like 7 Seconds and Youth Brigade and meld it together with the fury and hardness of Negative Approach and Agnostic Front. 4. Be

so moved by the music and the message that when we play, we fucking give everything we have, every night, and leave blood, sweat, and tears on the stage. And later on, we put in an addendum: 5. Start a vegetarian revolution amongst the youth and spread awareness of the exploitive and cruel nature of meat-eating and factory farming.[37]

It was Youth of Today who were the foundation for the emergence of youth crews, the name taken from Nevada straightedge band 7 Second's debut album, and a subculture primarily existing within the New York (and tangentially, Los Angeles) hardcore scene. Youth crews were hardcore and straightedge, and as Porcelly suggests in his quote, these (primarily) young men were implacably serious about both. Straightedge was no longer just a personal choice—as MacKaye had been insisting—but it was a moral and ethical one. But youth crews also intentionally brought a positive attitude, an optimism, to their moral messages. As Youth of Today's self-titled song describes, this new crop of straightedge kids was "Physically strong, morally straight—Positive youth, we're the youth of today." Their principles, their music, and even their fashion—which evolved into a jock-centered look of varsity jackets, Champion-brand sportswear, and sneakers—was a resistance against what Porcelly named the "violent, nihilistic, drunken mentality that was prevalent in the hardcore scene at the time."[38] There was a clear division between punks who were straightedge and those who weren't, as one *Maximum Rocknroll* reader made clear in his letter:

> You pump your money into corporations that kill people, pollute the earth, do animal testing, make sexist ads, ruin families, cause drunk driving, alcoholism. . . . How can you all be politically correct without being straight? It doesn't make sense.[39]

The moral resistance was clear—not only was the straightedge lifestyle mandatory, its morality expanded as well. To be straightedge now meant to be vegan, an environmentalist, and for animal rights. The music, at least when youth crews first began, stayed within the more traditional hardcore sound but took on these straightedge causes. Gorilla Biscuits (New York) sang about their pride in this new straightedge scene and their moral superiority, and Earth Crisis (New York) was more extreme in their views, singing "street by street/block by block/taking it all back" from "the youth immersed in poison," warning "violence against violence/ let the roundups begin," and Vegan Reich (Los Angeles) demanded "fuck you, shut your fucking mouth/we didn't ask for your opinion/we're telling you the way it is so sit back and listen," singing about (no surprise) veganism and animal rights, among other issues. Yet, as the youth crew scene began to splinter, so too did their morals and their music. A skinhead/white supremacist element crept into straightedge hardcore, as well as a heavier reliance on metal and thrash. It was the latter—the sonic infusion of heavy metal—that paralleled changes happening musically across the country.

Much like hardcore mutations creeping into Faith, and their album and label mates Void, the expansion of hardcore into the musical arena of heavy metal was occurring throughout the country (or, as Porcelly so eloquently said, "lame ass rock/metal direction"). With Black Sabbath a marked influence,[40] hardcore bands like Black Flag (Southern California), SSD (Boston), and Corrosion of Conformity (North Carolina) introduced a sonic sludge to their sound, significantly slowing down the tempo and adding lyrics of doom, gloom, and self-loathing. In part a reaction to the dissolution of the most celebrated of hardcore bands (including Minor Threat and Bad Brains in DC) and in part a contesting of the highly regimented and regulated (some would say maybe even formulaic) music of hardcore, the infusion of heavy metal by hardcore bands sought to "convey aggression and power without resorting to the cheap trick of velocity."[41] With Henry Rollins at the microphone, Black Flag's *My War* (1984) is one of the exemplars for this merging of metal and hardcore, from the oozing slowness of songs that were longer than six minutes to the thudding drumbeats of doom and the coupling of bass and guitar broken up by Greg Ginn's drawn-out guitar solos. Hardcore wasn't gone; it showed up in the A side of the album in speed and tempo, albeit with the nearly heretical addition of the guitar solo. But like the evolution of the band itself, on the B side, hardcore was supplanted by the sonic aesthetics of metal. Even the band's personal style matched their sonic shift, with long hair replacing shaved heads. And the lyrics of the songs tended toward the dark side of self-hatred in tracks like "Three Nights" and "Beat My Head against a Wall." By their second album of 1984 (*Slip*

It In), the marriage between hardcore and metal had been consummated. The sound was dense and aggressive, the lyrics purgative, and the affect powerful.

During the same year, SSD began its evolution from an instrumental straightedge hardcore band (influenced by Minor Threat and the DC straightedge scene and releasing the now-classic *The Kids Will Have Their Say* and *Get It Away*) to having a metal-infused sound. After switching labels, SSD turned toward lengthy guitar solos and longer songs in *How We Rock*, fusing hardcore and metal and continuing their metal/hardcore love affair on yet another label for 1985's *Break It Up*. And down in North Carolina, Corrosion of Conformity, who had begun as a hardcore band influenced by Judas Priest and Iron Maiden, Bad Brains, and Minor Threat alike, released 1984's *Eye for an Eye*, combining the inexperience and tornado of sound from hardcore with metal-inspired tempos and riff-rock influences. After losing vocalist Eric Eycke, the band released the even heavier *Animosity* featuring unbounded feedback loops, Black Sabbath–steeped guitar riffs, and the maniacal vocals of Mike Dean (their song "Holier" was later even covered by Metallica). By the 1990s, Corrosion of Conformity had left behind any vestiges of hardcore and were firmly embedded in heavy metal.

Those three bands serve as strong examples of the genre-mixing sound of hardcore and metal, and, as with the shifting sound in DC, they were not the only bands doing so: Killing Time, Sheer Terror, and Biohazard (New York), Outpatients (Massachusetts), Straw Dogs (formerly F.U.'s, from Boston), and Big Cheese and Discharge (England) were also combining the sonic elements of metal with hardcore, to name just a few.

Sonically closely related was the genre known as crossover thrash (not to be confused with thrashcore, despite some bands evolving from the latter to the former). Also situated within the lineage of heavy metal and hardcore, crossover thrash emphasizes technical aptitude and complexity with a more aggressive, velocity-based sound than its hardcore-heavy metal predecessors. But the sound also included metal essentials such as guitar solos and metal riffs, as well as longer and more technically varied compositions. The Cro-Mags (New York), who began as a traditional hardcore band, became the paradigm of crossover thrash with their 1986 *The Age of Quarrel*. In a hardcore scene already infused with a sense of anger, violence, and devotion, the Cro-Mags and their electric lead singer John Joseph combined the momentum and élan of hardcore with the unchecked bellicosity of thrash metal and mixed in their Hindu beliefs for good measure. Mixing assertive riffs structured on power chords with unyielding tempos, songs like "Show You No Mercy" and "Malfunction" highlight the ways in which hardcore and metal informed one another. By their 1989 album, *Best Wishes*, the Cro-Mags had completed their evolution into a crossover thrash band, prolonging their songs by minutes and adding guitar solos. Fellow New York hardcore band Agnostic Front was similarly crucial to the evolution of hardcore into crossover thrash, particularly with their equally genre-defining 1986 *Cause for Alarm*. Made in the midst of significant lineup changes, the album never veers from its hardcore intensity but adds a smattering of right-wing lyrics with constant drum kicks, double-bass beats, tight precision, wrathful vocals, and the heavy, volatile guitars of metal. "Out for Blood" may be the clearest crossover thrash song on the album, but the band remade "Your Mistake" from their first album into a near-total-metal cover of the original "Your Mistake," and "The Eliminator" (speed metal at its finest) and "Bomber Zee" had crossover appeal, played weekly on metal-centric college radio stations. Agnostic Front helped raise the sonic and conceptual hurdles between hardcore and metal.

Two other seminal crossover thrash bands should be mentioned, the first of whom, Suicidal Tendencies, perhaps seem an odd progenitor of the genre after the airplay on MTV of their best-known song, "Institutionalized"—and later on *Beavis and Butthead*. They started in Los Angeles as a hardcore band, even being voted "Worst Band/Biggest Assholes" in *Flipside* in 1982 (but by 1983 being voted "Best New Band") but embracing—some would say helping to create—crossover thrash with their 1987 *Join the Army*. With lead singer Mike Muir echoing the vocal stylings of Motörhead's Lemmy Kilmister, and the prolific use of the drum double kick, the album was indubitably both punk and metal but perhaps the geographically sunny origins of the band promoted a sound that was lighter and more playful than the crossover thrash of NYC's Cro-Mags and Agnostic Front. Speed meets doom meets melody meets aggression meets wicked guitar solos meets antisocial turmoil on this album that cracked the Billboard charts with songs that made their way into video games and even a music video. Finally, a discussion of crossover thrash would not be complete without Dirty Rotten Imbeciles from Houston, Texas, who billed themselves as the world's fastest band and whose 1985 *Dealing with It* is yet another mammoth prototype of the genre. The band combined the throbbing bass, metal-kissed riffs, and pure physicality of drumming from metal with the brevity of songs and velocity of hardcore, keeping the extreme aggression from both genres. Dirty Rotten Imbeciles' songs contained both the political and the humorous but filtered it through the ravages of thrash in "I Don't Need Society" and "Mad Man." Around the country (and across the pond), other crossover trash bands like Stormtroopers of Death (New York), Ringworm (Ohio), English Dogs (England), Dresden 45 (Texas), Attitude Adjustment (San Francisco), the Accüsed (Seattle), and Hogan's Heroes (New Jersey) continued to expand and fuse elements of speed metal, heavy metal, and hardcore.

It should also be noted that the influence of metal on hardcore was not unidirectional. Hardcore did branch out sonically into the aesthetics of metal, but metal did the same with hardcore. Iron Maiden, Slayer, Metallica, Megadeath, Anthrax, and Motörhead, for example, borrowed hardcore's obsession with speed, energy, and aggression. As Scott Ian from Anthrax said, "It did change everything. It affected all of our records that we made in the Eighties. If we weren't listening to bands like D.R.I., Discharge and Agnostic Front, we wouldn't have made the albums we made."[42] There seemed to be a direct lineage between Black Flag and Agnostic Front to Metallica and Slayer, as noted by many a metalhead themselves. And the ancestral lines continued into the form of metalcore in the 1990s and into the 2000s, where bands like Shai Hulud (Florida), Killswitch Engage and Converge (Massachusetts), All Out War (New York), Disembodied (Minnesota), and Atreyu (California) built on the sonic and aesthetic underpinnings of crossover thrash, centering the use of breakdowns, a hybrid of screaming and singing, heavy guitar riffs, aggressive verses, double bass drumming, melodic choruses, and the occasional use of blast beats.

Another strain of hardcore hybridity that can loosely be labeled posthardcore tends toward the more alternative rock music end of the spectrum. Bands of this kind were not only rooted in hardcore, they started out as hardcore bands in the vein of DC and posthardcore royalty Fugazi. Incorporating the sonic binaries of loud and soft, melodic and dissonant, as well as varied sonic textures and dynamics, this posthardcore offshoot embraced other genres of music like jazz and dub (an outgrowth of reggae, as discussed with DC posthardcore bands), retaining the energy and audacity of hardcore while thrusting the sound into discrete, and often more arty, musical arenas from which punk itself emerged. Perhaps the most famous of these national posthardcore bands are Hüsker Dü, the Replacements, and the Minutemen, who, in the words of music critic David Fricke, took "punk at its word, resubscribing to the freeing-up of forgotten energies and articulate rage it originally stood for."[43] The Minutemen, who, in their first incarnation as the Reactionaries, once opened for Black Flag, were raised on Creedence Clearwater Revival, matured into the Clash and the Ramones, and dabbled in English postpunk. Their lyrics were firmly rooted in the political nature their name suggests ("Sell or Be Sold," "Ain't No Picnic," "Viet Nam"), but they incorporated elements of jazz and funk, spoken word, and folk, along with hardcore's speed and dedication to minimalism. As bassist Mike Watt described in *Flipside* in 1985, "Punk rock doesn't have to mean hardcore or one style of music. It can mean freedom and going crazy and being personal with your art."[44] Their two pivotal albums, *What Makes a Man Start Fires?* (1982) and the double album *Double Nickels on the Dime* (1984), embodied this freedom, integrating polyrhythmic and syncopated drumming, melodic bass lines, scratchy guitars, and an overall beefed-up rock 'n' roll sound, pushing the limits of what hardcore could or should be.

Hüsker Dü, on the other hand, started in the hardcore scene in Minnesota, sustaining the hardcore banner of fast, intense, and loud before being lured to the more melodic side of rock though they preserved the sneering fury of hardcore and wed it with the lightness of pop. The union welcomed catchy hooks next to the agitating and oppressive clamor of guitar, using melody and pop as a counterpoint to the grinding of guitars and choppy fragments of language. Hardcore's speed and propulsion remained, but Hüsker Dü crafted songs into precious gems of 1960s bubblegum aesthetics, the pinnacle of which is the band's *Zen Arcade* (1984), often cited as the blueprint for the alt-rock genre that followed. The mainstream music industry took notice, and Warner Brothers signed the band in 1985 and released two more albums of pure melodic indie rock until they broke up in 1988.

Although not a self-proclaimed part of the hardcore scene, the Replacements (née Dogbreath and the Impediments) started as a garage punk band in Minneapolis and were in constant friendly competition with fellow Minnesotans punk-turned-alt-rock-gods Hüsker Dü, releasing their 1981 *Sorry Ma, I Forgot to Take Out the Trash* and their follow-up, 1981's EP *Stink* as a sloppy ode to hardcore. Their sound on these albums was in no way pure hardcore, but they were a semipassable mimic with brief, lethal outbursts of songs, albeit too messy in their playing and expressing more ennui than anger in their lyrics. By 1983's *Hootenanny*, the band had molted any remaining hardcore skin, dipping their sonic toes into pop, folk, and even (though perhaps ironically) country using humor as a shield against any critique. Their much-acclaimed 1984 *Let It Be* captured the raw, ragged, chaotic, and often untethered feeling of postadolescence, earning them a major-label record deal with Sire. The posthardcore revolution was hardly limited to these bands—Butthole Surfers, Sonic Youth, Naked Raygun, Saccharine Trust, Mission of Burma, Dinosaur Jr., Meat Puppets, just to name a few, all stretched beyond the occasionally limiting confines of hardcore to explore the more melodic and often more poppy sound of what became alternative rock.

Similarly situated in the alt-rock-to-hardcore continuum was the sonic transformation later labeled grunge, a slowed-down version of hardcore inflected with raw sonic aesthetics and influences of metal. Unlike the musical evolutions of hardcore on the East Coast, this metamorphosis was grounded in the Pacific Northwest, merging the intensity of hardcore with the melodies of rock and pop and the experimentation of art rock. Flipper, a hardcore band from San Francisco that had Dead Kennedy's Jello Biafra championing them, was crucial in the hardcore-to-grunge sonic shift, playing hours-long shows with distorted and dissonant guitars, sludge-like punk punctuated by pugilistic whines, buzzes, and drones of noise. Before there was a genre called grunge, Flipper married the acid rock and psychedelia San Francisco was famous for with hardcore, at once upsetting and thrilling hardcore fans with their slow and melodic, raucous brand of noise. They received massive recognition, not only in the obvious homage from Kurt Cobain wearing a DIY Flipper shirt in the booklet for *In Utero*, but also in their influence on other hardcore bands making that sonic jump—including the Melvins.

If Flipper was the original progenitor of what became grunge, the Melvins were its better-looking and more successful offspring. Devotees of hardcore in a small town in Washington State 150 miles outside Seattle, the band members felt oppressed by the confines of the genre's narrow dictates. As the founding member of the band Buzz Osborne said, "I realized by '84 or '85 that hardcore wasn't going to work for us. Even by then, I was sick to death of most of it. We wanted to do something that was more confrontational."[45] That confrontation was in the form of a massive tempo slowdown, still aggressive and primal but dripping in the grit of sludge and metal. As Soundgarden's Kim Thayil said, "The Melvins went from being the fastest band in town to the slowest band in town. . . . Everyone was trying to be punk rock, a kind of art-damage thing, and the Melvins decided to be the heaviest band in the world."[46] Their 1987 *Gluey Porch Treatments* is slow and lumbering with intermittent songs at the speed of hardcore, littered with squealing rages of feedback and ominous reverb and Osborne's sprawling yowls of vocals, disorienting the listener and refusing to conform. The still-together band inspired not only the Seattle sound of grunge but countless metalheads across the country. As with the other offshoots of hardcore, Flipper and the Melvins were hardly alone in their groundbreaking sonic upheaval. Fellow Seattle-hardcore-turned-grunge-forerunners Green River spurned the constraints of hardcore for the metal and rock noise that would turn into grunge, as did U-Men, whose frenetic and intense sound reigned over the Seattle underground music scene. In California, Tales of Terror also helped spur the dirty guitar revolution that birthed the mainstream—and wildly successful—grunge bands of Nirvana, Mudhoney, Soundgarden, and Pearl Jam. Dave Grohl's DC-to-Seattle/Scream-to-Nirvana journey reflects his and the larger sonic shift from hardcore to grunge.

DC Hardcore's Legacy

Hardcore as it was originally conceived in the late 1970s gasped its last breath by the mid-1980s; its demise was inevitable. As a product of the particular time and place it was formed, it is no wonder that as politics, culture, and the social context changed, so too did the aesthetics of its sound. Yet the kernels of hardcore remained, shifting, mutating, and reemerging as discrete sonic and social signifiers in an always evolving but never new musical landscape. Famous bands like Sonic Youth, Beastie Boys, Fishbone, Red Hot Chili Peppers, Nirvana, Slayer, the Roots, No Doubt, My Chemical Romance, politicians such as Beto O'Rourke, and contemporary DC punk bands like Rocket City Riot, Never Submit, Red Death, and Pure Disgust show the abiding influence of DC hardcore. Its seemingly outsized impact has made the scene—and the bands within the scene—an object of commodification despite their best attempts, with Minor Threat staving off unlicensed tees from Forever 21; Etsy stores brandishing homemade and bootleg DC hardcore pins, tees, and patches; and a secondary market for paraphernalia, zines, cassettes, and vinyl on eBay thriving. And the city that once tried to ignore DC hardcore and then cast it out or bury it under gargantuan white slabs of marble and culture with a capital C have, in recent years, come to embrace if not fetishize the scene. There was *Pump Me Up*, the exhibit literally institutionalizing DC hardcore (and go-go) at the Corcoran Gallery of Art,[47] a photo exhibition of the scene at the Center for Documentary Studies, a question-and-answer session with Henry Rollins at the Smithsonian, a panel on DC hardcore by the DC Humanities Council, and even an art opening in Los Angeles, *Banned in Babylon: The Art and Culture of Bad Brains*. Not only has the scene been memorialized through a wave of documentary movies—*Salad Days: A Decade of Punk in Washington, D.C. (1980–1990)*; *Punk the Capital: Building a Sound Movement*; *Positive Force: More Than a Witness*; *Finding Joseph I*; and Dave Grohl's episode on DC in HBO's *Sonic Highways*—but also these movies have been given the institutional seal of approval: screened at the Hirschhorn Museum, included at the Smithsonian National Museum of African American History and Culture, with reviews abounding in the *Washington Post, Rolling Stone, Variety, Paste*, and the *Hollywood Reporter*. Narrative books (*Dances of Days, Spoke, American Hardcore, Our Band Could Be Your Life*) and photo books (*Banned in D.C., Hard Art, DC 1979*) tell the stories of scene members from their own point of view. The cultural and academic significance of the scene has been and is still being actively memorialized in the form of archives—both at academic institutions (the University of Maryland's The Washington, D.C., Punk and Indie Fanzine collection and George Washington University's D.C. Music Archives) and government institutions (including the Martin Luther King Jr. Library's DC Punk Archives). And popular forms of DC hardcore dedication (if not nostalgia) remain, including flash sheets at local DC tattoo shops of black sheep or lightning striking the Capitol, a DC hardcore Facebook page and private Facebook groups where members trade memories and photographs, a walking tour of DC punk, and tourists snapping photos outside the Dischord house in Arlington. The power of the DC scene has in retrospect been commemorated—with both popular, commercial, academic, and even governmental acknowledgment of what a group of young kids with a few instruments and a mouth full of resistance can do.

It is clear that the legacy of DC hardcore remains vital and palpable both to the national music scene as a whole and the local identity of the DC metropolitan area. This book hopes to add to—and perhaps even help complicate—those crucial narratives about DC hardcore. By examining the way music communicates within the scene's social, political, and economic context, we can see the ways in which power and agency were—and in many ways still are—embedded, subverted, and realized in hardcore music, the musicians, and even the fans themselves.

Discography

Bad Brains. *Bad Brains*. ROIR, Vinyl, 1982.

Beefeater. *Plays for Lovers*. Dischord Records, Vinyl, 1985.

Beefeater, *House Burning Down*. Dischord Records, Vinyl, 1986.

The Clash. *The Clash*. CBS Records, Vinyl, 1977.

The Dictators. *The Dictators Go Girl Crazy!* Epic Records, Vinyl, 1975.

The Dictators. *Manifest Destiny*. Asylum Records, Vinyl, 1977.

The Dictators. *Bloodbrothers*. Asylum Records. Vinyl, 1978.

Embrace. *Embrace*. Dischord Records, Vinyl, 1987.

Government Issue. *Legless Bull*. Dischord Records, Vinyl, 1981.

Government Issue. *Make an Effort*. Dischord Records, Vinyl, 1982.

Government Issue. *Boycott Stabb*. Dischord Records, Vinyl, 1983.

Iggy and the Stooges. *Raw Power*. Columbia Records, Vinyl, 1973.

MacKaye, Ian, and Jeff Nelson. Linear notes. *Four Old 7"s on a 12"*. Dischord Records, LP, 1984.

Marginal Man. *Identity*. Dischord Records, Vinyl, 1984.

MC5. *Kick Out the Jams*. Elektra Records, Vinyl, 1969.

Minor Threat. *In My Eyes*. Dischord Records, Vinyl, 1981.

Minor Threat. *Minor Threat*. Dischord Records, Vinyl, 1981.

Minor Threat. *Out of Step*. Dischord Records, Vinyl, 1983.

The Ramones. *The Ramones*. Sire Records, Vinyl, 1976.

The Ramones. *Leave Home*. Sire Records, Vinyl, 1977.

The Ramones. *Pleasant Dreams*. Sire Records, Vinyl, 1981.

Richard Hell and the Voidoids. *Blank Generation*. Sire Records, Vinyl, 1977.

Rites of Spring. *Rites of Spring*. Dischord Records, Vinyl, 1985.

Scream. *Still Screaming*. Dischord Records, Vinyl, 1983.

Scream. *This Side Up*. Dischord Records, Vinyl, 1985.

The Sex Pistols. *Never Mind the Bollocks, Here's the Sex Pistols*, EMI, Vinyl, 1976.

The Slickee Boys, *Mersey, Mersey Me*, Limp Records, Vinyl, 1978.

Patti Smith. *Horses*. Arista Records, Vinyl, 1975.

State of Alert. *No Policy*, Dischord Records, Vinyl, 1981.

The Stooges. *The Stooges*, Elektra Records, Vinyl 1969.

The Stooges. *Fun House*, Elektra Records, Vinyl, 1970.

Teen Idles. *Minor Disturbance*. Dischord Records, Vinyl, 1981.

The Velvet Underground. *The Velvet Underground and Nico*, Verve Records, Vinyl, 1967.

Notes

Introduction

1. Greil Marcus, *The History of Rock n' Roll in Ten Songs* (New Haven, CT: Yale University Press, 2014), 10.

2. Despite this focus, I will explore the musical and cultural transformation of hardcore, including its foray into post-punk and emo, as well as the sociopolitical, economic, generational changes that spurred such a change, in the concluding chapter of the book. The primary focus of the succeeding chapters, however, is 1978–83.

3. This is not to undermine or ignore the existence and significance of other DC hardcore bands of the era, such as Youth Brigade, the Extorts, the Untouchables, Insurrection, Iron Cross, Void, Artificial Peace, and Red C.

4. Steven Blush, *American Hardcore: A Tribal History* (Port Townsend, WA: Feral House, 2010), 131.

5. Mark Andersen and Mark Jenkins, *Dance of Days: Two Decades of Punk in the Nation's Capital* (New York: Akashic, 2003), 26–33.

6. Jerry Williams, quoted in Blush, 139.

7. Quoted in Andersen and Jenkins, 55.

8. Howard Wuelfing, "Minor Threat," *Washington Post*, August 3, 1982, Style, B10.

9. George Hurchella, *Going Underground: American Punk 1979–1992* (Stuart, FL: Zuo, 2006), 63.

10. Sarah Weatherill, "DC Update," *Noise* #5, c. 1981, http://www.dementlieu.com/users/obik/arc/dc/dc_noise.html.

11. Although Garfield changed his moniker to Rollins in honor of Bad Brains' HR when he became the lead singer of Black Flag, he remained Garfield during his time in DC. He'll be referred to as Garfield in this book except for when discussing his post-DC band.

12. Quoted in Blush, 151.

13. Quoted in Andersen and Jenkins, 81.

14. Quoted in Andersen and Jenkins, 123.

15. Tom Lyle, interview by Dr. Strange, *ScannerZine*, www.scannerzine.com, accessed January 25, 2021, https://www.scannerzine.com/governmentissue.htm.

16. Aaron Leitko, "An Interview w/ Thurston Moore: Thoughts on Faith," accessed December 18, 2020, dischord.com/ faith-thurston-moore.

17. Blush, 164.

18. "The Faith and Void: The Glorious Dischord of 1980s harDCore Punk," *Guardian*, October 11, 2011.

19. Brent Burton, review of *Subject to Change Plus First Demo* by the Faith, *Washington City Paper*, September 30, 2011.

Chapter 1. DC Rising

1. Murray Forman, *The 'Hood Comes First: Race, Space, and Place in Rap and Hip-Hop.* (Middletown, CT: Wesleyan University Press, 2002), 2.

2. Sara Cohen, *Rock Culture in Liverpool: Popular Music in the Making* (Oxford, UK: Clarendon, 1991), 223.

3. Barry Shank, *Dissonant Identities: The Rock 'n' Roll Scene in Austin, Texas* (Hanover: Wesleyan University Press, 1994), 20.

4. George H. Lewis 1992. "Who Do You Love? The Dimensions of Musical Taste," in *Popular Music and Communication*, 2nd ed., ed. J. Lull (London: Sage, 1992), 144.

5. Forman, *'Hood*, 3.

6. Theodore Gracyk. *I Wanna Be Me: Rock Music and the Politics of Identity* (Philadelphia: Temple University Press, 2001), 9.

7. Forman, *'Hood*, 35.

8. Forman, *'Hood*, 9.

9. Forman, *'Hood*, 346.

10. A fight that persist today, as the federal government still maintains the purse strings in the form of the annual budget and the power of policy vetoes over DC, and local license plates proclaim "taxation without representation."

11. "Energy and National Goals: Address to the Nation, July 15, 1979," in *Public Papers of the Presidents: Jimmy Carter, 1979* (Washington, DC: GPO, 1980), 1235–41.

12. Quoted in Seymour Martin Lipset and William Schneider, *The Confidence Gap: Business, Labor, and Government in the Public Mind* (New York: Free Press, 1983), 15.

13. Bruce J. Schulman, *The Seventies: The Great Shift in American Culture, Society and Politics* (New York: Free Press, 2001), 218–20.

14. Campbell Gibson and Kay Jung, *Historical Census Statistics on Population Totals by Race, 1790 to 1990, and by Hispanic Origin, 1970 to 1990, for the United States, Regions, Divisions, and State*, Working Paper 56 (Washington, DC: US Commerce Department, Census Bureau, Population Division, 2002).

15. Dennis E. Gale, *Washington, D.C.: Inner City Revitalization and Minority Suburbanization* (Philadelphia: Temple University Press, 1987).

16. Denise Kersten Wills, "'People Were Out of Control': Remembering the 1968 Riots," *Washingtonian Magazine*, April 1, 2008, https://www.washingtonian.com/2008/04/01/people-were-out-of-control-remembering-the-1968-riots/.

17. Eddie Dean, "A Brief History of White People in Southeast," *Washington City Paper*, October 16, 1998.

18. National Capital Planning Commission, *1965–1985 Proposed Physical Development Policies for Washington, DC* Washngton, DC: National Capital Planning Commission, 1965, 35.

19. Washington DC Community Renewal Program, *Washington's Far Southeast '70 Report*, 1970: 38, 47.

20. Jeffrey R. Henig, *Gentrification in Adams Morgan: Political and Commercial Consequences of Neighborhood Change*, master's thesis, George Washington University, Washington, DC, 1982, 2.

21. Keith Melder, *City of Magnificent Intentions: A History of Washington, District of Columbia* (Washington, DC: Intac, 1997), 510–12.

22. Paul L. Knox, "The Restless Urban Landscape: Economic and Sociocultural Change and the Transformation of Metropolitan Washington, DC," *Annals of the Association of American Geographers* 81, no. 2 (1991): 189.

23. Knox, "Restless Urban Landscape," 191.

24. Knox, "Restless Urban Landscape," 202.

25. R. Beauregard, *Gentrification and the City* (Boston: Allen and Unwin, 1986), 35.

26. "Georgetown University: A Mostly White Enclave in a Black City," *Journal of Blacks in Higher Education*, Spring 2002, 55.

27. This is not to ignore the monumental importance of go-go to DC. Go-go will be discussed in more detail in a subsequent section of the chapter.

28. Maurice Jackson and Blair A. Ruble, eds., *DC Jazz* (Washington, DC: Georgetown University Press, 2018), xvii.

29. Maurice Jackson, "Jazz and the Struggle for Equality," *DC Jazz* (Washington, DC: Georgetown University Press, 2018), 16.

30. J. Freedom du Lac, "A Chord of Jazz History to Echo at Turkish Embassy," *Washington Post*, February 3, 2011.

31. As quoted in Anna Harwell Celenza, "Legislating Jazz," *DC Jazz* (Washington, DC: Georgetown University Press, 2018), 109.

32. Kip Lornell, *Capital Bluegrass: Hillbilly Meets Washington DC* (Oxford: Oxford University Press, 2020).

33. Hand Burchard, "The Birchmere for Bluegrass." *Washington Post*, January 28, 1983, WK14.

34. Melder, *City*, 467.

35. As quoted in Melder, *City*, 624.

36. John F. Kennedy, "Remarks to National Cultural Center Trustees and Advisory Committee, 14 November 1961," in *Public Papers of the Presidents of the United States: John F. Kennedy, January 10 to December 31, 1961* (Washington, DC: Office of the Federal Register, National Archives and Records, 1962), 719.

37. Nan Robertson, "Glittering Audience Attends Kennedy Center's Opening," *New York Times*, September 9, 1971.

38. Irvin Molotsky, "Culture Makes a Capital Gain," *New York Times*, September 6, 1980, 1.

39. J. Hillary Taylor, letter to the editor, *Washington Post*, January 26, 1948.

40. Gino J. Simi, letter to the editor, *Washington Post*, November 18, 1953.

41. Judith Martin, "Defining Culture in Advance," *Washington Post*, September 9, 1973.

42. Kip Lornell and Charles C. Stephenson, *The Beat! Go-go Music from Washington, DC* (Jackson: University Press of Mississippi, 2009, 94.

43. "Washington in the '70s: Share Your Memories," https://weta.org/tv/program/washington-70s.

44. Lornell and Stephenson, *The Beat!*, 19.

45. Lornell and Stephenson, *The Beat!*, 30–40.

46. James Avery, quoted in "Go-Going in Style: Getting Small with Trouble Funk," by Bill Bentley, *LA Weekly*, November 29, 1985, 67.

47. Lornell and Stephenson, *The Beat!*, 111.

48. Mark Andersen and Mark Jenkins, *Dance of Days: Two Decades of Punk in the Nation's Capital* (New York: Akashic, 2003), 4.

49. As cited in Andersen and Jenkins, *Dance of Days*, 14.

Chapter 2. The Racial Aesthetics of DC Hardcore

1. The Red Hot Chili Peppers, Nirvana, No Doubt, Rage against the Machine, Guns N' Roses, and the Weeknd are just a few of the musicians who credit Bad Brains' influence in their music. And their 1982 *Bad Brains* was declared the most influential hardcore album of all time by *Rolling Stone, Pitch Fork, L.A. Weekly,* Dave Grohl, Don Letts, and the Beastie Boys, among others.

2. Quoted in Steven Blush, *American Hardcore: A Tribal History* (Port Townsend, WA: Feral House, 2010), 139.

3. Kevin Fellezs, *Birds of Fire: Jazz, Rock, Funk, and the Creation of Fusion* (Durham, NC: Duke University Press, 2011), 4.

4. Langston Hughes, *Music and the Harlem Renaissance*, ed. Samuel Floyd (Knoxville: University of Tennessee Press, 1993), 9.

5. Quoted in Blush, *American Hardcore*, 134.

6. Blush, American Hardcore, 134.

7. Fellezs, *Birds of Fire*, 7.

8. Fellezs, *Birds of Fire*, 5.

9. Fellezs, *Birds of Fire*, 5.

10. Quoted in Don Howard, "Pay to Cum!," *Trouser Press*, 1983.

11. Quoted in Blush, *American Hardcore*, 134.

12. Scott DeVeaux, *The Birth of Bebop: A Social and Musical History* (Berkeley: University of California Press, 1997), 1–31.

13. Fellezs, *Birds of Fire*, 35.

14. Scott DeVeaux, *The Birth of Bebop: A Social and Musical History* (Berkeley: University of California Press, 1997), 168.

15. Ted Gioia, *The History of Jazz* (Oxford: Oxford University Press, 1997), 205.

16. Ben Sidran, *Black Talk* (New York: De Capo, 1981), 79.

17. DeVeaux, *Birth of Bebop*, 171.

18. Fellezs, *Birds of Fire*, 24.

19. Fellezs, *Birds of Fire*, 8.

20. Blush, American Hardcore, 139.

21. Mark Fleischmann and Greg Fasolino, "Bad Brains," Trouser Press (2002), https://trouserpress.com/reviews/bad-brains/.

22. Quoted in Blush, *American Hardcore*, 132.

23. Ron Eyerman and Andrew Jamison, *Music and Social Movements: Mobilizing Traditions in the Twentieth Century* (Cambridge: Cambridge University Press, 1998), 75.

24. See Simon Frith, Sound Effects: Youth, Leisure, and the Politics of Rock 'n' Roll (New York: Pantheon, 1981); Francis Davis, *The History of the Blues: The Roots, the Music, the People* (Cambridge, MA: De Capo, 2003); Robert Palmer, Deep Blues: A Musical and Cultural History of the Mississippi Delta (London: Penguin, 1988); Alan Lomax, The Land Where the Blues Began (New York: New Press, 2002).

25. Ian Hoare, *The Soul Book* (New York: Dell, 1976), 152.

26. Nina Eidsheim, *Voice as a Technology of Selfhood: Towards an Analysis of Racialized Timbre and Vocal Performance* (PhD diss., University of California, San Diego, 2008), 115.

27. Frank Tirro, *Jazz: A History* (New York: W. W. Norton, 1993), 48.

28. Frith, *Sound Effects*, 17.

29. David P. Szatmary, *Rockin' in Time: A Social History of Rock-and-roll* (Upper Saddle River, NJ: Prentice Hall, 1996), 6, 9, 13.

30. Fleischmann and Fasolino, "Bad Brains," 2002.

31. Marc Coleman, "Bad Brains Give You a Piece of Their Mind," *NY Rocker* no. 50 (1982).

32. Eric Carr, Review of "Bad Brains: Banned in DC," *Pitchfork*, September 2003.

33. Fellezs, *Birds of Fire*, 8.

34. Gene Santoro, "The Main Man," *Guitar World*, April 1987, 39.

35. Paul Richard, "Hanging Punk: Décor and Decadence From the Rock Scene," *Washington Post*, March 29, 1980, Style, C1.

36. Carlin Romano, "Punk Hits a Sour Note," *Washington Post*, August 23, 1979, C1.

37. Jon Pareles, "Rock around the Year," *Washington Post*, December 17, 1978, Book World, E9.

38. Harry Sumrall, "DC Punk: Blasting Away at Artistic Pretention," *Washington Post*, March 14, 1979, Style, B4.

39. Quoted in Mark Andersen and Mark Jenkins, *Dance of Days: Two Decades of Punk in the Nation's Capital* (New York: Akashic, 2003), 43.

40. Fellezs, *Birds of Fire*, 34.

41. "Interview with Brian Baker," Dayafterday.com, March 30, 2010, https://day afterdaydc.wordpress.com/2010/03/30/gettin-baked/.

42. Quoted in Andersen and Jenkins, *Dance of Days*, 55.

43. Andersen and Jenkins, *Dance of Days*, 73.

44. Andersen and Jenkins, *Dance of Days*, 55.

45. Fellezs, *Birds of Fire*, 7.

46. France Winddance Twine and Charles Gallagher, "The Future of Whiteness: A Map of the 'Third Wave.'" *Ethnic and Racial Studies* 31, no. 1 (2008): 15.

47. Twine and Gallagher, "Future of Whiteness," 63.

48. "Rap Session!," *Maximum Rocknroll* no. 8, September 1983.

49. W. E. B. DuBois, *Black Reconstruction in America 1860—1880* (New York: Free Press, 1992).

50. This song, despite MacKaye's protestations, was adopted by the white supremacist wing of the punk movement. The band asserts these readings are a complete misinterpretation of their intent. Whether or not this is so is, to some extent, irrelevant to this interpretation. The ability and audacity to speak about issues of (white) race already indicates a level of privilege afforded to these band members in a way not given to, say, Bad Brains.

51. "Rap Session!," maxiumumrocknroll #8, September 1983.

52. Winddance, Twine, and Gallagher, "Future of Whiteness," 7.

53. Susan McClary, *Feminine Endings: Music, Gender, and Sexuality* (Minneapolis: University of Minnesota Press, 1991), 21.

54. Robert Palmer, "The Church of the Sonic Guitar," *Present Tense: Rock and Roll and Culture*, ed. Anthony DeCurtis (Durham, NC: Duke University Press, 1992), 15.

55. Albin J. Zak III, *The Poetics of Rock: Cutting Tracks, Making Records* (Berkeley: University of California Press, 2001), 64.

56. Teen Idles ("Deadhead," 0:33–0:53) and Minor Threat ("Screaming at a Wall," 0:50–1:05, "Betray," 2:03–2:35, and "Little Friend," 1:13–2:05) also include breakdowns. Such an inclusion should be understood as a product of the relationship between Bad Brains and Teen Idles/Minor Threat, discussed in the previous section.

57. John Pidgeon, *Eric Clapton* (London: Panther, 1976), 65.

58. David Morse, *Motown* (London: Vista, 1971), 108.

59. George Hurchella, *Going Underground: American Punk 1979-1992* (Stuart, FL: Zuo, 2006), 34.

Chapter 3. The Sounds of Stratification

1. Quoted in Mark Andersen and Mark Jenkins, *Dance of Days: Two Decades of Punk in the Nation's Capital* (New York: Akashic, 2003), 19.

2. Andersen and Jenkins, *Dance of Days*, 70.

3. Pierre Bourdieu, *Distinction: A Social Critique of the Judgment of Taste* (Cambridge, MA: Harvard University Press, 1984), 11.

4. Bourdieu, *Distinction*, 18.

5. Lawrence W. Levine, *Highbrow Lowbrow: The Emergence of Cultural Hierarchy in America* (Cambridge, MA: Harvard University Press, 1988), 8–9.

6. Caroline Coon, "Punk Rock: Rebels against the System," *Melody Maker*, August 7, 1976, 24–25.

7. Theodore Gracyk, *Rhythm and Noise: An Aesthetics of Rock* (Durham, NC: Duke University Press, 1996), 213.

8. Simon Frith, *Sound Effects: Youth, Leisure and the Politics of Rock n' Roll* (New York: Pantheon, 1981), 213–14.

9. Frith, *Sound Effects*, 214.

10. Legs McNeil and Gillian McCain, *Please Kill Me: The Uncensored Oral History of Punk* (New York: Grove, 1996), 5.

11. McNeil and McCain, *Please Kill Me*, 18.

12. Iain Chambers, *Urban Rhythms Pop Music and Popular Culture* (London: Palgrave Macmillan, 1986), 178.

13. The costs associated with symphony-type instruments include the high price of the instrument itself, the maintenance of the instrument, and the money spent on lessons and music education. Socially, playing these instruments indicates either a vaster amount of leisure time (that is, the privilege of not working as a child or adolescent and having the time to practice an instrument) or a traditionally upper-class emphasis on the value of classical music or both.

14. See Paul Fussell, *Class: A Guide through the American Status System* (New York: Touchstone, 1992).

15. Bourdieu, *Distinction*, 19.

16. Some of these bands, as well as other hardcore bands not mentioned, certainly evolved and transformed sonically, which included adding nontraditional hardcore instruments and technology. However, such changes were frequently a result of the creation and fusion of hardcore subgenres, such as trash, metal, and grind, which happened in the mid-1980s, after what I am calling the heyday of hardcore in the DC scene.

17. Mark Prindle, "Interview with Ian MacKaye," 2009, http://www.markprindle.com/mackaye-i.htm.

18. Bourdieu, *Distinction*, 47.

19. The only exception is "I Don't Want to Hear about It," which goes F#/E/F#/B/E.

20. "Rap Session!," *Maximum Rocknroll* no. 8, September 1983.

21. "Lyle Preslar of Minor Threat Answers the Questions of Doom," gimmebad vibes.com. [Site has been taken down and redirects to https://topmusic.uno/, but the interview seems not to be found there.]

22. Steven Blush, *American Hardcore: A Tribal History* (Port Townsend, WA: Feral House, 2010), 151.

23. Paul Rachman, dir., *American Hardcore* (Los Angeles: Sony, 2007).

24. US Census, "1980 Census of Population, District of Columbia, Detailed Population Characteristics: Industry of Employed Persons by Class of Worker, Hours Worked, Sex, Race, and Spanish Origin. (Washington, DC: US Department of Commerce, US Census Bureau,1980.

25. See, for example, Theodor Adorno, "On Popular Music," *Studies in Philosophy and Social Science* 9 (1941).

26. As exemplified by the city's emphasis on classical music and the top sellers on the Billboard charts of 1979, 1980, and 1981 (Hall and Oates, Kool and the Gang, Captain and Tennille, Peaches and Herb, and Gloria Gaynor), as well as the explosion of progressive rock bands like Rush, Genesis, Yes, and Jethro Tull.

27. Frith, *Sound Effects*, 158–59.

28. Four instruments by the time of 1983's *Out of Step*, which incorporated two guitars for the first time.

29. Rachman, *American Hardcore*, 2007.

30. Michael Azerrad, *Our Band Could Be Your Life: Scenes from the American Indie Underground, 1981–1991* (New York: Back Bay, 2002), 129.

31. See Melissa Mohr, *Holy Sh*t: A Brief History of Swearing* (New York: Oxford University Press, 2013).

32. *Touch and Go* no. 15, July 1981.

33. Ian MacKaye, interview in *Barrelhouse*, http://www.webdelsol.com/Barre lHouse/ianmackaye.html.

34. Andersen and Jenkins, *Dance of Days*, 91.

35. Brian Baker interview, www.dayafterday.com, March 30, 2010, https://dayafter daydc.wordpress.com/2010/03/30/gettin-baked/.

36. Azerrad, *Our Band*, 128.

37. Mark Prindle, "Interview with Ian MacKaye," *Rebel Noise*, March 18, 2009, https://www.rebelnoise.com/interviews/ian-mackaye-2009.

38. Azerrad, *Our Band*, 128.

39. Blush, *American Hardcore*, 161.

40. Mark Prindle, "Minor Threat," MarkPrindle.com, http://www.markprindle .com/minora.htm.

41. Azerrad, *Our Band*, 128.

42. *Flipside* no. 34, 1982.

43. Bob Moore in *Noise* no. 5.

44. Skip Groff, "Buzz'n the Town: Killer Bees," Limp Records, accessed January 25, 2021, http://www.30underdc.com/discogs/limp3.shtml.

45. Pitchfork, "Top 100 Albums of the 1980s," https://pitchfork.com/features/lists-and-guides/the-top-100-albums-of-the-1980s/, November 20, 2002.

46. Baker interview.

47. Howard Wuelfing, "Minor Threat," *Washington Post*, August 3, 1982, Style, B10.

48. That is, their previously discussed relationship to realism and objective of destroying the middle-class romantic ideal.

49. "Rap Session!," *Maximum Rocknroll* no. 8, September 1983.

50. Blush, *American Hardcore*, 154.

51. Vic Bondi, Dave Dictor, and Ian MacKaye, "Rap Session," *Maximum Rocknroll* no. 8, September 1983.

52. Andersen and Jenkins, *Dance of Days*, 80.

53. Gwendolyn Audrey Foster, *Class-Passing: Social Mobility in Film and Popular Culture* (Carbondale: Southern Illinois University Press, 2005), 2.

54. Karen Bettez Halnon and Saundra Cohen, "Muscles, Motorcycles and Tattoos: Gentrification in a New Frontier," *Journal of Consumer Culture* 6, no. 1 (2006): 33–56. See also Peter Hitchcock, "Passing: Henry Green and Working-Class Identity," *Modern Fiction Studies* 40 (Spring 1994): 4.

55. Halnon and Cohen, "Muscles," 34–36. This includes the fashion styles of trucker hats, wife beater tank tops, and Timberland shoes, as well as Halnon and Cohen's focus, the reappropriation of the working-class symbols of motorcycles, muscles, and tattoos.

56. Hitchcock, "Passing," 5.

57. Gloria Stewart, "I'm a Revolutionary!," *Daily Mirror* (December 19, 1977), 12–13.

58. Franco Modigliani, "Reagan's Economic Policies: A Critique," *Oxford Economic Papers* 40, no. 3 (1988): 397–426.

Chapter 4. Masculinity as Music

1. Michael S. Kimmel, "Invisible Masculinity," *Society* 30, no. 6 (1993): 28–35.

2. Kimmel, "Invisible Masculinity," 30.

3. Ellen Willis, *Out of the Vinyl Deeps* (Minneapolis: University of Minnesota Press, 2011), 143.

4. Susan McClary, *Feminine Endings: Music, Gender, and Sexuality* (Minneapolis: University of Minnesota Press, 1991), 139.

5. McClary, *Feminine Endings*, 16.

6. Albin Zak III, *The Poetics of Rock: Cutting Tracks, Making Records* (Berkeley: University of California Press, 2001), 62.

7. J. D. Considine, "New Paths for Punk," *Washington Post*, August 16, 1984.

8. Steve Waksman, *Instruments of Desire: The Electric Guitar and the Shaping of Musical Experience* (Cambridge, MA: Harvard University Press, 1999), 5.

9. See Waksman, *Instruments of Desire*.

10. "100 Greatest Guitarists," *Rolling Stone*, November 23, 2011.

11. Waksman, *Instruments of Desire*, 223.

12. Theodore Gracyk, *Rhythm and Noise: An Aesthetics of Rock* (London: I. B. Tauris, 1996), 120–22.

13. Mark Andersen and Mark Jenkins, *Dance of Days: Two Decades of Punk in the Nation's Capital* (New York: Akashic, 2003), 73.

14. Richard Harrington, "Slamdancing in the Big City," *Washington Post*, July 19, 1981.

15. Jacques Attali, *Noise: The Political Economy of Music* (Minneapolis: University of Minnesota Press, 1985), 26.

16. This analysis is, I believe, still consistent with Waksman's cogent evaluation of the electric guitar as technophallus, which I employed here and in a previous chapter. In part, Waksman does contend that the elongated, phallic neck is a symbol of male sexuality, but the majority of his argument suggests that this gendered sexuality emerges from men's supremacy over technology, as well as its use in the performance of overt male sexuality (à la Jimi Hendrix and Robert Plant).

17. As quoted in Andersen and Jenkins, *Dance of Days*, 80.

18. These otherwise differences in time would be insignificant in a typical piece of music, but within the average length of an S.O.A. song (36 seconds to 1:16), seemingly minuscule variances have a greater importance relative to their length.

19. Because of the tempo of GI's songs and, indeed, most hardcore punk songs, sustaining any smaller of a rhythmic subdivision on the cymbals is nearly impossible.

20. See Raymond William, *The Long Revolution* (London: Cox and Wyman, 1961); Simon Frith, *Sound Effects: Youth, Leisure and the Politics of Rock n' Roll* (New York: Pantheon, 1981); Susan McClary, *Feminine Endings*.

21. See Matt Dean, *The Drum: A History* (Lanham, MD: Scarecrow, 2012); Kofi Agawu, *African Rhythm* (Cambridge: Cambridge University Press, 1995); Veronica Doubleday, "Sounds of Power: An Overview of Musical Instruments and Gender," *Ethnomusicology Forum* (2008): 3–39.

22. Richard Harrington, "Recent Releases from DC Rockers," *Washington Post*, June 26, 1983.

23. Michael Azerrad, *Our Band Could Be Your Life: Scenes from the American Indie Underground, 1981–1991* (New York: Back Bay, 2002), 13.

24. Harrington, "Recent Releases."

25. Robert Duncan, *The Noise: Notes from a Rock 'n Roll Era* (New York: Ticknor and Fields, 1984), 46.

26. This is not to argue that any of the band members was aware of the linguistic implications of their word choices; nor do I mean to contend that a strict phonological analysis of their lyrics is a productive or meaningful way to understand their resonance. However, this argument is meant to discuss the unconscious, socially constructed sonic meanings spoken language has.

27. Harrington, "Slamdancing."

28. It is important to note, however, that even with the scarcity of relationship- or sex-themed lyrics, the songs that do touch on such subjects are always heterosexual in perspective, reinforcing the assumption of heteronormativity both in both mainstream culture and in the subculture of DC hardcore punk rock.

29. Henry Rollins, live online discussion, *Washington Post*, January 11, 2006.

30. Mike, email communication, 2013.

31. Andersen and Jenkins, *Dance of Days*, 63.

32. Joseph Roach, *Cities of the Dead* (New York: Columbia University Press, 1996), 41.

33. Melissa Dittman, "Anger across the Gender Divide," *Monitor on Psychology* 34 (2003): 52.

34. Antonio Gramsci, *Selections from the Prison Notebooks of Antonio Gramsci* (New York: International, 1971).

35. Alfred Gell, *Art and Agency: An Anthropological Theory* (Oxford, UK: Clarendon, 1998), 7–17.

36. Or at least partially female; Steve Waksman's convincing analysis argues that the electric guitar should be understood as a technophallus, with its long neck symbolizing the phallus and its technological power quelled and reappropriated by masculine prowess. Indeed, I utilized this claim in analyzing the racialized hypersexualization of Bad Brains in chapter 3. However, much of Waksman's argument still dovetails with my own, particularly when we detach the physical instrument from the musician who plays it.

37. Mary Clawson, "When Women Play the Bass: Instrument Specialization and Gender Interpretation in Alternative Rock Music," *Gender and Society* 13 (1999): 201.

38. Judy Wajcman, "Reflections on Gender and Technology Studies: In What State Is the Art?," *Social Studies of Science* 30, no. 3 (2000): 454.

39. Jennifer M. Brown, "De-gendering the Electronic Soundscape: Women, Power and Technology in Contemporary Music," master's thesis, Southern Cross University, Lismore, Australia, 1995.

40. Zak, *Poetics of Rock*, 65.

41. Frith, *Sound Effects*, 161.

42. Philip Tagg, "Subjectivity and Soundscape, Motorbikes and Music," in *The Popular Music Studies Reader*, ed. Andy Bennett, Barry Shank, and Jason Toynbee (London: Routledge, 2006), 44–45.

43. It is not a coincidence that these professions, where yelling is not only allowed but also a requirement of the job, are nearly exclusively male-occupied realms.

44. Andersen and Jenkins, *Dance of Days*, 72.

45. Steven Blush, *American Hardcore: A Tribal History* (Port Townsend, WA: Feral House, 2010), 164.

46. As quoted in Azerrad, *Our Band*, 13.

47. Andreas G. Philaretou and Katherine R. Allen, "Reconstructing Masculinity and Sexuality," *Journal of Men Studies* 9, No. 3 (2001): 309.

48. A scant few women occupied cabinet positions during this time: In 1979 Patricia Roberts Harris was secretary of Health and Human Services and Shirley Hufstedler was the secretary of Education under Carter; Elizabeth Dole was secretary of Transportation and Margaret Heckler was secretary of Health and Human Services in 1983 under Reagan. However, when there were thirteen possible cabinet positions, a mere two women in those positions amounts to an egregious ratio.

49. Jennifer E. Manning and Ida A. Brudnick, "Women in the United States Congress, 1917–2013," Report no. RL30261 (Washington, DC: Congressional Research Service, 2013), 99.

Chapter 5. Do-It-Yourself Cultural Production

1. Thorstein Veblen, *The Theory of the Leisure Class* (Boston: Houghton Mifflin, 1973).

2. Thorstein Veblen, *The Theory of the Leisure Class* (Boston: Houghton Mifflin, 1973).

3. "Party N' Hearty in DC," *Touch and Go* no. 16, 1981.

4. Steven Blush, *American Hardcore: A Tribal History* (Port Townsend, WA: Feral House, 2010), 162.

5. Mike Heath, as quoted in Mark Andersen and Mark Jenkins, *Dance of Days: Two Decades of Punk in the Nation's Capital* (New York: Akashic, 2003), 23.

6. Andersen and Jenkins, *Dance of Days*, 35–36.

7. Howard Wuelfing, as quoted in Andersen and Jenkins, *Dance of Days*, 42.

8. Blush, *American Hardcore*, 321.

9. Tom Lyle, "80's DC Hardcore Scene Kids," January 26, 2020, https://www.facebook .com/groups/40186248140/user/1337572381.

10. Lyle, "80's DC Hardcore."

11. Michael Azerrad, *Our Band Could Be Your Life: Scenes from the American Indie Underground, 1981–1991* (New York: Back Bay, 2002), 151.

12. As quoted in D. A. Ensminger, *Visual Vitriol: The Street Art and Subcultures of the Punk and Hardcore Generation* (Jackson: University Press of Mississippi, 2011), 3.

13. As quoted in Blush, *American Hardcore*, 155.

14. Sean Reveron, "A 80's and 90's DC Punk Flyer Explosion!," *CVLT Nation*, December 7, 2015, https://cvltnation.com/168930–2/.

15. Ensminger, *Visual Vitriol*, 5.

16. Blush, *American Hardcore*, 335.

17. Ensminger, *Visual Vitriol*, 9–10.

18. Blush, *American Hardcore*, 336.

19. Ferdinand de Saussure, *Cours de linguistique générale* (Wiesbaden, Ger.: Otto Harrassowitz, 1989).

20. Alberto Melucci, "The Process of Collective Identity," in *Social Movements and Culture*, ed. Hank Johnston and Bert Klandermans, 41–63 (Minneapolis: University of Minnesota Press, 1995).

21. Email correspondence.

22. Email correspondence.

23. Some may argue that Chalk Circle, an all-female group composed of singer/guitarist Sharon Cheslow, drummer Anne Bonafede, guitarist/vocalist Mary Green, and a rotating bassist of Jan Pumphrey, Chris Niblack, or Tamera Lyndsay, should be considered. And although their music is certainly punk rock, it does not correspond with the hardcore sound. As Cheslow noted in David Malitz, "Revisiting Chalk Circle, D.C.'s First All-Female Punk Band," *Washington Post*, May 12, 2011, "initially we were all part of the DC punk/hardcore scene and people were very open minded. We all co-existed harmoniously until the hardcore sound became more codified."

24. As quoted in Andersen and Jenkins, *Dance of Days*, 93.

25. It should be noted that Cynthia Connelly had a substantial role in the cultural narrative production of DC hardcore as the unofficial scene photographer. Her photographs, and her accompanying book *Banned in DC: Photos and Anecdotes from the DC Punk Underground (79–85)* (New York, NY: Universe, 2005), compiled with Sharon Cheslow and Leslie Clague, helped shape the historical collective identity and narrative of the DC hardcore scene. Connelly also described helping Ian MacKaye lay out Minor Threat's first 7" sleeve, although, as she notes, her mother chided her for doing so without getting paid, making it a gendered form of unpaid labor.

26. As quoted in Blush, *American Hardcore*, 155.

27. As quoted in Greta Weber, "Zines Deserve a Better Place in DC Punk History. Here's Why." *Washingtonian*, August 2016, https://www.washingtonian.com/2016/08/04/zines-deserve-a-bigger-place-in-dc-punk-history-heres-why/.

28. As quoted in Blush, *American Hardcore*, 155.

29. Teen Idles' Nathan Strajcek was also a part of the creation of Dischord; however, by the time the label moved to its still-permanent address in Arlington in 1981, he was more and more disillusioned with the label, ultimately withdrawing completely.

30. And still does—Dischord Records continues to be the premier independent label in and for Washington, DC, releasing only local bands and shipping their music worldwide.

31. Stacy Thompson, "Market Failure: Punk Economics, Early and Late," *College Literature* 28, no. 2 (2001): 48.

32. Blush, *American Hardcore*, 150.

33. Ian MacKaye and Jeff Nelson, liner notes to *Four Old 7"s on a 12"* (Washington, DC: Dischord Records, 1984), LP.

34. As quoted in Andersen and Jenkins, *Dance of Days*, 88.

35. Although GI's *Legless Bull*, as well as two tracks for the DC hardcore compilation *Flex Your Head*, was with Dischord, all subsequent GI albums were released by various other labels. MacKaye, however, did produce 1983's *Boycott Stabb*, which was released by Fountain of Youth Records.

36. Jacques Attali, *Noise: The Political Economy of Music* (Minneapolis: University of Minnesota Press, 1985), 92.

37. Attali, 100.

38. Quoted in Daniel Sinker, ed., *We Owe You Nothing: Punk Planet, the Collected Interviews* (Chicago: Punk Planet, 2008), 8.

39. This is not to say, of course, that those differences in identity don't affect the interpretation or appreciation of the music. Clearly, divergences in social and personal histories shape not only what genres of music one is more likely to consume but also *how* one will consume and use said music; nor does this nullify the fact that recorded music itself never varies.

40. Michael Chanan, *Repeated Takes: A Short History of Recording and Its Effects on Music* (London: Verso, 1995), 13.

41. As quoted in Blush, *American Hardcore*, 329.

42. *Maximum Rocknroll* no. 10, December 1983.

43. Despite this complicated relationship between economic success and artistic authenticity, after Minor Threat broke up, Dischord Record has continued to be not only the most important DC record label, with more than seventy-five bands signed, but also one of the only independent labels that has not folded.

44. As quoted in Andersen and Jenkins, *Dance of Days*, 112.

Chapter 6. Straightedge

1. See Ross Haenfler's *Straightedge: Clean Living, Hardcore Punk and Social Change* (New Brunswick, NJ: Rutgers University Press, 2006), Robert T. Wood's *Straightedge Youth: Complexity and Contradictions of a Subculture* (Syracuse, NY: Syracuse University Press, 2006), Gabriel Kuhn's *Sober Living for the Revolution: Hardcore Punk, Straightedge and Radical Politics* (2010), and Beth Lahickey's *All Ages: Reflections on Straightedge* (Huntington Beach, CA: Revelation, 1997).

2. Wood, *Straightedge Youth*, 7.

3. This is not to presume that there is some sort of unifying doctrine of straightedge; indeed, the philosophy is marked by its individualistic approach to what clean living entails. Furthermore, straightedge has transformed significantly since Minor Threat's genesis; post-1983 straightedge is much more militant and explicit in its adoption of social justice causes, including vegetarianism, environmentalism, and issues of poverty. This section instead focuses on the idea of straightedge first espoused by Minor Threat and embodied by the DC hardcore scene before 1983.

4. As quoted in Michael Azerrad, *Our Band Could Be Your Life: Scenes from the American Indie Underground, 1981–1991* (New York: Back Bay, 2002), 121.

5. As quoted in Andrea Kurland, "Getting Deep with Ian MacKaye, the Godfather of DIY Culture," *Huck*, May 27, 2020, https://www.huckmag.com/art-and-culture/music-2/ian-mackaye-survival-issue-interview/.

6. Wood, *Straightedge Youth*, 96.

7. Mark Andersen and Mark Jenkins, *Dance of Days: Two Decades of Punk in the Nation's Capital* (New York: Akashic, 2003), 41–46, 60–63, 86–87.

8. As quoted in Wood, *Straightedge Youth*, 98.

9. Wood, *Straightedge Youth*, 100.

10. As quoted in Andersen and Jenkins, *Dance of Days*, 21.

11. It is important to note that not everyone with the DC hardcore scene was straightedge. Indeed, it is unclear exactly how many or what percentage of the scene identified as straightedge. However, as MacKaye himself noted, this did not negatively affect the scene: "People who were involved with Minor Threat and the DC hardcore scene, people who were supportive of the straightedge scene, were totally not straight at all, they just were into it and supported the idea that kids should see shows and that alcohol should not be the deciding factor. They respected our decision; they were our friends. And it was more about respecting each other's individual choices."

12. As quoted in Kurland, "Getting Deep."

13. As quoted in Lahickey, *All Ages*, 74–76.

14. Steven Blush, *American Hardcore: A Tribal History* (Port Townsend, WA: Feral House, 2010), 310.

15. As quoted in Lahickey, *All Ages*, 107–8.

16. Wood, *Straightedge Youth*, 75–76.

17. See Kathleen Gerson, *No Man's Land: Men's Changing Commitments to Family and Work* (New York: Basic Books, 1993); Michael S. Kimmel, ed., *The Sexual Self: The Construction of Sexual Scripts* (Nashville, TN: Vanderbilt University Press, 2007).

18. As quoted in Laura Barcella, "No Drugs, No Drink, No Problem—Straight Edge Then and Now," *The Fix*, July 9, 2014, https://www.thefix.com/content/straight-edge -fugazi-ian-mackaye-hardcore-sober-punk-laura-barcella2024.

19. Amy C. Wilkins, "Masculinity Dilemmas: Sexuality and Intimacy Talk among Christians and Goths," *Signs* 34, no. 2 (Winter 2009): 354.

20. *Maximum Rocknroll* no. 219, August 2001.

21. Andreas G. Philaretou and Katherine R. Allen, "Reconstructing Masculinity and Sexuality," *Journal of Men's Studies* 9, no. 3 (Spring 2001), 301–21.

22. As quoted in Azerrad, *Our Band*, 139.

23. Lois A. West, "Negotiating Masculinities in American Drinking Subcultures," *Journal of Men's Studies* 9, no. 3 (Spring 2001): 371–92.

24. As quoted in Blush, *American Hardcore*, 159.

25. Blush, *American Hardcore*, 159.

26. David Riesman, *The Lonely Crowd: Study of the Changing American Character* (New Haven, CT: Yale University Press, 1950).

27. National Institutes of Health, Division of Epidemiology and Prevention Research, *Drug Use among Ethnic/Racial Minorities*, NIH Publication No. 98–3888 (Rockville, MD: National Institutes of Health, Division of Epidemiology and Prevention Research, 1995), 1.

28. Megan E Patrick, Patrick Wightman, Robert F. Schoeni, and John E. Schulenberg, "Socioeconomic Status and Substance Use among Young Adults: A Comparison across Constructs and Drugs," *Journal of Studies on Alcohol and Drugs* 73, no. 5 (September 2012): 772–82.

29. As quoted in Wood, *Straightedge Youth*, 96.

30. As quoted in Andersen and Jenkins, *Dance of Days*, 113.

31. See Charis Eisen, Keiko Ishii, and Hidefumi Hitokoto, (2018). "Socioeconomic Status, Reactions to Choice Deprivation in Group Contexts, and the Role of Perceived Restrictions on Personal Freedom," in *Venture into Cross-Cultural Psychology: Proceedings from the 23rd Congress of the International Association for Cross-Cultural Psychology*, ed. Minoru Karasawa, Masaki Yuki, Keiko Ishii, Yukiko Uchida, Kosuke Sato, and Wolfgang Friedlmeier, https://scholarworks.gvsu.edu/iaccp_papers/153/; Nicole M. Stephens, Stephanie A. Fryberg, and Hazel Rose Markus, "When Choice Does Not Equal Freedom: A Sociocultural Analysis of Agency in Working-Class American Contexts," *Social Psychological and Personality Science* 2, no. 1 (2011): 33–41.

32. Barcella, "No Drugs."

33. As quoted in Lahickey, *All Ages*, 74.

34. R. W. Connell and James W. Messerschmidt. "Hegemonic Masculinity: Rethinking the Concept." *Gender and Society* 19, no. 6 (2005): 829–59.

35. As quoted in Azerrad, *Our Band*, 136.

36. Azerrad, *Our Band*, 136; Tim Lomas, Tina Cartwright, Trudi Edginton, and Damien Ridge, "New Ways of Being a Man: 'Positive' Hegemonic Masculinity in Meditation-Based Communities of Practice," *Men and Masculinities* 19, no. 3 (August 2016), 289–310.

37. For example, J. Patrick Williams, "Authentic Identities: Straightedge Subculture, Music, and the Internet," *Journal of Contemporary Ethnography* 35, no. 2 (April 2006): 173–200; Darrell Irwin, "The Straight Edge Subculture: Examining the Youths' Drug-free Way," *Journal of Drug Issues* 29, no. 2 (Spring 1999): 365–80; Jason Torkelson, "Life after (Straightedge) Subculture," *Qualitative Sociology* 33, no. 3 (May 2010): 257–74; Pam Nilan, "Straight Edge as an Australian Youth Subculture," in *Australian Sociological Association (TASA) Conference, University of Western Australia and Murdoch University*, December 2006 (Hawthorn, Australia: Sociological Association of Australia, 2006), 1–8; Michelle Weber, *Walking on the Edge: A Phenomenology of the Straight Edge Music Subculture*, Phd diss., California State University, Fullerton, 2004.

38. Haenfler, *Straightedge*, 76.

39. This refers to the store Hot Topic, which is dedicated to selling a mainstream, fashion-based, detoothed version of punk and goth, primarily to teenagers. Other examples of such commodification include the leather jacket and the biker subculture, the flannel and grunge, and "girl power" as a mantra of the Spice Girls and Britney Spears appropriated from Riot Grrrl, and commercialization includes rave subculture (to EDM money-making machine), hip-hop (to mainstream music mogul), and even drag subculture (*Rupual's Drag Race*, *We're Here*, etc.).

40. Examples include the criminalization of graffiti that emerged from hip-hop culture, the focus on illicit drug use in the rave subculture, the deviancy of BDSM subculture, and the illegal use of public property in skateboarding subculture.

41. For example, the environmental movement and LGBTQ movement's inclusion and dilution in the Democratic party platform and the Tea Party movement in the Republican party.

42. As quoted in Lahickey, *All Ages*, 99.

43. As quoted in Daniel Dylan Wray, "Ian MacKaye Doesn't Do Many Interviews, but This Is One of His Most Enlightening," *Loud and Quiet*, accessed January 4, 2021, https://www.loudandquiet.com/interview/ian-mackaye-dischord/.

44. Sidney Tarrow, *Power in Movement* (Cambridge: Cambridge University Press, 1994), 85.

45. Jack Goldstone, "More Social Movements or Fewer? Beyond Political Opportunity Structures to Relational Fields," *Theory and Society* 33, nos. 3–4 (June 2004): 357.

46. As quoted in Blush, *American Hardcore*, 154.

47. Review of *Minor Disturbance*, punknews.org, January 25, 2008.

48. As quoted in Wray, *Loud and Quiet*.

49. Quoted in Wood, *Straightedge Youth*, 96–97.

50. As quoted in Azerrad, *Our Band*, 136.

51. As quoted in Azerrad, *Our Band*, 135–36.

52. Haenfler, *Straightedge*, 9.

53. As quoted in Lahickey, *All Ages*, 99.

54. As quoted in Azerrad, *Our Band*, 136.

55. Which MacKaye, over and over again, insists that it was; he maintains that straightedge, as well as his music, was in no way a demand, a rallying cry for communal identity, or an explicit attempt to enact political change. As he noted to Beth Lahickey in her collection of interviews on straightedge, "In my mind I wasn't interested in it being a movement. It ran conversely to my initial idea that it was a concert of individuals, as opposed to a movement. I felt like a movement had to have some sort of aim" (Lahickey, *All Ages*, 102).

56. Ron Eyerman and Andrew Jamison, *Music and Social Movements: Mobilizing Traditions in the Twentieth Century* (Cambridge: Cambridge University Press, 1998).

57. Alberto Melucci, "The Process of Collective Identity," in *Social Movements and Culture*, ed. Hank Johnston and Bert Klandermans (Minneapolis: University of Minnesota Press, 1995), 115.

Chapter 7. Embodying (White, Middle-Class) Masculinity

1. As quoted in Mark Andersen and Mark Jenkins, *Dance of Days: Two Decades of Punk in the Nation's Capital* (New York: Akashic, 2003), 89.

2. *Now What*, July 10, 1981, Michelle Smith Performing Arts Library, D.C. Punk and Indie Fanzine Collection, Collection 0195-SCPA, University of Maryland, College Park.

3. *Punk Planet* 41, 2001, https://archive.org/details/punk_planet_41/page/n1/mode/2up.

4. Michel Foucault, *Discipline and Punish: The Birth of the Prison* (New York: Random House, 1977), 143.

5. Michel Foucault, *The History of Sexuality*. Vol. 1, *An Introduction* (London: Allen Lane, 1979), 94.

6. Hippie subculture is the notable exception.

7. Kobena Mercer, *Welcome to the Jungle: New Position in Black Cultural Studies* (New York: Routledge, 1994), 249.

8. Richard Harrington, "Slamdancing in the Big City," *Washington Post*, July 19, 1981, G1–2.

9. Quoted in Blush Steven Blush, *American Hardcore: A Tribal History* (Port Townsend, WA: Feral House, 2010), 25.

10. Blush, *American Hardcore*, 47.

11. It is important to note that in the comprehensive photographic history of the DC hardcore scene, the few females who were in the scene were almost never wearing chains, combat boots, or spiked leather cuffs. This style was almost exclusively in the male domain.

12. Andersen and Jenkins, *Dance of Days*, 73.

13. Artificial Peace was a short-lived DC hardcore band that contributed songs to the DC hardcore sampler "Flex Your Head" and put out one split 7" LP under Dischord's label. Soon after they formed in 1981, the band dissolved, with members joining other local bands, including GI and a post-'83 DC punk band, Marginal Man. In fact, as the lead singer of Marginal Man, Steve Polcari, also often performed shirtless, as documented in his March 11, 1983, show at Georgetown University's Hall of Nations (Cynthia Connolly, *Banned in DC: Photos and Anecdotes from the DC Punk Underground [79–83]* [Washington, DC: Sun Dog Propaganda, 1988]).

14. Harrington, "Slamdancing."

15. Karen Bettez Halnon and Saundra Cohen, "Muscles, Motorcycles and Tattoos: Gentrification in a New Frontier," *Journal of Consumer Culture* (2006): 41–43.

16. Including Bert Queiroz of the Untouchables, members of Black Market Baby, Danny Ingram of Youth Brigade, Dante Ferrando of Broken Cross, Deadline.

17. Halnon and Cohen, "Muscles," 41 (first quote), 42 (second quote).

18. Lynne Luciano, *Looking Good: Male Body Image in Modern America* (New York: Macmillan, 2002).

19. As quoted in Andersen and Jenkins, *Dance of Days*, 34.

20. As a sidenote, denim has a long and storied history of and correlation with iconic and conventional masculinity. For the cowboy, the biker, the blue-collar worker, and the teenage rebel, jeans have come to symbolize a certain masculine potency, a ruggedness and power that seems to bridge the gap between the seemingly disparate cultural paradigms of manliness.

21. All these photographs are chronicled in Cynthia Connelly's photographic history, *Banned in DC*.

22. George Hurchella, *Going Underground: American Punk 1979–1992* (Stuart, FL: Zuo, 2006), 63.

23. Risto Moisio, Eric J. Arnould, and James W. Gentry, "Productive Consumption in the Class-Mediated Construction of Domestic Masculinity: Do-It-Yourself (DIY) Home Improvement in Men's Identity Work," *Journal of Consumer Research* 40, no. 2 (2013): 298–316.

24. See Sally Ann Ness, *Body, Movement, and Culture: Kinesthetic and Visual Symbolism in a Philippine Community* (Philadelphia: University of Pennsylvania Press, 1992); Cynthia J. Novack. *Sharing the Dance: Contact Improvisation and American Culture* (Madison: University of Wisconsin Press, 1990).

25. Richard Harrington, "Stiff Little Fingers," *Washington Post*, October 21, 1980.

26. Harrington, "Slamdancing."

27. Paul Rachman, dir., *American Hardcore: The History of American Punk Rock 1980–1986* (Los Angeles: Sony Classic Pictures, 2006), DVD.

28. Tayana L. Hardin, "Josephine Baker and the Shadow of Spectacle," *Dance Chronicle* 38, no. 2 (2015): 179–203.

29. "Hardcore Mettle: Bad Brains' Strange Survival Tale," *SPIN*, November 29, 2012.

30. Andersen and Jenkins, *Dance of Days*, 37.

31. Simon Frith, *Sound Effects: Youth, Leisure, and the Politics of Rock 'n' Roll* (New York: Pantheon, 1981), 19.

32. Frith, *Sound Effects*, 19.

33. Blush, *American Hardcore*, 32.

34. In part, of course, because the quality of video was shoddy, because it was shot by a fan without the assistance of professional equipment or the now-ubiquitous iPhone.

35. Rachman, *American Hardcore*.

36. As quoted in Blush, *American Hardcore*, 156.

37. Rachman, *American Hardcore*.

38. Ryan Kearne, "An Incomplete Oral History of Henry Rollins' D.C. Years," WJLA, https://wjla.com/news/entertainment/a-brief-oral-history-of-henry-rollins-s-brief-career-in-d-c--8387.

39. Andersen and Jenkins, *Dance of Days*, 96.

40. *Maximum Rocknroll* 1, no. 3, November–December 1982.

41. William Tsitsos, "Rules of Rebellion: Slam Dancing, Moshing, and the American Alternative Scene," *Popular Music* 18 (1999): 397.

42. Email communication.

43. Email communication.

44. Email communication.

45. Email communication.

46. As quoted in Andersen and Jenkins, *Dance of Days*, 92.

47. Andersen and Jenkins, *Dance of Days*, 93.

48. Joseph Roach, *Cities of the Dead* (New York: Columbia University Press, 1996), 41.

49. Kenneth Eldred, "Noise at the Year 2000," Fifth International Congress on Noise As an International Problem, Stockholm, Sweden, August 21–28, 1988.

50. The Noise Control Act of 1972, 42 USC 4901 (passed October 27, 1972).

51. Maureen E. Loughran, *Community Powered Resistance: Radio, Music Scenes and Musical Activism in Washington, DC* (PhD diss., Brown University, 2008), 152.

52. Michael Azerrad, *Our Band Could Be Your Life: Scenes from the American Indie Underground, 1981–1991* (New York: Back Bay, 2002), 151–52.

53. As quoted in Andersen and Jenkins, *Dance of Days*, 66.

54. Quoted in Azerrad, *Our Band*, 125.

55. "Rap Session!," *Maximum Rocknroll* no. 8, September 1983.

Chapter 8. The Transformation of Hardcore

1. As quoted in Steven Blush, *American Hardcore: A Tribal History* (Port Townsend, WA: Feral House, 2010), 175.

2. As quoted in Paul Rachman, dir., *American Hardcore* (Los Angeles: Sony, 2007).

3. As quoted in Mark Andersen and Mark Jenkins, *Dance of Days: Two Decades of Punk in the Nation's Capital* (New York: Akashic, 2003), 124.

4. As quoted in John Dugan, "End on End: Rites of Spring," *Stop Smiling Magazine* 37 (the DC Issue), November 3, 2008, http://stopsmilingonline.com/story_detail .php?id=1170.

5. As quoted in Louis Pattison, "Rites of Spring and the Summer that Changed Punk Rock," *Guardian*, November 27, 2012, https://www.theguardian.com/music/ musicblog/2012/nov/27/rites-spring-summer-punk-rock.

6. As quoted in Andersen and Jenkins, *Dance of Days*, 153.

7. Chad Stone, Danilo Trisi, Arloc Sherman, and William Chen, "A Guide to Statistics on Historical Trends in Income Inequality" (Washington, DC: Center on Budget and Policy Priorities), April 17, 2004.

8. US Census Bureau, Historical Poverty Tables, https://www.census.gov/data/ tables/time-series/demo/income-poverty/historical-poverty-people.html.

9. Email communication.

10. Email communication.

11. Email communication.

12. Email communication.

13. Email communication.

14. According to Andersen and Jenkins (*Dance of Days*), Pickering began sending out photocopied letters, thanks to the free copy machine and stamps at her internship, to members of the first-wave hardcore scene that read "Be on your toes. This is . . . REVOLUTION SUMMER," inspiring the name.

15. As quoted in Blush, *American Hardcore*, 175.

16. As quoted in Andersen and Jenkins, *Dance of Days*, 173.

17. Andersen and Jenkins, *Dance of Days*, 181.

18. This label "emocore" is nearly universally rebuffed by every single band given that label. MacKaye himself called the label "the stupidest fucking thing I've ever heard of." Despite that, the genre label has stuck and, like many musical categories, has widened so much in the past thirty-plus years as to make it nearly unrecognizable. In DC, emocore was a necessary shorthand to distinguish hardcore from posthardcore.

19. Jim H. "Beefeater," *Vinyl Mine Blog*, August 27, 2004, https://vinyljourney.blog spot.com/search?q=Beefeater.

20. As quoted in Blush, *American Hardcore*, 175.

21. Louis Pattison, "Rites of Spring and the Summer That Changed Punk Rock," *Guardian*, November 27, 2012.

22. Ian McCaleb, review of "Rites of Spring," https://trouserpress.com/reviews/ rites-of-spring/.

23. Scream, interview, *Flipside* no. 36, December 1982.

24. Indeed, neuroscientists have discovered that the part of our brain that tracks and processes melody, the rostromedial prefrontal cortex, is the same area of the brain that stores emotion, as well as short- and long-term memory.

25. Joseph Neff, "(Re)Graded on a Curve: Rites of Spring, *Six Song Demo*," review of *Six Song Demo*, by Rites of Spring, *Vinyl District*, November 18, 2013, http://www .thevinyldistrict.com/storefront/2013/11/regraded-curve-rites-spring-six-song-demo/.

26. Jim H. "Beefeater," *Vinyl Mine Blog*, August 27, 2004, https://vinyljourney.blog spot.com/search?q=Beefeater.

27. *Touch and Go* no. 21, April 1983.

28. Gunnston, *This Is Albatross: Reunions, Breakups, and Interviews Blog*, January 28, 2012, https://thisisalbatross.com/interview-marginal-man.html.

29. See Kenny Inouye and Andre Lee's comments in *End Times* no. 1, 1983.

30. *Inside View* no. 2, 1983.

31. Andersen and Jenkins, *Dance of Days*, 167.

32. Jacques Attali, *Noise: The Political Economy of Music* (Minneapolis: University of Minnesota Press, 1985), 5.

33. As quoted in Andersen and Jenkins, *Dance of Days*, 191.

34. Andersen and Jenkins, *Dance of Days*, 166.

35. See, for example, Andersen and Jenkins, *Dance of Days*; Blush, *American Hardcore*; Rachman, *American Hardcore*.

36. Johanna Fateman and Kathleen Hanna, eds., *The Riot Grrrl Collection* (New York: Feminist Press at CUNY, 2013); Sara Marcus, *Girls to the Front: The True Story of the Riot Grrrl Revolution* (New York: HarperPerennial, 2010),

37. As quoted in Anthony Pappalardo, "Break Down the Walls: How the Youth Crew Aesthetic and Ethos Disrupted Punk's Status Quo," *Hundreds*, June 12, 2017, https://

thehundreds.com/blogs/content/how-the-youth-crew-aesthetic-ethos-disrupted-punk-status-quo.

38. Pappalardo, "Break Down the Walls."

39. *Maximum Rocknroll* no. 103, December 1991.

40. Void's name was taken from Black Sabbath's "Into the Void," and Henry Rollins has discussed the important influence of the band on Black Flag's second album.

41. Michael Azerrad, *Our Band Could Be Your Life: Scenes from the American Indie Underground, 1981–1991* (New York: Back Bay, 2002), 40.

42. As quoted in David Konow, "Exploring the Roots of the Mid-80s Metal/Punk Crossover with Kerry King, Scott Ian, and Gary Holt," *Vice*, October 9, 2015, https://www.vice.com/en_us/article/6vgykd/crossover-metal-punk-roots.

43. David Fricke, "Double Nickels on the Dime," album review, *Rolling Stone*, January 22, 1997, https://www.rollingstone.com/music/music-album-reviews/double-nickels-on-the-dime-94788/.

44. As quoted in Azerrad, *Our Band*, 76.

45. *Revolver* staff, "How Melvins Invented Sludge: 'Ugly Spawn of Punk and Metal,'" *Revolver*, October 31, 2019, https://www.revolvermag.com/music/how-melvins-invented-sludge-ugly-spawn-punk-and-metal. See also J. J. Anselmi, *Doomed to Fail: The Incredibly Loud History of Doom, Sludge, and Post-metal* (Los Angeles: Rare Bird, 2020).

46. "The Father the Son and the Holy Grunge," *Guitar World*, February 1995.

47. Where, it should be noted, this author taught at its in-house Corcoran College of Art and Design and where Ian MacKaye came to speak to a small group of my students studying the intersection of popular culture, intersectionality, and politics.

Index

SHAYNA L. MASKELL is an assistant professor in the School of Integrative Studies at George Mason University.

MUSIC IN AMERICAN LIFE

Only a Miner: Studies in Recorded Coal-Mining Songs   *Archie Green*
Great Day Coming: Folk Music and the American Left   *R. Serge Denisoff*
John Philip Sousa: A Descriptive Catalog of His Works   *Paul E. Bierley*
The Hell-Bound Train: A Cowboy Songbook   *Glenn Ohrlin*
Oh, Didn't He Ramble: The Life Story of Lee Collins, as Told to Mary Collins
    Edited by Frank J. Gillis and John W. Miner
American Labor Songs of the Nineteenth Century   *Philip S. Foner*
Stars of Country Music: Uncle Dave Macon to Johnny Rodriguez
    Edited by Bill C. Malone and Judith McCulloh
Git Along, Little Dogies: Songs and Songmakers of the American West   *John I. White*
A Texas-Mexican *Cancionero*: Folksongs of the Lower Border   *Américo Paredes*
San Antonio Rose: The Life and Music of Bob Wills   *Charles R. Townsend*
Early Downhome Blues: A Musical and Cultural Analysis   *Jeff Todd Titon*
An Ives Celebration: Papers and Panels of the Charles Ives Centennial Festival-
    Conference   *Edited by H. Wiley Hitchcock and Vivian Perlis*
Sinful Tunes and Spirituals: Black Folk Music to the Civil War   *Dena J. Epstein*
Joe Scott, the Woodsman-Songmaker   *Edward D. Ives*
Jimmie Rodgers: The Life and Times of America's Blue Yodeler   *Nolan Porterfield*
Early American Music Engraving and Printing: A History of Music Publishing
    in America from 1787 to 1825, with Commentary on Earlier and Later
    Practices   *Richard J. Wolfe*
Sing a Sad Song: The Life of Hank Williams   *Roger M. Williams*
Long Steel Rail: The Railroad in American Folksong   *Norm Cohen*
Resources of American Music History: A Directory of Source Materials
    from Colonial Times to World War II   *D. W. Krummel, Jean Geil, Doris J. Dyen,
    and Deane L. Root*
Tenement Songs: The Popular Music of the Jewish Immigrants   *Mark Slobin*
Ozark Folksongs   *Vance Randolph; edited and abridged by Norm Cohen*
Oscar Sonneck and American Music   *Edited by William Lichtenwanger*
Bluegrass Breakdown: The Making of the Old Southern Sound   *Robert Cantwell*
Bluegrass: A History   *Neil V. Rosenberg*
Music at the White House: A History of the American Spirit   *Elise K. Kirk*
Red River Blues: The Blues Tradition in the Southeast   *Bruce Bastin*
Good Friends and Bad Enemies: Robert Winslow Gordon and the Study
    of American Folksong   *Debora Kodish*
Fiddlin' Georgia Crazy: Fiddlin' John Carson, His Real World, and the World
    of His Songs   *Gene Wiggins*
America's Music: From the Pilgrims to the Present (rev. 3d ed.)   *Gilbert Chase*
Secular Music in Colonial Annapolis: The Tuesday Club, 1745–56   *John Barry Talley*
Bibliographical Handbook of American Music   *D. W. Krummel*
Goin' to Kansas City   *Nathan W. Pearson Jr.*

Sacred Steel: Inside an African American Steel Guitar Tradition   *Robert L. Stone*
Gone to the Country: The New Lost City Ramblers and the Folk Music Revival
    Ray Allen
The Makers of the Sacred Harp   *David Warren Steel with Richard H. Hulan*
Woody Guthrie, American Radical   *Will Kaufman*
George Szell: A Life of Music   *Michael Charry*
Bean Blossom: The Brown County Jamboree and Bill Monroe's Bluegrass
    Festivals   *Thomas A. Adler*
Crowe on the Banjo: The Music Life of J. D. Crowe   *Marty Godbey*
Twentieth Century Drifter: The Life of Marty Robbins   *Diane Diekman*
Henry Mancini: Reinventing Film Music   *John Caps*
The Beautiful Music All Around Us: Field Recordings and the American
    Experience   *Stephen Wade*
Then Sings My Soul: The Culture of Southern Gospel Music   *Douglas Harrison*
The Accordion in the Americas: Klezmer, Polka, Tango, Zydeco, and More!
    Edited by Helena Simonett
Bluegrass Bluesman: A Memoir   *Josh Graves, edited by Fred Bartenstein*
One Woman in a Hundred: Edna Phillips and the Philadelphia Orchestra
    Mary Sue Welsh
The Great Orchestrator: Arthur Judson and American Arts Management
    James M. Doering
Charles Ives in the Mirror: American Histories of an Iconic Composer   *David C. Paul*
Southern Soul-Blues   *David Whiteis*
Sweet Air: Modernism, Regionalism, and American Popular Song
    Edward P. Comentale
Pretty Good for a Girl: Women in Bluegrass   *Murphy Hicks Henry*
Sweet Dreams: The World of Patsy Cline   *Warren R. Hofstra*
William Sidney Mount and the Creolization of American Culture
    Christopher J. Smith
Bird: The Life and Music of Charlie Parker   *Chuck Haddix*
Making the March King: John Philip Sousa's Washington Years, 1854–1893
    Patrick Warfield
In It for the Long Run   *Jim Rooney*
Pioneers of the Blues Revival   *Steve Cushing*
Roots of the Revival: American and British Folk Music in the 1950s   *Ronald D. Cohen
    and Rachel Clare Donaldson*
Blues All Day Long: The Jimmy Rogers Story   *Wayne Everett Goins*
Yankee Twang: Country and Western Music in New England   *Clifford R. Murphy*
The Music of the Stanley Brothers   *Gary B. Reid*
Hawaiian Music in Motion: Mariners, Missionaries, and Minstrels   *James Revell Carr*
Sounds of the New Deal: The Federal Music Project in the West   *Peter Gough*
The Mormon Tabernacle Choir: A Biography   *Michael Hicks*
The Man That Got Away: The Life and Songs of Harold Arlen   *Walter Rimler*

The University of Illinois Press
is a founding member of the
Association of University Presses.

———————————————————————

Composed in 10.5/13 Minion Pro
with ITC Franklin Gothic Std display
by Lisa Connery
at the University of Illinois Press
Manufactured by Sheridan Books, Inc.

University of Illinois Press
1325 South Oak Street
Champaign, IL 61820-6903
www.press.uillinois.edu